Preparing to Preach

BY

DAVID R. BREED, D. D.

PROFESSOR OF HOMILETICS IN WESTERN THEOLOGICAL SEMINARY,
PITTSBURGH, PA.

HODDER & STOUGHTON
NEW YORK
GEORGE H. DORAN COMPANY

PREFACE

This volume is not intended as a comprehensive treatment of the subject of homiletics, and much is necessarily omitted which should be considered by those who are "preparing to preach." I have endeavored, however, to cover the ground which is traversed in the preparation and delivery of the ordinary sermon—the staple of the preacher's pulpit work.

I have profited by certain criticisms which intelligent Christian laymen sometimes pass upon the methods and manners of certain preachers and have included some suggestions which are generally omitted from similar publications, such as those which will be found under "The Attack Upon the Text," "Pulpit Manners," and elsewhere.

It is my sincere prayer that the book may be helpful to my brethren in the ministry, especially to those for whose sake it has been more particularly prepared, as indicated in the title.

DAVID R. BREED.

INTRODUCTORY:
THE ESSENTIAL ELEMENT

INTRODUCTORY: THE ESSENTIAL ELEMENT.

The essential element is the prophetic.
    The nature of prophecy.
    The true sermon defined.
    The exact form changes with the age.

I. The message.
    Derived from the Word of God.
    Spiritual interpretation.
    Study indispensable.
    Fidelity the paramount condition.

II. The man.
    Possessed by the message.
    Dangers of mere professionalism.
    The true preacher a "Seer."

Read Behrend's " Philosophy of Preaching." I and II; Shedd's "Homiletic and Pastoral Theology," Chap. I; Horton's "Verbum Dei," Lect. I; Jefferson's " The Minister as Prophet."

INTRODUCTORY: THE ESSENTIAL ELEMENT.

The essential element in preaching is the prophetic element. Within the Scriptural meaning of these terms the preacher is a prophet. He bears a message from the Most High God. He speaks with divine authority.

In this respect the fundamental principles of homiletics are abiding and unalterable. They were the same in New Testament times as in Old Testament times. They have not been changed since.

The true sermon is a prophecy. It is derived from revelation; it is the product of spiritual illumination; it is prepared in humble prayer and delivered in conscious reliance on the Holy Spirit. It is the result of a supernatural process; devoted to a supernatural work; made effective by a supernatural influence.

But the exact form of preaching, like all prophecy, changes with the changing age. Argument, exhortation, illustration and application become superannuated and are superseded. Others are introduced born of the new needs and new aspirations. So there comes to be a new homiletics. The prophet is a prophet still; but he is a prophet of his own age to his own age. If it be not so the age will disown him. If it be so the age will welcome him, listen to him, and follow him.

Such are the principles upon which we proceed in this volume. We exalt preaching as a form of prophecy. We exclude, of course, from these terms all those features of prophecy which are derived from direct inspiration—such as the predictive factor. But there is much remaining. So long as Christianity is regarded as a supernatural religion the essential elements of prophecy will remain, namely, these: a veritable message from God, received under supernatural conditions, delivered in the name of its Divine Author by one who is wholly given to its sincere proclamation.

It appears then that the prophetic element is composed of two integral parts. *The preacher is a man with a message.* The man without the message is in no true sense a preacher. The message without the man is not, in the largest sense, preaching. We consider each in order.

I. *The Message.* The preacher's message is derived from the Word of God as contained in the Holy Scriptures. It is nothing more nor less nor other than a portion of these Scriptures explained, illustrated, and applied.

The words of the Scriptures possess for every believer a certain force and meaning which they do not possess for the unbeliever—a spiritual "savour." They are "quick and powerful" as the Authorized Version puts it, or "living and active," according to the Revision. But if such be the case with the private Christian, what of the preacher? If he has diligently followed the Apostolic example and "continued steadfastly in prayer and in the ministry of the Word" (Acts 6:4), should not his standing be unique and his influence transcendent? Should not his proclamation of the truth evoke such commendation from those who hear him, as one has written concerning the heralds of the "Gospel of Mystery?"

> "Their banners blaze and shine
>   With Jesus Christ's dear name
>   And story, how by God's design
>   He saves us in His love divine
>   And lifts us from our sin and shame.

INTRODUCTORY

"Their music fills the air,
　Their songs sing all of heaven;
　Their ringing trumpet-peals declare
　What crowns to souls who fight and dare
　　And win, shall presently be given.

"But all the banners bear
　Some words we can not read,
　And mystic echoes in the air,
　Which borrow from the song no share,
　　In sweetness all the songs exceed."
　　　　　　　　　　　(Saxe Holm.)

But "mystery" though it be, there is no mysticism about
it. Illumination does not add to the Word nor alter it.
It does no violence either to the laws of speech or the
laws of the understanding. It simply quickens the spiritual perceptions so that the meaning which was before
hidden becomes clear. It does for the preacher what
Jesus did for His disciples when He "opened their minds
that they might understand the Scriptures." (Luke
24:45.)

But still further. In order to this deeper understanding of the Scriptures and the proclamation of their message there is need not of less study, but of more. Illumination is indeed supernatural; but it is neither unnatural or miraculous. It creates no new faculties; it
supplies no lack of learning. Hence the need of diligent
study upon the part of the preacher, and of constant
painstaking care. He must devote himself to all branches
of learning which may contribute to his usefulness, and
the very art of sermonizing must be mastered. The message is the product of illumination; but the more consecrated learning it conveys the more instructive and influential it will be. God never chose men for His special
service because they were ignorant or stupid, and to put
any sort of premium on illiteracy is to reflect upon the

two greatest religious teachers of all mere men in the Old Testament and the New respectively—Moses and Paul. We do well to emphasize the advice given long ago by Cowper, and

> "Lay not careless hands
> On skulls that can not teach and will not learn."

The best preaching then is done by the preacher who has gathered the best materials, provided he has disposed them in due subserviency to the governing principle. Dr. Robertson Nicoll well sums up the matter in these words:

"What is supremely important to a minister is that he should have a message. Other things are by no means to be despised. Nearly all wise Christians are of the opinion that the education of preachers, so far from being lowered, ought to be made much more thorough than it is. I do not need to dwell on this, but rather to insist upon the other side, that the preacher without a definite message, no matter how well furnished otherwise, is necessarily impotent." "Further," he continues, "this message is always a secret given by the Holy Ghost and blessed by the Holy Ghost. No book, no earthly teacher, can ever impart that hidden wisdom without which a minister must be a thing of nought."

The author of "Verbum Dei" well expressed the truth in announcing his theme for the Yale lectures of 1893. "Every living preacher must receive his communication direct from God, and the constant purpose of his life must be to receive it uncorrupted and to deliver it without addition or subtraction."

The musician who is an expert performer upon the cornet sometimes suffers a serious misfortune in what is called "losing his lip." The cause can not be fully explained; but the fact remains that for some strange reason the lips refuse to take the shape which is necessary to the control of the instrument. In this condition the musician can make a great variety of sounds, but he finds himself absolutely incapable of producing a single musical tone, much less of evolving a melody.

The preacher may suffer a similar but much more serious misfortune. Then there will be "words, words, words," but none of the melody of the gospel. And the sermon will fail—not as a piece of rhetoric perhaps, but as a message from God to dying men.

But how different, how very different, when the preacher is true to his prophetic commission. His God does not desert him. Again and again the truth is flashed upon his mind in startling beauty and overwhelming power, and as he presents it to his people the same Divine Spirit which brought it home to his own heart and conscience brings it home to the hearts and consciences of his hearers. He is clothed with that peculiar "authority" of which Dr. Shedd speaks so forcibly in his lecture on "Eloquence and Exegesis"—"the first and indispensable requisite" in sermonizing. He manifests a "high celestial dogmatism" and "human weakness becomes immortal strength." His hearers recognize the unusual elevation of his thought, the purity of his motive, and the validity of his appeals. They feel that in some very strange but very real way there is divine import and almighty urgency behind it all. The preacher has become to them far more than a teacher or lecturer; more than a mere scribe or doctor of the law. He is a prophet; he speaks for his God!

II. We proceed now to the second factor—*The Man.* All that may be said in this connection is forecast in a single sentence: *The man is not simply to possess the message; he is rather to be possessed by it.* In this respect there is no substantial difference between the inspired prophet of Bible times and the uninspired prophet of all times—the origin and gravity of the message are controlling. Henry Ward Beecher has very justly said: "A preacher is in some degree a reproduction of the truth in personal form. In the preacher the word becomes again as it was when first spoken by prophet, priest, or apostle. It springs up in him as if it were first kindled in his heart and he were moved by the Holy Ghost to give it forth. He *is* so moved." The preacher says with Paul, "Necessity is laid upon me; for woe is unto me if I preach not the gospel." (I. Cor. 9:16.) He says with Peter: "Whether it is right in the sight of God to hearken unto you rather than unto God, judge ye. For we can not but speak the things which we saw and heard." (Acts 4:19, 20.) The message is stronger than the man. He is condemned if he conceals it. He is constrained to tell what has been communicated to his soul. The message makes the man, rather than the man the message; and *the man thus made is a preacher*.

And yet herein lurks a subtle, sometimes a fatal temptation—*the preacher's personality*. How often it outgrows its limitations! How imperious it sometimes becomes! Forgetting for the time being that the message is not our own, and feeling and acting as though it were our own, we attempt to exercise control over it rather than to permit it to freely control us. The preacher thrusts himself into the first place. He hides the very Savior with his own obtrusive personality. The inspired prophets themselves sometimes succumbed to this temptation and forfeited their inspiration. Moses went down before it at Meribah. Elijah weakened under it when he fled from Jezebel. Peter played the gospel false in its power when he dissembled at Antioch. When we yield to it we, too, "speak unadvisedly with our lips" and the Master is dishonored.

In such a case the preacher may seem to be even more earnest than before—just as Moses was. His earnestness may even degenerate into positive violence; but it is professional not prophetical earnestness. There is much flame but little heat; loud thundering but no lightning. And this mere professional earnestness is the bane of the pulpit. Just because it is able to simulate so closely the baptism of fire, it becomes both to pastor and people one of the most serious of delusions. Even the Pharisee— both in pulpit and pew, shrewdly abandons his self-adulation for "God be merciful to me a sinner," and the publican becomes the model after which his pious formulas are constructed. Professional earnestness is devoted to all the externals of Church life. It multiplies machinery; it labors for congregational aggrandizement; it vehemently urges the evangelical faith and champions the doctrines of orthodoxy. But in it all the preacher's personality is to the fore and, exalting his office rather than his God, he cries with Moses, "Hear now, ye rebels, shall WE bring you forth water out of this rock." (Numb. 20:10.) Strangely enough the water often flows, even in such a case. The dishonored God will not dishonor the prophet's commission and the prophet's rod; but the prophet himself has lost a prophet's reward.

There must be upon the man's part, then, a conscious self-surrender. Like John the Baptist, the truth which he is sent to proclaim must take such possession of him that he shall refuse to be identified except by and in his message and become, as it were, only a "Voice"—the voice of something other than himself, intangible, mysterious, and mighty. Let us sum it all up in the eloquent words of Bautain, the great professor of the Sorbonne:

"He should blot himself out in the presence of the truth and make it alone appear. This will happen naturally, spontaneously, whenever he is profoundly impressed by it and identifies himself with it, heart and mind. Then he grows like it, great, mighty, and dazzling. It is no longer he who lives, it is the truth which in him lives and acts. The man vanishes in the virtue of the Almighty, and this is the speaker's noblest, his true glory. Then are wrought the miracles of eloquence which turn men's wills and change their souls, and such is the end at which the Christian orator should aim. Oh, ye who have taken the Lord for your inheritance and who glow with the desire to announce to men the Word of God, ask urgently of Him the grace to forget yourselves and to think of Him—of Him only!"

In defining the term, "the prophetic element," we were careful to exclude the predictive factor, as it appears in the prophets of the Scriptures. But after all that has been said we perceive that something very akin to it is the true preacher's most signal characteristic. It bears the same relation to predictive prophecy which illumination bears to inspiration; it is the product of illumination in connection with the predictive portions and general predictive character of the Word of God. The preacher has no such vision as the inspired prophet. The future does not rise before him in distinct detail and elaborate reality. Nevertheless he often manifests an unusual foresight, indulges hopes which others deem chimerical, and anticipates events of which others never dreamed. *He becomes a seer.* He meditates so long upon the methods of the Divine Providence, he is brought into such loving sympathy with the development of the Redeemer's plans that he is able to forecast the trend of Providence, at least in its general features, and to organize for the oncoming of the Kingdom. He counts upon agencies that men of the world despise; he relies upon the promises; he takes God into the account.

This is the crown of the prophetic element in preaching. It is the same divine message which we have discussed, looking to the great future. It is the same self-surrendered man projecting himself into the coming years. O, what wonders it accomplishes for God and humanity! It sails a "Mayflower" across the untried ocean—sweet pledge and promise of the season that shall be when the May flowers are succeeded by the summer harvest. It sends a "Morning Star" far, far away to lands that sit in darkness, bright harbinger of rising day and of the Sun of Righteousness. The log college, the missionary hay-stack, the "Ride that saved a continent" —what are these but meager illustrations of the many times and many ways in which prophetic saints have

> "Viewed the triumph from afar
> And seized it with their eye "

Surely Peter put no limitations on the language of the Prophet Joel, when he quoted him upon the Day of Pentecost: "And it shall be in the last days, saith God, I will pour forth of My Spirit upon all flesh; and your sons and your daughters shall prophesy, and your young men shall see visions and your old men shall dream dreams." (Acts 2:17.) In view of such an inspiring deliverance we conclude by reiterating the words of Moses, when it was told him that Eldad and Medad did prophesy in the camp: *Would that all Jehovah's people were prophets that Jehovah would put His Spirit upon them.* (Numbers 11:29.)*

---

*The quotations from the Scriptures in this volume are all from the American Standard Revision, except those employed by others and taken from the Authorized Version.

CONTENTS

PART I.
THE STUDY.

THE TEXT: ADVANTAGES; ACQUISITION.

Sermons classified.
> Topical; textual; expository.

I. Advantages of preaching from a text.
> Divergent views.
> The special advantages.
> Failure of "Lectureships."

II. Acquisition of texts.
> False methods.
> The homiletical temptation.
> Suggestion the fruitful source, as promoted by:
>> 1. Devotional reading of the Bible.
>> 2. Other sermons and religious literature.
>> 3. Providential circumstances.
>> Keep a text-book.

Read Watson's "Cure of Souls;" Pattison's "Making of the Sermon," Chap. II; Horton's "Verbum Dei," Lect. I.

I

THE TEXT: ADVANTAGES; ACQUISITION

THE usual classification of sermons with reference to the text and the one which we shall employ is the following: topical, textual, and expository.

Topical sermons are those in which the subject alone is derived from the text. Textual sermons are those in which the subject and main divisions are derived from the text. Expository sermons are those in which the subject, main divisions and most of the details are derived from the text.

In the topical method there is more opportunity for the display of rhetorical ability and pulpit oratory. There is also an opportunity to discuss certain themes which are not strictly speaking "Scriptural," in that the very subject is brought to notice in the Bible. But this method has this positive disadvantage that the preacher is apt to become decidedly unscriptural, to forget his message, and to discourse upon unsuitable themes.

The textual method is closely allied to the expository and the line of demarkation can not be sharply drawn. In the expository sermon more attention is generally given to special words or expressions, with more particular and extended explanation. The disadvantages of these methods is apparent; they do not afford the range of the topical method. But they have this great advantage, the preacher who employs them deals with distinctively Scriptural themes. It is well to employ all three methods, with the preponderance of the textual.

I. *Advantages of preaching from a text.* It is held by some that the use of a text furnishes no positive advantage. Certain writers have claimed that "a slavish adherence to a text cramps the liberty of preaching." Voltaire is quoted by many as saying that for a preacher to speak at length upon a brief quotation and to make his whole discourse bear upon that, "appears to be trifling little worthy the dignity of the ministry. The text becomes a kind of motto, or rather enigma, which the discourse develops." Some have also said that the use of the text, especially of the short text, is often fatal to the most intelligent treatment of the Scripture itself. The Bible is chopped into fragments and sadly abused by the dislocation of its parts. Its real meaning and intent can not be discovered, so it is said, by taking a few isolated words from some consistent book, and using them in whatever way the preacher may himself desire. It is still further urged that the use of texts renders the preacher monotonous and unnatural; that he is not himself. His intellect as well as moral nature is cramped by the process, and upon this very account he becomes somewhat uninteresting, and therefore some authorities would give the preacher considerable liberty in this matter, and not oblige him upon every occasion to speak from a definite passage selected from the Scripture. Prof. Hoyt claims that "preaching must be the unfolding and application of some truth in harmony with Scripture," but it need not necessarily be in the very words of Scripture, because, as he inquires, "Must the sermon always have a text? Does it fail to be God's message without a text? Surely not," and he quotes the words of Vinet, "What gives a Christian character to a sermon is not the text, but the spirit of the preacher. It may be very Biblical without a text, and with a text not

Biblical at all." The same author says that the "pulpit may need to speak of some special need or duty of society, and find it difficult to find a single passage of Scripture proper, teaching the exact phase of the truth. Then do not hesitate to unfold and apply what you hold to be the law of Christ, without a text. Far better to do this than to have the only connection between Scripture and sermon that of sound."

We believe, however, that the use of a text has such a manifest advantage that it is not proper at any time to preach without its use. This is the position taken by most thoughtful writers upon this subject. Prof. Dabney, writing in 1870, declares that the preacher's only work is to expound and apply to the people an authoritative message from God. Dr. Slattery declares "the text will never grow obsolete. There is a dignity in its use which belongs to the realm of historical good taste," a taste which is sanctified by the whole history of preaching. And Dr. Horton, in his "Yale Lectures on Preaching," gives great emphasis to the same idea. He tells us that the aim of his lectures "is to show that preaching must be the deliverance of a word of God, received immediately from God." He calls this a "neglected truism," but he recurs to it again and again. He says "the man is set apart to address his fellow-men, sometimes men who are his peers in knowledge and ability. Why should they listen to him? There is no reason why they should unless he has been in the secret cell of the Oracle and has heard God speak, and practically they will not unless the authentic command is in him, and 'Thus saith the Lord' introduces all he teaches." The chief advantage, therefore, of the use of a text can be no better expressed than in the words of Chas. H. Parkhurst, "There is an Almightiness behind it." Kern expresses the truth in somewhat different language when he says, "The chief advantage of the text is that the preacher's theme is given to him." And Dr. Oswell Dykes expresses it in still another form, but equally emphatic, "A good sermon is not one sought after, but one given."

Other advantages might be mentioned, but they are not of great value as compared with this. The preacher, as we have seen, is a prophet; he conveys a message to men which he has himself received through diligent study of the Word of God and the illumination of the Holy Spirit; and as a matter of fact, that preaching has not long endured which has proceeded upon any other plan. Religious "lectureships," as they are sometimes called, have usually been dismal failures. They might have succeeded for a while in enlisting the interest of a number of people, but they were unable to hold a congregation for any great length of time. Dr. Horton says: "The lecturer has a sphere of his own, but it is not the preacher's. The lecturer may under inspiration become a preacher, but woe to the preacher if under some supposed influence he becomes merely a lecturer. He will not have staying power. An encyclopedia is exhausted in time. Long before it is exhausted the hearers are exhausted with receiving it. The world rightly declines to hear two lectures a week from the same man throughout the year." The preacher holds his place in the community, and holds the audiences that wait upon his preaching, because he is supposed to expound the inspired Word of Almighty God, and those preachers who do it the most carefully and the most faithfully have the largest and most permanent influence. Such is the advantage of a text.

II. How are texts to be acquired? This question might be very easily answered if all that the preacher desired were simply some small section of the Bible concerning which he could say something of some character to a certain set of people; but if that is involved in the text which has been applied above, then the acquisition of texts means very much more than this. Dr. Watson (Ian Maclaren) in his "Cure of Souls" has a very amusing but very just description of the preacher whose notion of acquiring texts is of this inferior sort. He says: "As it is the duty of this artisan to furnish two sermons for next Sunday, he goes out, say on Tuesday, into the Bible as into a woodyard, and selects with due deliberation suitable material, and then bit by bit he constructs the discourse, measuring, sawing, planing, and joining in a very deft manner, and finishing with a polish composed of one part spirit, crude and fiery, and three parts thick, sweet oil." He then goes on to show that this artisan has a set of very simple designs which answer all his purposes—conventional designs upon which he can construct a sermon on almost any text.

The very expression "the acquisition of texts" possesses then a peculiar meaning. Texts are never acquired by a homiletical search-warrant. Of course, passages of Scripture may be easily found, as we have intimated; but texts that are texts indeed are not found by simply hunting for them. To treat the Bible as a mere compendium of texts is foolish and wrong; it yields no worthy fruits. It has a bad effect upon the hearer, to begin with. Campbell Morgan says, "There are thousands of people who have been brought up in somewhat close relationship to the Christian Church who nevertheless think only of the Bible as a book of texts from which sermons are preached, or which are quoted in proof of some theological position." This is very true. But whose fault is it? How has it come about?

We are dealing, however, with the preacher, and Dr.

Morgan says of him, "To think out a sermon which seems religious and then to hunt for some Biblical text upon which to hang it, is little short of profane." Dr. M. B. Riddle says: "The most pernicious habit is that of studying passages of Scripture mainly, if not exclusively, for homiletical purposes. To treat the Word of God as a collection of texts for sermons is putting dishonor upon it. To use it as if this were its character is to get away from its full and true meaning. He who seeks to find in it little save sermon material will soon find himself short of good sermon material. What he thinks he finds will prove to be inadequate, and very often incorrect."

One of the most specious temptations to which the preacher is exposed is this very homiletical temptation. Just because it is so closely associated with his work and with his own devotion to his great calling he is the more liable to fall before it. Where then lies the danger, and how is it to be avoided? The danger lies in this—that he reads the Word of God only that he may apply it to others. He avoids it by reading first of all for his own soul's sake. The preacher who seldom reads his Bible except for some sort of a homiletical purpose, may quite unconsciously excuse himself from his own private study upon the ground that he is professionally engaged with the Bible much of his time; but such a preacher is not likely either to feed his own soul or to feed the souls of others. The texts upon which he discourses will not be chosen in the right spirit, nor handled in the most profitable manner. His work will be professional and perfunctory, not warm, personal, practical, and spiritual.

How then, we ask again, is he to acquire his texts? There are a variety of ways, all of them included in the one word "suggestion." The suggestion, however, is of God. Texts may come to the preacher in the course of his general reading or of his pastoral duties, or in connection with special circumstances transpiring about him. But from whatever source they arise they are given to him, and in that sense they are not of him. It is far better then for one to put himself in the way of texts finding him, than for him to attempt to find texts. Dr. Watson says: "It is not the man who selects the text. It is the text which selects the man." "As the minister was busy with study, or as he sat by the bedside of the sick, or as he walked the crowded street, the truth, clad in a text, suddenly appeared and claimed his acquaintance. It seemed to him that they had met in the past, as one is haunted by the idea that he has known some one before he has ever seen him, and he will be right; for there is a pre-established harmony between that particular truth and his own soul."

1. The very best of all sources from which texts are acquired is the devotional reading of the Bible. The minister beyond all others should give time to the private reading of the Word of God, without any direct and positive thought of employing that Word except for his own spiritual nourishment and comfort. He is looking for nothing but the message of God to his own soul. If the private Christian, who is charged with no professional Christian service, should be encouraged thus to read the Word of God, much more so the minister; else he may some day take up the lament of the preacher of old, "They made me keeper of the vineyards, but mine own vineyard have I not kept." And yet in the course of this devotional reading of the Bible, when he has no conscious thought of reading for homiletical purposes, the best texts will suggest themselves to him; that is to say, those that are best for him to employ. The words of Scripture have struck a responsive cord in his own soul.

They have found his weakness, his need, his sin. They have brought to him strength, consolation, salvation; and his first thought concerning them may be, after he has applied them to himself, "These words might be of vast service to others also." He has acquired a text.

But this text must be worked into his life before it can be worked out for his pulpit. This does not mean that he is never to preach upon the evil of sins which he has not himself committed, nor upon heights of virtue which he has never himself attained; but that in some way he must have been made spiritually susceptible to the message which he is to bring to his people. Dr. Horton tells of one whom he calls a noble preacher in England, who declared that the turning point in his ministry came when he discovered this principle. "He noted carefully which parts of his discourse were accountable for such success as attended his preaching, and presently he observed that only those things produced any effect which had passed through the alembic of his own experience, and had been in fact real transactions between himself and God. Thenceforward he began to base his preaching upon that foundation," and tides of blessing followed his work.

2. But texts may be acquired from other sources of a somewhat similar character. They are still acquired from the Scripture, and still acquired from one's own devotional use of the Scripture, but they come to the preacher indirectly. He may obtain his texts from reading or hearing other preachers' sermons. A discourse which he will not repeat, either in whole or in part, contains the suggestion of which we have spoken. A verse of Scripture may have been quoted with a bare reference, or with a slight use made of it; but it comes home to the heart and mind of the reader or listener. A world of truth is opened before him in connection with the quota-

tion. The suggestion is pregnant with meaning, and he has acquired a text. The like may happen in the reading of a hymn, or some article upon a certain phase of religious experience or activity. But the point is this, that however indirectly the suggestion may come, it is always connected with some passage of Scripture, and is always commended to the preacher's own self, his own need, and his own growth in grace. A single illustration may be given of the way in which this may be done. A well known British preacher discoursed before a certain audience composed of ministers and students for the ministry upon this subject, "The Joys of the Ministry." The text which came into the mind of one of his hearers was not mentioned in his discourse, but it was suggested by it. The supreme example of the Lord Jesus Christ, "who for the joy that was set before Him endured the cross, despising shame." In connection with the discourse upon the "Joys of the Ministry," the joy of Jesus Christ in His ministerial work, His service for humanity, loomed up large and brilliant. It was to the hearer's mind the supreme example of the subject with which the speaker was engaged—the joy of Jesus Christ.

3. Texts may be acquired from providential circumstances. Yet again the suggestion of the circumstances is always connected with some passage of Scripture. That transpires in our own day which transpired in the day of the sacred writers, but with its own peculiar local and temporal coloring. The preacher recurs, in connection with the circumstances of to-day, to the circumstances of old. Some text is borne in upon his mind with new meaning and power, and he acquires it, to his own profit and the profit of those who shall listen to him. Mr. Spurgeon was much given to the treatment of texts associated with current incidents. Upon the occasion of the

stances of old. Some text is borne in upon his mind with new meaning and power, and he acquires it, to his own profit and the profit of those who shall listen to him. Mr. Spurgeon was much given to the treatment of texts associated with current incidents. Upon the occasion of the taking of one of the British censuses, which is always done by a large number of enumerators upon a single day, he preached from Ps. 87: 5, 6, "Yea, of Zion it shall be said, This one and that one was born in her; and the Most High Himself will establish her. Jehovah will count, when He writeth up the peoples, this one was born there."

The preacher who accustoms himself to improve such circumstances will be in the way of exercising great power over the congregation to which he ministers. It is well for the preacher to have a text-book in which he shall enter the names of such texts as suggest themselves to him, with such thoughts concerning them as may come to him from time to time. These texts should be entered with considerable space between them to allow room for additional notes. It will be well also if every other page is left blank for the same purpose. It is not usually well for a preacher to write upon a text when it is first suggested to him, but to prove it by waiting, ruminating upon it, and gathering around it those thoughts and illustrations which may be suggested in connection with it, in much the same way in which the text has suggested itself. He will recur to these thoughts whenever he opens his text-book to review those passages of Scripture which have been entered in it. And the text which gathers power, and presents itself to his own mind with more and more force as the time passes on, will be the text which he can use to the best advantage and preach with the best results.

THE PREACHER'S DUTY BY HIS TEXT

THE PREACHER'S DUTY BY HIS TEXT.

His chief duty is to preach its meaning.

1. No text has more than one meaning.
2. The preacher is under obligation to find it.
3. Having found it he must abide by it.
4. Yet several different sermons may be preached from the same text.
   (1) Its meaning may be enlarged.
   (2) It may have various uses and applications.
   (3) Its general principle may be variously employed.
   (4) It may be viewed obliquely.
5. The misuse of the text.
   (1) Intentional—"Accommodation."
   (2) Unintentional.
6. The preacher must maintain his intellectual integrity.

Read Dabney's "Sacred Rhetoric," Lect. V; Garvie's "Guide to Preachers,' III; Slattery's "Present Day Preaching," I; Broadus' "Preparation and Delivery of Sermons," Part I, Chaps. I and II.

II.

THE PREACHER'S DUTY BY HIS TEXT.

The preacher having chosen his text, what is his chief duty by it? The answer may be given in a single sentence—to preach its meaning. Dr. Dabney says: "The exact mind of the Spirit in the text must be ascertained before you presume to preach upon it. A proper apprehension of the preacher's mission will make him intensely honest and prayerful in his study." Dr. Pattison says: "In the matter of the selection of a text the preacher should do his utmost to be conscientious. Let him lay down the rule that he has no right to take a text unless he means to use it." The common proverb indeed requires the preacher to "stick to his text;" but the proverb does not adequately express the rule. There are several particulars embraced in it, as follows:

1. No text has more than one meaning. The meaning may not always be clear at first sight, and it may not be very clear after considerable study. There also may be differing interpretations with regard to its meaning; but no one can dispute the statement that the meaning, when really discovered, is a single meaning, and in the very nature of the case it can not have a second one.

2. The preacher's obligation is to find that single meaning. He can not take the second step until he has taken this. Before anything is done by him in the way of sermon construction his mind must be settled with regard to what the text means. This may involve consider-

able breadth of study—a good knowledge of the original languages, correct rules of exegesis, acquaintance with Bible history and customs, and the like. By such means as the preacher can command he must search for the meaning of the text, and if after a time he is not satisfied that he has found it, the text should be abandoned and another chosen.

3. Having found the meaning of this text, he must abide by it whatever befall. He may not seek to modify it in any way; he may not attempt to relax the conditions which it imposes upon the faith or life of those to whom his sermon is to be addressed. He must not seek to neutralize this special text by something which he imports into it from his understanding of some other text of Scripture. This is not to say that he is not to interpret Scripture by Scripture; only that he is not to set aside the plain meaning of one text by something which he thinks he finds in another. He must not admit to his own mind, much less to his sermon, what he thinks the text might mean, or might be made to mean, much less what he supposes it ought to mean.

A young student of law entered the office of a distinguished attorney in New York City. Upon a certain occasion the attorney was engaged in preparing for a very important suit which was to be tried in several weeks. He directed his student to search certain authorities with regard to the law, as he himself was somewhat uncertain with regard to its character and its application to the case in hand. After a lapse of several days he inquired what progress his assistant had made in his work. He received very little satisfaction. Several more days passed by. He made the same inquiry, with the same result. Somewhat surprised, and not a little indignant, he inquired what his student had been doing, and was answered:

"Well, sir, I have found a good many references in this case, but I do not think I have discovered anything of service to you. It seems to me that the law ought to be thus and so, but I can not find that it is." The older man turned upon him and ejaculated with vehemence, "My dear young friend, I do not care to know what the law ought to be: all I wished you to learn for me was what the law is." And is it not so with the preacher of the Word of God? Should he not be at all times chiefly concerned with knowing what the law of God is, not what it ought to be?

4. This does not mean that only a single sermon can be preached upon a given text. On the contrary a number of sermons may be preached from it.

(1) The single meaning may be very much enlarged as the preacher proceeds with his study. More and more light may break forth from it upon his mind, so that having preached one sermon upon it he may preach yet another. The subject may be the very same, but the truth will have addition and amplification beyond anything which he set forth in his former sermon, so that virtually his second sermon will be both different and better.

(2) The single meaning of the text may have a number of applications, and therefore may be employed in several ways, and a number of different sermons prepared upon it. These applications will depend, for example, upon the different people to whom it is addressed, the different places in which it is delivered, and the different occasions that shall call for its presentation.

(3) The single meaning may embody a certain definite principle, which principle may be legitimately employed in a number of ways—the meaning of the text being duly recognized. There are many such texts in the Bible. "Whatsoever a man soweth, that shall he also

reap," (Gal. 6:7) contains such a broad, general principle. As presented by the Apostle Paul it referred to
the matter of Christian liberality; but there is no reason
why the principle should be limited to such an exercise.
The warning of Amos 4:12, "Prepare to meet thy God,"
referred to the temporal judgments which were to befall
the nation in case it did not repent. But the deep meaning of the text may be used at any time when the principle which it embodies is employed, to warn sinners in
their indifference or their antagonism to the will of God.

(4) There may be an oblique view of the meaning of
the text which shall furnish a peculiarly rich and prolific
sermon, though it is not that view which presents itself
to the reader upon the first consideration. And yet the
oblique view may be even more faithful to the deeper
meaning of the passage than the first and more direct
view itself. This oblique view is characteristic of the
sermons of Bushnell. His celebrated sermon upon "Unconscious Influence" is a fine illustration. His text is
John 20:8, "Then went in also that other disciple." The
subject which he derives from it is a legitimate subject.
Peter's influence over John, all unconscious to himself,
certainly appears in the passage, but unconscious influence
is not its immediate and direct teaching.

Archdeacon Perowne in his essay upon the interpretation of texts, sums up this subject in a most interesting
and appropriate way. He says: "In interpreting a text
seek to ascertain the exact and proper meaning of the
words in which it is couched. An interpretation is sometimes put upon a text by a preacher which the English
words, apart from any reference to the original, on
careful consideration will not bear. A thoughtful and intelligent hearer will find himself asking: 'Can this really
be the meaning of the text? I know nothing of Greek

or Hebrew, but as it stands in my English Bible I do not see how this can be got out of it.' Our very familiarity with the Bible may prove a snare to us in this respect. Its words and phrases which we have known from childhood are stereotyped in our memories, and sometimes in the inexact form which popular tradition has given them. There are such things as conventional readings as well as conventional interpretations of texts, —readings which are inadequate representations of our English version, but which have become so familiar to the preacher by frequent repetition that he is in danger of regarding them as the *ipsissima verba* of his text."

5. A text may be entirely suitable and well chosen, but treated in a very unsuitable way. It may be misused by the preacher, intentionally or unintentionally. The first of these is, of course, very much the more culpable. Yet sometimes the preacher deliberately disregards the single meaning of the text and the purpose for which it was written, using it in another sense and for a purpose altogether foreign to that for which it was originally employed. Sometimes the preacher makes full confession of this misuse. He may even say to his congregation, "This text means thus and so, but I propose to employ it this morning in a different sense." This misuse of the text is commonly called "Accommodation." It is so thoroughly well understood, and so frequently treated in books upon homiletics, that it is not necessary for us to employ much time in its consideration. Accommodation, however, is a very much broader thing than is commonly understood. It is more than the misuse of a single text, principle, or doctrine of the Scripture. It is the misuse of its entire trend and teaching. Dr. Dykes well says: "This question of accommodation of Scripture and its limit is commonly discussed in connection with

the choice or use of a text. In truth it is a much wider question. It concerns the whole employment of Scripure for edification, both in its narrative portions and above all in its typology."

There are some who would permit accommodation under certain circumstances. They say that such a use of a text is sometimes permissible. Dr. Pattison, for example, alludes to the sermon of Henry Melville upon the occasion of the burning of the Royal Exchange in London. His text was the passage in Revelation 18:17, which describes the mourning of the merchants, made rich in the mystic Babylon, over her fall; "In one hour so great riches is come to nought." But it is doubtful whether such a use of a text should ever be countenanced. Certainly one of the worst forms of accommodation is the allegorical, where literal words are used in a metaphorical sense. Quite a considerable list of such texts may be found in Broadus, Part I., Chapter II. Because this is often done, even by ministers of reputation, the temptation is all the greater for the young preacher, and he must the more carefully guard himself against it. That man assumes a fearful responsibility who alters in any way the meaning of the Word of God. It is not difficult to find a text suitable to almost any emergency, containing at least the principle which is involved; and when there is a special occasion which calls for some special lesson it were better for the preacher to confine himself to such texts, or if a text suitable to his purpose is not to be found, to deliver an address without one, and without calling it a sermon.

There is, however, a certain form of accommodation which really is not accommodation at all. This has been already foreshadowed above in what has been said with regard to the principle contained in the text and its various uses. Dr. H. Clay Trumbull was singularly expert in such a use of texts. This appeared particularly while he was an army chaplain. The texts used by him in preaching to the soldiers in the field are most appropriate, and also most legitimate. For example, he preached on a certain Thanksgiving-day at the front, when a battle seemed to be imminent, from Ps. 23:5, "Thou preparest a table before me in the presence of mine enemies." Again, after a defeat of the Northern arms, and when it seemed likely that the disaster might be repeated, he preached from Ps. 60:12, "Through God we shall do valiantly; for he it is that shall tread down our enemies." And on one occasion he preached, with reference to the disinclination of some at home to take active part in military service, from Numbers 32:6, "Shall your brethren go to war, and shall ye sit here?" More than a third of this last sermon was explanatory of the text and its surroundings, yet so strong was it in its argument for patriotism and loyalty to the government that it was printed, by special request of the colonel of the regiment, for general distribution.

We are inclined to think, however, that the unintentional misuse of the text is more frequent than its intentional misuse. The text is misinterpreted, and yet the preacher is honest and earnest in his very misinterpretation. It may be well to note some of the reasons for this misinterpretation of the text and its consequent misuse.

(1) Beyond all question the most frequent source of such misuse is this, that the text has not been carefully read, and read in its connection. In dealing with students in the theological seminary and their mistaken work, it has often been sufficient to say to them, "Let me read that text to you," and by its deliberate, careful,

and emphatic reading the meaning has been made to appear, and the student has said with some surprise, "I did not so understand it, but now I see the error I have committed." Ministers of considerable experience are sometimes subjects of the same fault. Because of that traditional or conventional meaning of the text which has been fastened upon it, the preacher often jumps to conclusions which it would have been impossible for him to reach had he read his text as though it were totally unfamiliar to him, and he must be at pains to discover what it contains.

The text "Behold, I stand at the door and knock," Revelation 3:20, has been interpreted by many to refer to the Savior as standing at the door of the un-regenerate sinner's heart. One of our Christian hymns is written upon this understanding of it. No doubt the Savior does assume such an attitude at the door of the sinner's heart, but the epistle from which this declaration was taken was addressed to professing Christian people—to the Angel of the Church in Laodicea. The beautiful hymn by Bishop Howe, beginning "O Jesus, Thou art standing" is a correct interpretation:

> "Shame on us, Christian brothers,
> His name and sign who bear,
> O shame, thrice shame upon us,
> To keep Him standing there!"

Yet the writer has heard this hymn ridiculed in a meeting of ministers by one who did not himself understand the passage upon which it was founded.

Sometimes, strange to say, a text is misinterpreted by omitting a single word, regarded as somewhat unimportant, but by which omission the meaning of the text is altogether altered. Rom. 8:28, "We know that

to them that love God all things work together for good,
even to them that are called according to His purpose," has been quoted omitting the word "together,"
thus making the text say that which is not strictly true,
namely, that all things work for good. The text does not
teach the working of single circumstances in behalf of
the called of God, but of that holy conspiracy of events
whereby God over-rules all things for the good of His
people.

Sometimes the misinterpretation of the text is conventional: a meaning has been fastened upon it by common but mistaken use, which is accepted even by the
preacher without further consideration. This is notably
the case in Gen. 31:49, "Jehovah watch between me
and thee, when we are absent one from another."
This is used as though the speaker meant that Jehovah
was to watch between those that were separated in order
to bring them together again, which is exactly what the
text does not mean. And the word "Mizpah" in the same
connection, by which name Laban called the heap of
stones which he and Jacob gathered together for a witness tower, has been in the same conventional way misapplied.

It is, therefore, very important that the text should
be read carefully, and that its exact phraseology should
be minutely understood. One of the worst faults that
a preacher can commit is to err through sheer care-
lessness.

(2) The text is unintentionally misinterpreted by
failing to note the peculiarities of Scripture language.
Oriental speech is different in many ways from our
Western forms. For example, hyperbole is frequently
employed, much more frequently than among Western
nations, by whom it is generally discountenanced. In

Bible phraseology, language may sometimes mean more than is borne upon the surface, and sometimes less, according to circumstances. When the Savior says that in order to follow Him we must "hate" father and mother, He is not to be understood as He would have been had He not Himself used an Orientalism. Just so when He bids us when we make a feast to "call not" our friends and rich neighbors.

It is to be remembered also that the translation of one language into another is always attended with imperfection. At times something is lost thereby, and at other times something is added. This is unavoidably so. Because there often is, on the part of the sacred writer, a struggle to express thought. It is impossible for his own language to convey in full the ideas that are surging through his mind. He uses the best words at his command to make his ideas clear and intelligible, but even so there is something left to the imagination of the reader. Now when these words of the original writer are translated into another language, the lack is even greater.

There are also peculiarities of an idiomatic character, in which there is a certain flavor that can not possibly be conveyed in another language because the idioms of one language do not correspond with those of another. Take, for example, the parable of the Good Samaritan. There are words in it which illustrate the intensive meaning which was attached to a verb in the Greek by the prefixing of a preposition. We have no corresponding method of doing this in the English. For example, the Good Samaritan instructed the innkeeper, when he was about to leave the wounded man, whom he had brought to the inn, as expressed in English, "Take care of him." Yet the verb is in the intensive form by the prefix of the preposition 'ἐπι. The Good Samaritan instructed the innkeeper to take very tender care of him.

So also the Greek word φιλέω with the prefix κατά means not simply "to kiss," but to kiss frequently. And in that other parable of the Savior of the Prodigal Son, we are told that the father "fell on his neck and kissed him." In this case the sense is communicated by the margin, which renders the word "kissed him much."

Let us note in passing that herein lies one of the advantages of original study of the text in the languages in which it is written, and the importance of the preacher knowing these languages in a deeper and better way than in the mere ability to translate them into English. And the preacher who has some knowledge of the original should never fail to study his text in that language before he attempts to write upon it. If he is ignorant of the original language he should do the next best thing by seeking the concordance or commentary that will give him the best understanding of the original flavor and meaning.

(3) A third source of the unintentional misuse of the text proceeds from the disregarding of the context. And by the context we do not mean those verses that are immediately associated with the text. It may be longer or shorter. It may be a paragraph or the entire book. It is very important that the preacher should obtain the author's viewpoint, and understand in what connection the truth was spoken, upon which he proposes to preach. Sometimes the preacher is misled by chapter and verse divisions, or by the paragraphs which he finds in the Bible which he is accustomed to use. Fortunately for the preacher of to-day, the new version is paragraphed much more satisfactorily than the old version ever was, but the chapter and verse divisions remain. Sometimes the preacher takes a text, confines himself to it, does not look far enough into the context for its meaning, and so preaching only upon that which the text itself seems to

convey, he misses its meaning altogether. For example, I Peter 1:5, which reads in the King James Version, "Who are kept by the power of God through faith unto salvation," and which seems to be very plain in its meaning, so that the preacher need scarcely look further in order to interpret it, may be misused simply because the preacher has neglected to observe that Peter in his epistle is addressing the Christians who had been Jews of the Dispersion, scattered through Asia Minor. His entire epistle, therefore, has a Jewish coloring, and in the verses from which this text is taken there is immediate reference to the ancient hope of Israel, as it was associated with the promise of the land which had been given unto them, and into which they entered after the bondage in Egypt. But the hope of Israel has been displaced by a larger and better hope, which Peter calls in the third verse a "living hope." Therefore in the fourth verse the "inheritance incorruptible, and undefiled, and that fadeth not away" is in his mind set over against the corruptible inheritance of the land of Canaan, although he makes no explicit mention of it. Likewise "the power of God" whereby we are "kept through faith unto salvation" is set over against that power of God by which ancient Israel was defended from all their enemies. Of course the text "Who are kept by the power of God through faith unto salvation" becomes much more significant and luminous when once the preacher has obtained the viewpoint of the writer.

In addition to the three sources which have been mentioned, we may state in general terms that the text is misinterpreted unintentionally for lack of sufficient knowledge of Bible history, Bible geography, Bible customs, and the various nations with whom the Jews were brought into contact. It may also be misinterpreted because those very figurative expressions and symbolic passages, with which the Scripture abounds, are pressed too far, particularly those in the Old Testament which look forward to their completion and fulfillment in the New Testament. A very safe rule for us to adopt with regard to this matter is to go no farther in our construction of the figures of the Old Testament than the New Testament itself does. Where it is made plain in the New Testament that a certain type or symbol of the Old Testament foreshadowed a definite principle or duty, we may so employ it; but to proceed farther is to involve ourselves in danger, and it may even go so far as to beget a strange fanaticism. It might also be said that most of the fads and isms and fanciful theories of the religious life which have been produced since the gospel was first preached, have been the result of improper allegorizing.

6. The preacher's duty by his text also involves a duty which he owes to his own self. He is to maintain his own intellectual integrity. It is not necessary for him to attempt to deduce from a text its conventional or traditional meaning, when he himself is not altogether sure that it is indeed the meaning of the text. This is a form of intellectual dishonesty; it is immoral, and no one is required to be immoral in order to be orthodox. Let us be true to what we believe God says. Let us preach nothing of which we are not fully sure; and if we are in serious doubt concerning any matter let us wait for light and seek the wisdom which God in due time may impart to us.

TEXTUAL ANALYSIS.

TEXTUAL ANALYSIS.

Textual analysis defined.
    Its value to the preacher.
    First of all dependent on illumination.
Rules—
    1. Note the meaning of every word.
    2. Note the relation of words to each other.
    3. Note peculiar forms of speech.
    4. Compare parallel passages.
    5. Classify the thoughts.
    6. Paraphrase.
    7. Select a subject.   Special rules.
    8. Note the relation to the general subject.
    9. Divisions of the subject.
   10. Recapitulate.

Read Phelps' " Theory of Preaching," Lectures V and VI;" Garvie's " Guide
to Preachers," III ; Campbell Morgan's " The English Bible."

III.

TEXTUAL ANALYSIS.

How shall the preacher obtain that full and exact meaning of his text of which we have spoken in the preceding chapter? We proceed to answer.

Textual analysis for homiletical purposes is the careful examination of all the parts of a given passage of Scripture with a view of determining, (1) their separate meaning, (2) their mutual relations, and (3) the specific meaning and import of the passage as a whole.

This work is not to be confounded with textual criticism of any kind. It employs its results, but does not make use of its processes. We do not study about the Bible in order to ascertain what its true text may be; but we take the text which has been furnished to us by the most competent authorities and dissect it in order to obtain our homiletical material. This corresponds in a measure to what is known in ordinary rhetoric as "invention"—the search for seed-thought and its discovery. It is the way to sermonizing. The sermon is its final product.

Textual analysis is the condition and groundwork of all good preaching. Dr. Campbell Morgan says with regard to it, "I can not too earnestly urge the importance of studying the Bible analytically and of refusing to abandon a passage until its real sense is understood." We are to "preach the Word." All good preaching is Scriptural. In fact that which is not Scriptural is unworthy the name. It is the purpose of textual analysis to find what is in Scripture for the preacher's use.

The lack of the analytical faculty is a frequent source of failure in the pulpit. Either the preacher runs short of homiletical material, or he supplies the lack by departing from the Scripture in whole or in part and resorting to other sources. A young minister once remarked to an older one, "I fear that I shall not be able to continue in the pulpit." "Why so?" "Because I have exhausted all my material. I have preached upon *all the subjects* I can think of." "Suppose, then," said the elder, "you now begin to *preach upon texts.*" The young man perceived his mistake and was led to apprehend the proper method to his immediate relief and his subsequent manifest growth.

On the other hand, no preacher can fail, however modest his abilities, who adopts the method of textual analysis and diligently pursues it in the preparation of every sermon. His homiletical material will increase more rapidly than he can employ it. Many passages of Scripture will yield not simply a single sermon, but will suggest a number. Familiar texts will bring forth unfamiliar lessons and reveal new truths. They will urge themselves upon the preacher's mind with unusual force and present aspects of which he never dreamed. His congregation will be continually edified and often remark as they once did of the Savior, "We never saw it on this fashion." (Mark 2: 12.)

In what then does the art of textual analysis reside?

First of all, it is derived from the blessing of the Holy Spirit, whose aid the preacher may confidently invoke. He will seek that illumination of which we have already spoken, which, while it is distinguished from inspiration, is often productive of similar results. There is no new truth revealed, but such light is shed upon the old truth that it has the meaning and power of a fresh revelation.

In order to this the preacher will endeavor to find that meaning of his text which is concealed from the undevout, the "natural man," but which is made known to the spiritually-minded, simple-hearted student of the Word of God. This is always its simplest and most natural meaning, only it is not seen by eyes that are willfully blinded nor understood by minds that are unwilling to be taught.

We seek therefore the illumination of the Holy Spirit. How are we to do so? When may we hope to obtain it? When we employ the means that are in accord with the method of His operation; when we honor the Word of God; and then endeavor to ascertain its meaning according to the recognized laws of human speech.

The analysis of the text may proceed upon the following plan. Begin at once with the text itself. The preacher need employ no commentary whatsoever, at least until his own analysis has been completed, when he may seek further help in the development of his sermon work. He may bring to his aid at the first only a reference Bible, a Bible dictionary, a concordance and maps. He then proceeds to study the passage under review, in the following order:

I. First note the meaning of every word; its meaning in the original language. If he can not himself read the original, there are certain works at hand from which he may derive the original signification of the word. He is not to be satisfied with the English equivalent of the word; because it is often impossible accurately to translate the word of another language, so that its exact sense and, more particularly, its precise flavor shall be perceived. This rule also applies to those words in the Greek which are translations or substitutes of certain words in the Hebrew. He is to note the meaning of every word. There are none so insignificant that he can afford to pass them by. Sometimes it would seem as though the word had no special meaning apart from that which is ordinarily associated with it in the reader's mind. This was particularly true of the King James Version, where the same care was not exercised which has been shown in recent revisions of the Bible, particularly the American Standard Revision. For example, the word "will" is sometimes an auxiliary verb used only to indicate the future tense. At other times it is the translation of a word which means "to will" or "to desire." For example, John 7: 17, "If any man will do His will" in the old version is made clear by the translation of the revision, "If any man willeth to do His will, he shall know of the teaching, whether it is of God, or whether I speak from myself." So with the word "now." Sometimes it is a conjunction. "Remember now thy Creator in the days of thy youth." (King James Version.) In such a case no particular importance is attached to it. At other times it is an adverb and means "at this very present time." Romans 8: 1, "There is therefore now no condemnation to them that are in Christ Jesus." These distinctions also appear in a great many passages where words that ordinarily appear of trivial consequence are invested with great meaning. There are some special words which must be minutely examined; for example:

(1) The different names of God, and the force which they possess in the original—"Jehovah," "God Almighty," etc.

(2) The terms which are applied to the people of God—"believers," "disciples," "saints," etc. A serious

mistake has been made by certain men in interpreting Acts 19: 1, where the word "disciples" is used, and where it is supposed they were Christian disciples, as they were not; but only disciples of John the Baptist.

(3) Terms defining peculiar relations, such as "covenant," "promise," "sons," "portion," "heirs," etc. For example, the word "promise" when it is preceded by the definite article, ("the promise"), has a very different meaning from that which obtains when it stands alone.

(4) Terms defining special conditions—"flesh," "spirit," "natural," "spiritual." If the preacher has already learned to define his Scripture terms with precision, he will not likely be led astray with regard to such words.

(5) It is of great importance that the analyst should give good attention to the various forms of words—tenses, moods, cases and so on; derivative words, figurative expressions, and the like.

II. Note the relation of each word to every other word. The special meaning of the passage is often determined by this relation. The very meaning of a particular word may be changed when it is brought into special relation with some other word; for example:

(1) The same word in the original translated by two different words in English.

(2) Different words in the original translated by the same word in English.

(3) The same word occurring twice in the same passage, and manifestly so used, as the careful student will discover, for a special purpose. For example, in the fourth chapter of John we have an account of the Savior's conversation with the woman of Samaria. The word "well" occurs in this passage five times. It is translated by this same English word in every case, but two different Greek words are employed. The one which the wo-

man uses indicates only a pit or cistern in which water is contained. The one which Jesus uses indicates the source of a perpetual spring. The greater part of the force of His teaching in this case depends upon understanding the meaning of these two words, though they are the same word in the English translation. The woman says, "Thou hast nothing to draw with, and the well is deep." Jesus replies, "The water that I shall give him shall become in him a well of water springing up unto eternal life." Again, in the parable of the Prodigal Son, the Greek word "μακρὰν" is found twice. It is the same word in the Greek. It may be an adjective in one case and an adverb in the other, or an adverb in both cases. We can not determine this from the exact form of the word. It is rendered into English as though it was at first an adjective and afterwards an adverb, but the form in the Greek is exactly the same. But this same Greek word is translated in the one case "took his journey into a *far* country," and in the other case "while he was yet *afar off.*" The careful student will be led to believe inasmuch as it is the same word in the Greek, that while the prodigal was still in the far country his father saw him, and not after he had made a long and tedious journey towards his home. These are but meager illustrations of the advantage which ensues from a careful study of every word in the form in which it is found in the Scripture.

III. Note peculiar forms of speech, especially those that are characteristic of the author of the passage—hyperbole, antithesis, allegorical expressions, forms of speech peculiar to the author's age of the world or the community in which he lived, and expressions which are favorite ones with the author. A large number of illustrations might be given; the Apostle Paul's reference,

for example, to Roman citizenship and Roman customs;
the favorite "straightway" of the Evangelist Mark, and
the philosophic expressions of the Apostle John. Wher-
ever such peculiar expressions are found they should be
examined and their meaning and force distinctly understood.

IV. The passage is to be compared with parallel
passages. Scripture is its own best interpreter. There
are very few passages of Scripture which are absolutely
repeated in two places. In very many instances passages
which seem much alike are found to possess features that
are very unlike, as for example the two miracles of the
draft of fishes, and therefore when placed in contrast
with each other afford unusual instruction.

We should understand what a parallel passage really
is. Many are misled by the mere sound of words, or
by the fact that one passage contains some reference to
a certain virtue or doctrine which the other also possesses.
Many so-called "Bible Readings" are founded upon this
kind of parallelism, which really yields nothing of any
special importance. But parallel passages are those which
convey analogous truth. Their comparison is of immense value. Often it is indispensable. Sometimes the
teaching of one passage may be disputed, and therefore
the preacher may be left in the dark with regard to certain elements of its teaching until it is placed side by side
with another passage in which the viewpoint is much
the same, or the lesson to be taught is much the same,
when the ambiguity entirely disappears, and the uncertainty of its meaning is removed. The parable of the
Prodigal Son, for example, has given rise to much dispute as to whom the Savior referred in the younger son
and the elder son. All sorts of interpretations have been
offered with regard to this question. Some have even

supposed that by the younger son the Savior referred to the human race, and by the elder son to the angels. A strictly parallel passage, however, is found in the parable of the Two Sons in Matt. 21, to whom the father addressed the command, "Son, go work to-day in the vineyard." In this case the Savior Himself indicated to whom He referred when He said, "Verily I say unto you, that the publicans and the harlots go into the Kingdom of God before you." We turn again, therefore, to the parable of the Prodigal Son, and we find that it is introduced with the words: "Now all the publicans and sinners were drawing near unto Him to hear Him. And both the Pharisees and the scribes murmured, saying, This man receiveth sinners, and eateth with them." The parallel passage, taken in connection with the introduction to the parable of the Prodigal Son, determines who the Savior had in mind.

The value of a careful use of parallel passages can not be overestimated. If one would be a Scriptural preacher, he must needs employ them, and much of his skill will be determined by the use which he makes of them. But they should always be consulted by the sermonizer before his sermon is begun.

V. Write down all the ideas conveyed by the passage. Classify them—teachings, truths, duties, graces, and so on. Arrange them in proper order. Show their mutual relations. Summarize and unify them. This may take considerable time, but it should be done by all means.

VI. Paraphrase the passage. This is not always necessary, but it is of special use in the introduction to a narrative or descriptive sermon, in which the historical incidents which are associated with it are to be set before the congregation. It is not sufficient for the preacher to repeat the story in the very words of Scripture. He is so to rehearse them as to interpret them, modernize them —setting the situation before his hearers as it would appear to their own eyes at the present day. Moreover, it indicates his understanding of the passage. What God has said to him in the words of Scripture, he says back to God again, as it were, in his own language, so indicating his understanding of it. The sermonizer is now prepared to begin the construction of his discourse.

VII. Select so much of the given passage as will furnish a complete subject. The passage itself, therefore, should be complete; not an imperfect or fragmentary statement. It may be a question, but if so it must be a question which plainly suggests its answer, or with the answer as given, if it be so. Take, for example, the text from James 4: 14, "What is your life?" It is not infrequently preached upon, but it is not a suitable text because it is fragmentary, incomplete. The question may be answered out of the preacher's own mind in a great many different ways, and may be so answered as to be false to the passage in which the question is contained. Let us add to it the following words of the passage: "What is your life? For ye are a vapor that appeareth for a little time, and then vanisheth away." This is complete, but in view of the passage from which it is derived it has not that measure of completeness which it should possess for the preacher. Let us add to it again. "Come now, ye that say, To-day or to-morrow we will go into this city, and spend a year there, and trade, and get gain: whereas ye know not what shall be on the morrow. What is your life? For ye are a vapor that appeareth for a little time, and then vanisheth away." This is still better, but not yet so full as it should be. The entire connection from the thirteenth verse to the fifteenth. should be included in the text, adding to what we have already quoted

the words, "For that ye ought to say, If the Lord will,
we shall both live, and do this or that." Indeed, it would
not be amiss for the preacher to add the sixteenth and
seventeenth verses also. It is not meant hereby that the
preacher must always select a number of verses, or a
somewhat extended text. Some texts are complete which
contain very few words. The number of words is not
important.

While a short text can more easily be borne in mind
by the listener than a long one, it is quite sure to pass out
of the mind if it be so short that it does not convey a
clear and comprehensive thought. If the text is very
brief, as it may sometimes be, it should be fully illuminating and suggestive. Some such texts are proposed by
Dr. Slattery, for example, "The God of hope," "Redeeming the time," "Called to be saints," "Christ pleased not
Himself," etc. Garvie says a text need not be one verse,
it may be more or less; just as much or little as may
serve the purpose for which it is chosen, and as the literary, historical, or logical character of the passage from
which it is taken may demand. A whole parable or a
whole psalm, if possessing the necessary unity, may be
the text, yet a single verse may be sufficient to suggest
a subject. Dr. Hoyt, while expressing his decided prefer-
ence for short texts because, as he says, they allow for
"emphatic repetition" and are "more likely to result in
concise and effective sermons," yet expresses himself in
the very terms we have employed. "The text should be
a complete thought of Scripture. Respect for the sacred
writers demands this, for the inspiration of Scripture is
not only speculative theory. To cut up the Scripture
like so much merchandise, in lengths to suit the user, is
treating it as we should be ashamed to treat any other
book."

The tendency of the pulpit generally seems to be rather in favor of shorter texts than of longer ones, but we think it is a mistaken tendency. Very frequently the preacher's sermon would have been better if his text had been longer. The abbreviation of a passage of Scripture is often its positive mutilation. It does not appear to carry the meaning with which it is invested when the complete thought of the sacred writer is given to the congregation.

The text should be comprehensive as well as complete. This means not only that it is a finished thought, but that it is a thought inclusive of a certain number of thoughts closely related one to the other, or intimately associated in their bearing on doctrine or life. John Claude, who may be called "The father of Protestant homiletics," among the excellent things which he says in his essay upon the composition of a sermon, remarks that a text should "include the complete sense of the writer whose words they are" upon the subject presented in the passage. He says: "For example, should you take these words of 2 Cor. 1:3, 'Blessed be the God and Father of our Lord Jesus Christ, the Father of mercies and God of all comfort,' and stop here, you would include a complete sense, but it would not be the apostle's sense. Should you go further and add 'who comforteth us in all our affliction,' it would not then be the complete sense of St. Paul, nor would his meaning be wholly taken in unless you went on to the end of the fourth verse. When the complete sense of the sacred writer is taken you may stop." This comprehension is required in a text, else it is virtually as incomplete as that kind of text to which we referred in section one. The presentation of the truth is fragmentary, though the text itself may contain a complete thought, and being fragmentary it is incorrect. But in order that the text should be compre-

hensive it must not be too simple or axiomatic, as for example the text, "All unrighteousness is sin." Here there
is a single proposition which the preacher will find difficult to elaborate in any way. Nor must it be too large
and inclusive, as for example the text, "God is love."
Those texts that limit the broad and general statements
in some statement which is still comprehensive and suggestive, usually furnish the richest sermons, as for example; in connection with the love of God, "God com-
mendeth His own love toward us, in that, while we were
yet sinners, Christ died for us."

The text being determined, the preacher will then
proceed to express his subject. It should be derived
from the passage; it should have immediate reference to
it; it should embrace in epitome all that is to be embraced
in the sermon. It should be a veritable theme, not a mere
title. It should not be complex, but simple, and it should
be intelligently expressed.

VIII. Note the relation of this special subject which
is derived from the text to the general subject of the
passage from which the text is taken: it should be in harmony therewith. If one is to write upon the text, "What
is your life? For ye are a vapor that appeareth for a
little time, and then vanisheth away," his sermon must
be in keeping with the trend of the entire paragraph,
which was written to prevent self-confidence and our
foolish boasting, and to teach humble dependence upon
the pleasure of Almighty God.

IX. The value of the analysis which the preacher has
made will now appear in the division of his subject. The
material which he has derived from the passage by his
minute study of it will furnish him with his divisions and
his application. This matter, however, will be more particularly treated in a subsequent chapter.

X. Finally, the preacher should recapitulate, not simply to repeat what has already been said, but to gather up that which he has derived from his text in intelligent, practical terms, wherein the distinct lesson of the text is enforced and the duty of observing it.

Let us sum up what has been said above in the following words from Dr. Shedd: "Originality is not the power of making a communication of truth, but of apprehending one. Two great communications have been made to him: the one in the book of nature and the other in the book of revelation. If truth has been conveyed he is the most original thinker who is most successful in reading it just as it reads and expounding it just as it stands. If truth has been imparted by special revelation he is the original thinker who is most successful in its interpretation—who is most accurate in analyzing its living elements, and most genial and cordial in receiving them into his own mental and moral being." So he says: "There has been no creation but only a development, no absolute authorship but only an explication. Yet how fresh and original has been the mental process! There has been all the enthusiasm, all the stimulation, all the flow of life and feeling that attends the discovery of a new continent or a new star.

> "Then feels he like some watcher of the skies
>   When a new planet swims into his ken;
> Or like stout Cortez, when with eagle eyes
>   He stared at the Pacific and all his men
> Looked at each other with a wild surmise
>   Silent, upon a peak in Darien."

PLANNING THE SERMON.

PLANNING THE SERMON.

I. Importance of arrangement.
  1. To the preacher.
  2. To the people.
II. Fundamental qualities.
  1. Unity.
  2. Organization.
  3. Progress.

Read Howson's "Hints," in Bishop Ellicott's "Homiletical and Pastoral Lectures;" Dyke's "Christian Minister," Chap. XXI; Slattery's "Present Day Preaching," I.

IV.

PLANNING THE SERMON.

When the text has been finally determined and the passage from which it is taken carefully analyzed, the preacher will begin the formal work of sermon construction. He will attempt to arrange his thoughts upon some consistent and orderly plan.

I. The importance of logical arrangement. It has been said again and again by writers upon rhetoric that it is arrangement which makes a discourse, and some have counseled it with a degree of iteration most emphatic. It is indeed true that there is no such thing as a discourse in the proper sense of that word without arrangement, and more than this—without *proper* arrangement. A collection of ideas, however well they may be separately expressed, is no more a discourse than a collection of materials, however good, is a building, or a company in uniform, however fine, is an army. It is perhaps a frequent fault in sermonizing that the material is misarranged even when some attempt has been made to arrange it. Dean Howson, in one of his admirable essays, divides sermons into two classes, borrowing as he says an image from natural history. He calls them "vertebrate" and "molluscan," and continues, "I have heard some discourses from the pulpit which might have been turned round with little disadvantage, and preached from the end almost as well as from the beginning; but sermons of the molluscan kind produce little impression on the congregation for this reason, that it is impossible to attend to them." And again: "In a good sermon there must be a skeleton, though the skeleton need not be seen. By all means make use of abundant drapery if you please, but be sure there is a true skeleton underneath. The richest drapery placed upon a mere stick is only a scarecrow." Slattery says, "The amorphous thing called a sermon may arouse a certain flutter of passing emotion, as a bell which has been ringing for twenty minutes, but it is not likely to leave any important lesson behind." He draws a parallel between Robertson upon one side of the Atlantic and Phillips Brooks upon the other. He says: "Brooks always said vital and illuminating things through his sermons, but there was not the angular structure of Robertson's sermons which tells of strength and growth. The sermons that people will read are some indication of what sort of sermons will help people in our day." So Robertson continues to be read more than Brooks, although the latter was in his time the greater pulpit orator, and filled a larger place.

1. Arrangement is important to the preacher himself to begin with. It stimulates his thought, it promotes ideas and so affects the preacher's own interest and enthusiasm in his subject. "It grows upon him." The very arrangement of his ideas provokes the incoming of other ideas, and leads to that careful discrimination in the relation of ideas which alone deserves the name of thought.

2. It is equally important also to the audience. It renders the preacher's discourse both more intelligible and more instructive. The listener is very much more likely to be pleased and profited when he is able to mark the stages of growth which are found in the sermon plan. Every one admires orderly thinking. There is a pleasure in procession, the "getting somewhere." In this age of

the world we like to get there rapidly, without being delayed too long upon the way. It is a day of fast locomotion, and so long as the locomotion is not perilous it is every way profitable. Even so in sermonizing.

But the audience is more than pleased; it is also persuaded. Some have even declared that arrangement is the first element in eloquence rather than "magnetism," so-called, or manner, or any such thing. Cicero defined eloquence as "the continuous movement of the soul." Certainly if eloquence consists in carrying the audience, it can not be accomplished without proper arrangement.

And once more the importance to the audience resides in the fact that the impression created by such a sermon is more likely to be abiding. A well arranged sermon is the only kind of discourse which is ever remembered. It is true that the audience may remember brilliant sayings or striking epigrams, introduced into the body of a discourse which is poorly arranged, but they will not remember its governing thought. Whereas, while they may never be able to recall particular details of the persuasive sermon, its movement and purpose will abide and it will have done its work in the instruction of their minds and the molding of their characters.

II. On what principle then is a sermon to be arranged? What are the fundamental qualities of discourse? They are usually given as three, though they are not always stated in the same terms. By all writers unity is put first, and there is no disagreement with regard to the term. The second is usually called order, and the third movement, or proportion, or something of the like. We prefer to designate them as, (1) unity; (2) organization; and (3) progress. Let us define them.

1. Unity. Some writers seem to have some difficulty in defining this term, though all have evidently the same

idea of what it really is. Hoyt does not really define it at all, although he says it is singleness of idea, not sameness of idea, and proceeds through several sentences with his explanation. Slattery says unity "implies diversity within itself. When the diversity is so arranged as to lead straight on to the center and pith of a subject" that is unity. We define unity as that quality of a discourse whereby each part bears the same or a similar relation to the subject, and also to every other part. Unity forbids our growing figs upon thistles, or in any other way bringing those things together which are unrelated. A "monster" in the old mythology was a being with incongruous organs, like the centaur or the minotaur. It was not physiologically possible for a man's head and shoulders to rest upon the body of a horse, nor is it rhetorically possible to bring together such incongruities in a discourse, and the sermon in which this is done is monstrous. Therefore, in planning the sermon it must be so arranged as that the parts shall be fitly associated together. The sermonizer should frequently ask himself, Does this idea proceed from the same general source as the other ideas of my sermon? and can this idea be properly associated with that one? and do both this and that one tend to the same general end?

And yet it must be observed that unity is not uniformity. That would be like imagining a man who was all arms, or a wheel which was all spokes. Indeed, there can be no unity without diversity and without variety. Just as a tree, which is a complete unity, consists of its roots, trunk, branches, leaves, and fruit; so also a sermon. Dr. Dykes has a very fine and somewhat extended passage on the subject of unity in which he considers it under several heads. The substance is as follows:

(1) Unity of theme: by which he means a proposi-

tion which states with precision the subject of his discourse. It is the germinal idea around which materials shall gather. Such a theme, he says, will much assist the purity of the preacher's discourse, more particularly if he sets it down in writing in the form of a proposition.

(2) Unity of aim. By this he refers not simply to the design which the preacher has in producing his sermon, but also to its scope. It is an address spoken for some practical purpose, and the very planning of its construction is determined by the object which the preacher has in view. He reminds us that many subjects lend themselves to a multiplicity of uses, but that the preacher must select one use out of the number, and keep himself to that. His unity of aim should be apparent particularly near the end of the discourse, in which the preacher is sometimes tempted to divide the force of his application between a variety of "lessons" which he thinks may be derived from his consideration of the subject.

(3) Unity of tone. He means by this the pitch or key of feeling of the speaker, and his manner of speaking. This will appear in his arrangement and in his material. This tone is not a monotone, but what musicians call a "crescendo," increasing in volume and effect. The musical term also suggests that any part of the discourse should never strike the listener as in violent disharmony with the rest.

2. Organization. We define organization as the orderly arrangement of material, subject to some dominating idea or principle. This domination should appear throughout the entire sermon. It is derived, of course, from the text, and from the general subject which the preacher obtains from his text; but it should control all the separate parts of the discourse. In this respect the sermon, with its various ideas, is like an army in that it

is not only arranged in some suitable form, but is also arranged subject to certain elements of control. Slattery says "the real sermon ought, of course, to have a commanding idea, but this idea ought to be broken up into sections so that people will feel that they are not perpetually coming to a point, and then running off to do it again in a little different way, but that they are gradually filling the different angles of the idea with significance."

Organization, then, is something different from order. Order is mathematical; organization is logical. It is at this point that many sermonizers commit an unconscious error. They suppose that they have proper arrangement because they have embodied in their discourse a collection of separate ideas to each of which they have attached certain numbers in order—first, second, third, and so on. But though there be separate ideas, and though they be arranged in order and numbered consecutively, and though there may be a certain relation between them consistent with unity, yet there is no apparent control or government which causes them to be arranged as they are, and promotes their larger efficiency.

If a preacher is not able to organize his thoughts as suggested, they are very likely to run wild, and unity itself will be disturbed, if not indeed destroyed, so that the relation between unity and organization is intimate and reciprocal. Dean Howson says: "It is quite a mistake to suppose that the poor and the ignorant do not feel the power of order in that which is addressed to them. They do feel the power though they may not understand the reason," and he quotes Vinet, who, however, uses the term "order" in the sense of organization. "Order is the characteristic of a true sermon. A sermon can not exist in any other way. Without order one would not know what to call it." The preacher then should ask himself with reference to his quality of the discourse, Why this remark in this place? Why not in some other place? What particular purpose does it serve? Will it be apparent to those to whom I preach that my purpose is being served by it? Does it obey orders, so to speak? Is it suggested by the main idea? Is it compelled by it, is it subservient to it? Oh, the value and beauty of such arrangement as this would indicate!

3. Progress. This is our word for the third quality of the discourse. There must be positive advance as the sermon proceeds, both intellectual and spiritual. It must move on from the less to the more profound, from the simple to the abstruse, from the lower level to the higher levels. It is this positive procession of ideas that constitutes what we call "thought." There is no moving in a circle, no vibration like that of a pendulum; no mere "marking time."

A certain most interesting trick is performed by some traveling magicians, in the course of which a seed is planted in a pot, in the sight of the audience, which quickly germinates and in a few moments sends up a stock, develops branches, bursts into bloom, and bears fruit which rapidly ripens and is distributed among the audience. Such, indeed, is the very "trick" in proper discourse. Only the ripening of a sermon takes much more time.

The simpler seed thoughts are introduced in the opening of the sermon that come to fruitage in the close. The people are encouraged to think, and think deeply, and thence the preacher proceeds to those higher things which are not readily apprehended even by the Christian mind. If now the separate divisions of the sermon manifest no such progress, it is indicative of the fact that both the unity and the organization are at fault, for the right unity and the right organization will tend toward the right progress. The sermon is not properly planned if the three elements do not appear. Beecher once remarked in his characteristic way that some sermons reminded him of the sausages in a meat shop. They had unity and organization of a certain kind, but no procession. Cut them off at any point, and the same thing was furnished. Let it not be so with our sermons. Let each successive part be bigger, weightier, more persuasive than the preceding, and all tending to some great conclusion.

THE ATTACK UPON THE TEXT.

THE ATTACK UPON THE TEXT

It introduces the introduction.
  The preacher's first words.
  Answer to the inquiry of the audience.
The subject to be at once announced.
  Newspaper work.
Examples from great preachers.

Read the sermons of the preachers quoted in the chapter, or other sermons, noting the illustrations or violations of the rule.

V.

THE ATTACK UPON THE TEXT.

What is ordinarily called the "Introduction" is supposed to be the first thing in the sermon. This term is defined in the dictionary as "a preliminary treatise," and with such a treatise many a preacher begins his discourse.

But what of those words with which this "preliminary treatise"—if there be one—is itself introduced? How shall the sermon start off?

The preacher having chosen his text and set himself to prepare his sermon upon it, should ask himself: "What shall I first say? How shall I in the presence of my hearers attack this text?" In order to answer that question he must ask himself another: My text having been announced, what is the probable attitude of my congregation with regard to it? And this second question can be best answered by his asking himself again, What is my own state of mind and my own attitude toward the text when I hear it announced by a preacher other than myself? The answer will no doubt occur to him upon very little consideration. His own attitude under such circumstances, and so likewise the attitude of the congregation to which he may be called to preach, is generally—we might say always—one of inquiry. The question may not be distinctly framed by them, but it certainly is in their minds, "What does that mean?" "How will the preacher use this text?" "What does he propose to tell us with regard to it?" and "How will he tell us?" The preacher must at once respond to this spirit of inquiry. Such questions as these must be answered before he proceeds to the discussion of his theme. This is his "attack upon the text."

Very much depends upon the way in which the preacher shall attack his text. It may mean the command of the full attention of the congregation from the start, or it may mean the incipient loss of their interest and attention, which consequently it will be very hard to regain.

He is not, therefore, to engage in some digression which the minds of the congregation will not readily associate with the text, or which they may not readily perceive to be pertinent to his subject. Least of all should he begin with some figure of speech, or some illustration for which he has not prepared the minds of his congregation. He should relate no anecdote, and it is doubtful if he should even refer to the context from which the text is derived, the people to whom it was addressed, or the author from whom it proceeded. All these things may be suitably done in a little while, but they are not to be done in the very first sentences of a discourse. Some preachers wander from their text at the very outset. Instead of beginning with its very words and that which they believe they contain, they begin at a distance from the text and approach it by ways and means which the congregation can not possibly apprehend.

The text is to be attacked, therefore, by bringing its meaning and the mind of the hearer together at once. The preacher should tell them in his very first sentences exactly that which he believes the text contains, and exactly that which he proposes to do with the text in his discourse. Generally this is done by the immediate announcement of his subject. Indeed, this is the best way in which to attack the text, provided the subject is stated in succinct terms, easily comprehended, readily associated with the text, and foreshadowing all the various parts of the sermon which are to follow. Sometimes, however, it is not fully convenient nor entirely practicable for the preacher to announce his subject. He has a clear idea of what the subject is, but he can not express it in a few words, and if he were definitely to announce a subject it would require too much circumlocution. In such a case he omits the mention of a particular subject, but he does substantially the same thing—he tells the people that which he proposes to talk about.

There are some who seem to imagine that the bare announcement of the text is sufficient, as though in quoting it the preacher was indicating to his congregation just that which he proposed to teach. But that this is not altogether true will appear upon a little thought, and even if it were entirely true it is not sufficient; because the text is God's word to the preacher, and the preacher must translate it into his own language. It is what God has inspired to be said; but it is necessary that the preacher in discoursing upon this text should express his sense of that which God has said; his own understanding of the Divine Word as though he were to say, "I understand this to mean thus and so, to set forth such and such principles, to encourage such and such graces," and so on.

Sometimes the text is of such a character that, though it be properly selected and properly interpreted, an explanatory statement is needed before the preacher can state definitely that which he finds in it. In such a case it may be well for the preacher, before calling attention to the particular words which he employs as his text, to read the paragraph in which it is found, to indicate, without mentioning its words, that his text is to be taken from a portion of this paragraph, and then to inform his people that he desires to explain something before the text itself is announced. This something which he must explain may be found in the occasion, in some peculiar providential circumstance, or in some slight obscurity, not of the text itself, but of the propriety of its use. Such a necessity, however, is comparatively rare, and it will be but seldom that the preacher will have need of any preparatory statement or explanation. Ordinarily he should attack his text as has been indicated.

There is only one kind of literature in which suspense is admissible; that is romance. The best novel is usually considered the one in which the plot is the longest concealed, and in which it is the most difficult for the ordinary reader to determine what the author means by his arrangement of scenes and characters. In all other literature, of whatever name or nature, that author is the best rhetorician, and gives most satisfaction to his readers, whose purpose is made distinctly clear from the beginning. Newspaper work, perhaps, corresponds more closely to sermonizing in this respect than any other form of literary work. The very name indicates it; the daily journal is issued to convey news to the people, and the gospel is "good news." Occasionally there is an editor who seems to think that the proper way in which to introduce news is by obscure headlines, catchwords, or something that is only suggested by the body of the article; but the best editors are not given to such mistakes. Those newspapers that are most in favor with the reading public are those in which the headlines distinctly announce the news that is to be given beneath them, or if the article be of an editorial character the political or social subject that is to be discussed. A certain editor's advice to his correspondents is not out of place in this connection. He told them through the columns of his own paper that if they had some item of interest to communicate it was well to introduce it with some careful and elaborate piece of rhetorical work, in which they should exert themselves to render their composition as elegant and classical as possible. This introduction was to be followed by the plainest possible statement of the facts in the case, without ornamentation or embellishment, and with no figures of speech or illustrations that did not make the matter more distinctly clear. He again advised them to follow this statement with a peroration in which their most elegant writing should be done. All their flights of fancy were to be reserved for the peroration, all their most elaborate work. "Then," he added in conclusion, "cut off the introduction and the peroration, and send us the rest."

The attack upon the text must, therefore, be in the simplest and plainest language which the writer can command, the simplest and plainest to be found in his whole sermon. It should be modest and unpretentious, and directed immediately toward the meaning of the text. This is sure to bring the audience into sympathy with the preacher. They feel that he is intent upon delivering them a message, and that a message from the Word of God. Their interest is at once aroused and their attention is sure to be secured. Preachers sometimes fail to do this simple work in the attacking of their text, because they appear to think that it reflects upon their ability as rhetoricians and as orators. The very reverse is the case. A young boy, who was attending a certain academy, was requested by his father to go with him to hear a distinguished speaker upon an important subject. The lad, in his boyish way, replied, "Well, father, is he an eminent man?" The father, little imagining what was in the boy's mind, and supposing that he would be the more inclined to go if his answer was in the affirmative, replied, "Yes, my son, he is a very eminent man." "Then," said the boy, "please do not ask me to go." The reason for the boy's reply is apparent. He supposed that eminent men always began their addresses, as well as continued them, in language which a boy could not understand nor appreciate.

While this method of attacking the text belongs distinctly to the New Homiletics, it may be observed that it is the method adopted by many of the most distinguished and useful preachers of the past. Let us observe a few examples.

Archibald Alexander. Text, Jude 21, "Keep yourselves in the love of God." Subject, "Keeping alive the love of God." His first sentences are, "The phrase 'love of God' has two significations in the New Testament. First, it imports God's love to us; secondly, our love to God."

Frederick William Robertson. Text, John 16:31, 32: "Jesus answered them, Do ye now believe? Behold the hour cometh, yea is now come, that ye shall be scattered every man to his own, and shall leave Me alone; and yet I am not alone, because the Father is with Me." Subject, "The Loneliness of Christ." First sentences: "There are two kinds of solitude; the first consisting of insulation in space; the other of isolation of the spirit. The first is simply separation by distance."

Charles H. Spurgeon. Text, 2 Corinth. 8:9, "For ye know the grace of our Lord Jesus Christ, that, though He was rich, yet for your sakes He became poor, that ye through His poverty might be rich." Subject, "The Condescension of Christ." First sentence, "The apostle in this chapter was endeavoring to stir up the Christians to liberality."

Thomas Chalmers. Text, Isaiah 27:4, 5: "Fury is not in Me: who would set the briers and thorns against Me in battle? I would go through them, I would burn them together. Or let him take hold of My strength, that he may make peace with Me; and he shall make peace with Me." Subject, "Fury not in God." First sentences, "There are three distinct lessons in this text. The first, that fury is not in God: the second, that He does not want to glorify Himself by the death of sinners— "Who would set the thorns and briers against Me in battle?" The third, the invitation, "Take hold of My strength, that you may make peace with Me; and you shall make peace with Me."

Edward M. Goulburn. Text, James 3:2-4, "For in many things we offend all. If any man offend not in word, the same is a perfect man and able also to bridle the whole body. Behold we put bits in the horses' mouths, that they may obey us; and we turn about their whole body. Behold also the ships, which though they be so great, and are driven of fierce winds, yet are they turned about with a very small helm, whithersoever the governor listeth." Subject, "The Government of the Tongue." First sentences: "The apostle is speaking in these verses of the government of the tongue. And he says of the government of the tongue two distinct things which are not to be confounded together"—which two things he briefly explains are these: The government of the tongue is an index of a man's whole moral state, and also a determining instrument.

These illustrations furnish a distinct variety of subjects and of texts; but in every case the preacher goes to work at once to enlighten his hearers. There is no suspense. Their inquiry is immediately met. There is no better homilete in our own day than W. L. Watkinson; and this method of attacking the text is most characteristic of his pulpit style. Here are some of his opening sentences. Texts, Rom. 7:17 and 1 Cor. 15:10, "Note, first, the significance of these passages." Text, Mark 12:34, "First, 'the Kingdom of God'—let us briefly inquire into the meaning of this phrase." Text, 1 Tim. 6:19. "In speaking of a life that is life indeed, St. Paul implies that all life is not such; but that many live a false life."

Let us learn this lesson.

THE INTRODUCTION.

THE INTRODUCTION

The Classic Custom.
   The Method in the New Homiletics.

I. Purposes of the Introduction.
   1. To engage interest in the subject.
   2. To prepare the mind to understand, appreciate and accept.

II. Qualities of a good Introduction.
   1. Germane.
   2. Single.

III. Sources.
   1. Cognate to the theme.
   2. The Occasion.
   3. The Context.

IV. Special Faults.
   1. Anticipation.
   2. Apology.

Read Lyman's "Preaching in the New Age," Chap. V; Watson's "Cure of Souls," Chap. I; Shedd's "Homiletics," Chap. VIII.

VI.

THE INTRODUCTION.

We use this term "Introduction," in the sense already explained, namely, that of a preliminary treatise. The lack of proper sermon preparation usually appears more emphatically in the introduction than in any other portion of the discourse; and it may almost be said that a bad introduction is worse than any other bad feature in formal discourse. While many of the best preachers of the past, as we have shown, proceeded at once to the attack upon the text, yet the Old Homiletics usually provided for a somewhat elaborate introduction, and one that was not always germane to the discourse. Cicero himself, though a master of rhetoric in very many respects, positively advised an introduction in character foreign to the general subject of the oration, and it is said of him that he often wrote such introductions when he did not know in advance to what oration or essay they might be attached. It was in his mind an avenue of approach sometimes very circuitous, and leading through a variety of scenery, so as to furnish somewhat of a surprise when its end was finally reached. He calls it the "aditus ad causam." But Cicero himself was a frequent illustration of the violation of his own principles. Some of his best orations begin without any introduction in the sense in which the word is sometimes understood. For example his oration against Catiline begins abruptly, "When, O Catiline, do you mean to cease abusing our patience?" Other illustrations will suggest themselves.

Following, however, what appeared to be the classic models, the preachers of a former generation sought to introduce their sermons in much the same way. Vinet directs the preacher to lead the audience very carefully to his real subject by its partial concealment. His introduction should lie near to his subject, but should not be directly connected with it. This sort of an introduction, however, is ruled out by the New Homiletics. Dr. Dykes significantly says that "time is precious, and none of it should be wasted on introductory matter, unless it is judged requisite for certain very important reasons." The main thing, he says, is to create an impression on the audience from the first that you have something to say worth hearing, and are so much in earnest that you mean them to listen to it. Dr. Shedd says, "There is not ordinarily any need of an exordium in sacred eloquence" for the reasons which the classic authors sought to connect with it. Dr. Dabney says, "A formal exordium is not to be too much insisted upon." Bishop Quayle says: "The preacher must come at his theme at once. He must not deal in prolix preludes. He must leap like a man from a moving train and touch the ground on a dead run. He must instantly throw a challenge to a man's brain. He must flash his sword at the outset of the fray. Then the auditors will not care to drowse." These quotations are sufficient to show that what is ordinarily called an introduction is not popular with the best authorities upon this subject. In very many cases the attack upon the text, as it has been already defined, is a sufficient introduction of itself, and the preacher's sermon would in many cases be much better if nothing were added to it.

Dr. Watson says that there should be something of

an introduction to a sermon, "especially when a man is young—an introduction which used to extend back to the creation of the world and the purposes of God, and now embraces the latest results of criticism on the book from which the text is taken. Whether our fathers liked to approach a subject through an underground passage of theological archæology may be doubtful; but it is certain that their children have no wish to arrive at an ethical principle of prophecy through a museum of the higher criticism. This generation desires to be ushered into the subject of the day without wearisome preliminaries, and nothing will more certainly take the edge off the appetite than a laborious preface. Very likely it must be written, or else the minister would not get further, but it ought then to be burned as having served its purpose. It is really getting up steam, and it is no use inviting passengers on board till the vessel is ready to start."

Introductions are sometimes prolonged by including in them that which might much better be reserved for the body of the discourse, and in sermon preparation the preacher should always ask himself in advance whether that which he regards as introduction is really introduction in any proper sense, or whether, with some slight modification, it might not better be inserted at a later point.

Giving these considerations all the weight which they should have, it is yet important that we should consider the purposes of an introduction and its proper qualities.

I. What, then, are the purposes of an introduction? Sometimes the only purpose which an introduction serves, or which the preacher seeks to serve thereby, is simply to "kill time." It not infrequently happens that he has considerable good material, sufficient to interest the audience for a certain space of time, say fifteen minutes, but he is in doubt about being able to properly prolong the discussion of his theme beyond that point. In order, therefore, that he may not seem to have nothing to say, and desiring to reserve the best that he has to say, he labors through an introduction which he knows possesses but little value, except to prolong his sermon to what he regards as the necessary half-hour. It would be far better in this case for the preacher to err upon the other side, if indeed it be an error, and preach but fifteen minutes. It is always a serious mistake to talk when one has nothing to say.

The proper purposes of an introduction are the following:

1. To engage interest in the subject which the preacher purposes to discuss. Such is the chief purpose which Cicero attached to an introduction, claiming that he had learned from the Greeks to "adopt such an exordium as to make the hearers favorable to us, willing to be informed, and attentive." It is doubtful, however, if even Cicero would have made this statement had he been a modern preacher, inasmuch as modern audiences are supposed to be interested in any subject which the preacher may present. There is a vast difference between a speech in the Roman Forum and a speech delivered in a Christian church. However, it is well, in introducing a subject which might possibly arouse antagonism, to allay the prejudices with which the preacher might otherwise contend. There are some subjects presented even from the Christian pulpit which are not altogether palatable, and it is well that the preacher should disarm criticism at the start. This is not to be done, however, by magnifying the theme, nor by emphasizing the importance of the subject in advance, but by saying

something with regard to it that will show it to be well worth considering; by promoting that spirit of inquiry with regard to it about which we have already spoken, or by indicating that it is to be pursued in a spirit of charity and conciliation.

2. The second purpose of an introduction is to prepare the mind to (1) understand the truth which is to be presented, (2) to appreciate its importance, and (3) to accept its conclusions. These three things belong together, and the preacher should have them in mind in every introduction which he writes. Inasmuch as it is his purpose to prepare the people to understand his subject, this is the place for such preliminary remarks as are necessary to its full definition. Fundamental instruction is given in the introduction with regard to the terms employed, either in the Scripture from which the preacher quotes, or in his own discussion of the theme, and for that general clearing of the ground which shall make the whole discussion intelligible. As it is his purpose in the introduction to prepare them to appreciate the subject, he must have it in mind that the appreciation is not to be for his own work, in argument, illustration, or anything of that kind; or even in his conclusions, so far as they are personal to himself; but to appreciate the truth which lies behind it all. The people must be prepared to consider it worthy, timely, practical. He is to prepare them to accept it. This will appear rather in the spirit in which the introduction is written than in anything which it may contain. Nowhere in the whole discourse is it so important that the preacher display a kindly spirit, intent upon winning the souls that are before him. He must not place himself in a hostile attitude, but in a most friendly one toward his congregation. His introduction is for this very purpose, that he and

they may come to terms at once, and be disposed to enter into a discussion that shall be mutually friendly and forbearing.

II. What qualities, then, are in order to these purposes? What are the qualities of a good introduction? We answer:—

1. It should contain nothing foreign to the purpose of the discourse. For this very reason it is sometimes advisable that the introduction should not be prepared at the beginning of the preacher's writing, as is so frequently done, but that it should be reserved until the sermon has been otherwise completed, or nearly so. It very frequently occurs that a preacher in the preparation of his sermon begins with an introduction which he supposes, at the outset, to be exactly adapted to the discourse which is in preparation, but as he proceeds his viewpoint is somewhat altered; thoughts occur to him which he did not anticipate, and he even reaches a somewhat different conclusion than that at which he expected to arrive when he began: yet his introduction remains, and his discourse is out of joint. He is like a traveler who starts for some distant point, but is diverted by certain circumstances so that he arrives at a different place than that which he expected to enter. Dr. Watson in his "Cure of Souls" has certain characteristic rules for the preparation of a sermon which he states succinctly in the following words: (1) selection, (2) separation, (3) elimination, (4) meditation, (5) elaboration, and (6) revision. The second process of which he writes, "separation," should be the characteristic of a good introduction. It should distinctly set by itself the course of thought which the preacher intends to pursue. This would greatly aid him in its delivery. "A sermon," says Dr. Watson, "ought to be a monograph, not an encyclopedia." A monograph is the result of separation.

2. A good introduction should be single, not complex. There should be just one door to the edifice which he is constructing, with not even what we call a "storm-door" in front of it. It should therefore be brief. Dr. Howe remarked, with regard to a certain preacher, that he was so long "laying the cloth" that he did not feel certain that any meal would be served. Preachers should remember that our age is impatient of the superfluous. "All noble art," says Dr. Lyman, "begins with rejection. Cut away all the marble which is not statue." Said Michael Angelo—

> "The more the marble wastes
> The more the statue grows."

"Do not hammer the head off the nail." Robert Louis Stevenson aptly remarks that "to add irrelevant matter is not to lengthen, but to bury." Such a remark pertains more to the introduction than to any other portion of the discourse. There are some preachers whose sermons are chiefly introduction, and there are a few whose sermons are all introduction. Some of them are masters of their art in a certain way, because there is such a thing in both rhetoric and theology as "Introduction," which means the elaborate preparation for some study or group of studies which is to be pursued at length. So there is a small but important class of preachers who construct most profitable sermons by talking at great length about a text without ever discussing the truth which the text contains. The people, however, are thereby led to reflect upon it for themselves, and upon their own reflection, to appreciate it. But such work is not at all to be counseled. It belongs to unusual minds.

III. The sources of a proper introduction are very hard to determine—so much in this case depends upon the theme. The sources from which the introduction to one sermon may be gathered are altogether different from those upon which the introduction to another sermon may be drawn; yet a few suggestions with regard to this matter may not be out of place.

1. The introduction should be taken from those sources which are cognate to the theme. If the text is one which refers to the phenomena of nature, then nature is a suitable source from which to derive one's introduction; and so with regard to other matters.

2. The occasion may sometimes furnish a suitable source for the introduction. The sermon may relate to some special exigency of the times, or to some special movement in society, or to some special activity on behalf of the Church, in which case the occasion will furnish the introduction.

3. Sometimes it is to be derived from the context, particularly so if it is necessary to consider the context in order to the full understanding of the passage which the preacher has selected.

IV. The special faults which are found in introductions have been in a measure already noted, but there are two remaining against which the preacher should be particularly guarded.

1. The most frequent fault, and one which may be said to be the very worst possible, is Anticipation. It is always destructive of interest and often destructive of profit. By "anticipation" we mean the introduction of any kind of material in advance of its proper place, and before the audience is prepared to understand or to receive it. Dr. Dabney well says with regard to this matter: "The introduction must not embody a thought which is essential to the main discussion. This is an error of structure to which the inexperienced and impulsive writer is prone. Approaching the work of composition with a

mind fired by the subject, he finds those ideas which are cardinal to it prominent in his thoughts, and he can scarcely refrain from pouring out some one of them the moment he begins. The consequence is that when he proceeds in earnest to deal with his proposition he will find he has anticipated essential matter. He has now only the choice between a bald repetition of his first idea, or else a leaving of his argument fragmentary. A stone which is absolutely necessary to close his arch has been already laid in the threshold." This is exactly the way in which anticipation comes about. The preacher has been long engaged in thought with regard to the subject which he is about to present. He has thought it through very carefully and it has grown upon him. He has added one thing to another until he has reached certain conclusions which have been a source of profit to his own soul; but he does not consider that it would be better for him to lead his audience over the very way in which he has himself traveled; that, in fact, they can reach his conclusions by no other method. Forgetting all this, he places in the very introduction of his discourse those considerations which in his own study of the subject came at the close.

Anticipation is of two kinds: (1) It may be logical, in which case those conclusions which are the result of argument are given before the argument itself; (2) It may be spiritual, in which case duty is enforced, or truth is commended, before the ground upon which that duty rests has been stated, or before the reasons for the belief of that truth have been given. Both are common and equally disastrous.

2. A second serious fault in an introduction is Apology. We may speak with regard to this matter without qualification. *An apology is never to be made.*

Sometimes the preacher will feel it well to make an explanation, not so much by way of excusing himself, as by way of rectifying some mistake, or what not, upon his part; but even such an explanation had better be made at the close of a sermon than at its beginning. An apology is never in place, least of all in an introduction. It ministers nothing but weakness to the preacher's discourse. If he himself feels that it is inadequately wrought out, or presented without due preparation, he will only make its defects the more apparent by an apology, in directing the attention of the congregation to them. Frequently, however, his apology is a sheer mistake. That for which he apologizes really needs no apology, and if nothing of the kind is offered it may come with greater beauty and power to the listener than the preacher had himself expected.

The preacher may be tempted to present an apology either for the subject or for himself, but he should never present any subject for which it is necessary for him to apologize. And the apology for one's self is an excuse which a preacher has no right to make. If he has done the best that he could do under the circumstances, let him speak in humble reliance upon God, and in the expectation of a blessing upon his best. He can do no more.

The old proverb says, "Well begun, half done." So we may say with regard to the introduction. If it is clear, clean, and direct, if it serves those proper purposes for which it is prepared, the sermon which follows it is likely to be acceptable.

A plain worshiper, who had been much upon the sea in the days of the old sailing vessels, remarked with regard to the sermons of a certain minister that they were "clipper-built." Those who recall the special design of such vessels will understand his reference. The peculiar quality of the old clippers was in the formation of their prows, rather than in the general form of the vessel. The "cut-water" was sharp, clean, and projected backward upon lines which offered the least possible resistance to the waves. Therefore they were fast sailers, while at the same time capable of carrying considerable freight. And the introduction to the sermon is the "cut-water;" it, too, should offer the least possible resistance. It should be no burden upon the attention of the congregation, but rather the reverse. A scow may carry more freight than a clipper, but its sailing qualities are so imperfect that it is capable of making but a single passage while the other vessel is making half a dozen. The clipper is the more effective, and there are some sermons weighted with an immense amount of learning, thought, and argument, which are not effective, only because they are not "clipper-built."

SERMON BODY.

SERMON BODY.

Variety advisable.

I. There should be divisions.
Proper character.
When they should be stated in advance.

II. Number of divisions.
The text governs.

III. Nature of divisions.
1. Comprehensive.
2. Coordinate.
3. Flowing.
4. Distinct.
5. Unconventional.
6. Original.

IV. Order of divisions.
Rhetorical rather than logical.

Read Kern's "Ministry to the Congregation," XIV; Pattison's "Making of the Sermon," XI; Beecher's "Yale Lectures," Vol. I; IX.

VII.

SERMON BODY.

We call that portion of the sermon which follows the introduction "sermon body." This really is the sermon. The introduction should possess no value except as an introduction. The same remark may be made with regard to the conclusion, as we shall presently see. The special value which attaches to this discourse, as sermon work, relates to the sermon body. This portion of the sermon has been called by different names by different writers upon the subject, such as the "argument" or the "discussion" and a variety of other terms; but we prefer to discard them altogether because they are not applicable to all sorts of sermons.

This remark should be made before we consider the character of the sermon body—that the preacher should cultivate variety therein. He is sure to be ultimately wearisome to his congregation if his sermons are all built upon the same plan, or upon plans that closely resemble each other; and yet in every sermon there should be some plan. The principal thing which is to be urged with regard to it is that it should present the development of some theme. There should be positive thought in it, by which the hearer shall be carried along from one position to another unto the culmination.

I. Should there be divisions in the sermon body? There is but one reasonable answer to this question. By all means.

It is true that certain objections have been made to the ordinary practice with regard to this matter. It has been said, for example, that it interrupts the flow of thought. There are those who claim that a preacher should go where his thoughts carry him in the composition of a sermon. Again it is said that it is unfavorable to the unity of a discourse, that when divisions are multiplied unity is impaired. Again it is said that it strains the play of the emotions and defeats the best purposes of the orator, which should include the play upon the feelings of those to whom he speaks. It is said that it deadens a discourse, deprives it of life, and reduces it to a mechanical production. These objections do not seem to possess great weight, and very much may be said to set them entirely aside. Dr. Watson well says that educated people resent a sermon where A comes in the middle of the alphabet, or S precedes M, and they are not appeased by the fact that they have had all the letters somehow. He adds that it is well worth saying that even the people without culture are dissatisfied with a disorderly sermon. It is disheartening to follow a guide whose progress is a zigzag.

We ought, however, carefully to inquire what it means that a preacher is counseled to divide his sermons into the firstly, secondly, thirdly, and so on. It certainly does not mean that he has a number of separate ideas whose separation he wishes to make emphatic, nor that he imagines a certain number of doctrines or duties should be presented from his text, in the presentation of which he affixes a certain number to each. If a preacher has no other idea of the divisions of a sermon than that which such a consideration would imply, he is very much at fault. There should be no divisions at all in a discourse unless they mark positive gradations in the thought which

3603.

the preacher presents. There is a ceratin law in the mental process which we can not set aside. There is a certain positive order in all rationality. This law requires us to think and speak methodically. It is the demand of our own minds, and it is the demand of the minds of those whom we address, and it is this which furnishes the underlying principle of divisions in a sermon. We are not then to gather up the different parts of a discourse and patch them together in any way so as to make a something which we call a whole, but we are to put them together in such shape that the whole when it is completed is a comprehensive unity, and not a mere conglomeration. It has been well suggested that the work of the painter is a fine illustration of this process. He does not attempt in every picture of some person to show the skeleton, but he must know where the skeleton is, and there must ever be one in his imagination. The great masters were as careful students of anatomy as any surgeon of the present day. They studied from the nude with the most painstaking care, but only in order that their figures when draped should represent things of life. Phillips Brooks practiced what he preached when he declared that the true way to get rid of the boniness of a sermon was not by leaving out the bare bones of the skeleton, but by clothing it with flesh.

It is not necessary then that the divisions should be always stated, but it is important that the hearer should always be able to recognize the processes of the thought. Ordinarily, however, it is better that the divisions should be stated; it is a positive help to the understanding of the process of the thought which the preacher can scarcely afford to omit.

It is not generally well to state them in advance. This is a kind of anticipation which may seriously interfere with the profit of the preacher's work. The audience is apt to run ahead of his thought, and sometimes to connect that with his divisions which he himself is not likely to mention. More than this, there is a certain skill in the surprise power which resides in a division which is not expressed until the preacher is ready to treat it, which he does well to cultivate. If the subject is of such a character that there is some obscurity connected with its statement, or it is likely to be misunderstood or misapplied, it may be well to state the divisions in advance, but this should be the exception and not the rule. Let us illustrate this by a couple of examples. A preacher is engaged, let us say, with the text taken from 1 Sam. 4:22, "The glory is departed from Israel; for the ark of God is taken." It will be remembered that these were the words of the dying wife of Phinehas when she heard of the disaster which had overtaken the Israelites in their battle with the Philistines. The preacher's subject is "The Climax of Calamity." He proposes to show the sense in which the ark of God may be taken to-day. But the text is such, and the theme is such that the congregation may be left in a state of unnecessary and undesirable suspense. There is an obscurity in the text in this —that the audience will not at once see why the glory departed from Israel when the ark of God was taken. The preacher therefore announces his divisions in advance. He says that he will consider the subject in connection with four questions as follows:

(1) What does it mean that the ark of God is taken? (2) Why is the ark of God taken? (3) What is involved in the taking of the ark of God? (4) How is the ark of God restored? It will be seen that the announcement of these divisions in advance will be of great assistance to the preacher in the discussion of his theme, and in no

way involve that anticipation against which he is warned. But suppose the preacher intends to speak concerning the raising of Lazarus from the dead, in connection with the criticism of the unbelieving Jews, as the company proceeded to the sepulcher (John 11:37), "But some of them said, Could not this man, who opened the eyes of him that was blind, have caused that this man also should not die?" The preacher's theme is "Between the House and the Grave," as indicative of the point at which our doubts and misgivings are most likely to arise. He announces his divisions as he treats them, one at a time. (1) The unbelieving Jews here make a tardy confession of what Christ had already done. He had opened the eyes of one that was born blind. (2) Here is a sinister implication of what Christ might have done. He might have caused that Lazarus should not die. (3) Here is woeful doubt and ignorance of what Christ was about to do. He would raise Lazarus again from the dead. The very concealment of these points adds to the beauty and force of the sermon as it proceeds. The preacher, therefore, is to be his own judge in the matter, and no rule can be given of an inflexible character with regard to the statement of divisions in advance. Beecher once said, "When you have finished your sermon, not a man in your congregation should be unable to tell you distinctly what you have done, but when you begin a sermon no man in the congregation ought to be able to tell you what you are going to do."

II. What should be the number of divisions in a sermon? Certainly no fixed rule can be given with regard to this matter. Not only will the number depend upon the text which is treated, and the subject which is announced; but it will also depend in a measure upon the preacher's own habit. Some men do better work with fewer divisions, and others seem to require more. John Bright contrasted his oratory with that of Gladstone in the following words: "Gladstone goes coasting along, turning up every creek and exploring it to its source before he can proceed upon his way, but I have no talent for detail. I hold my course from headland to headland through the great seas." Ordinarily, we believe that it is better that the divisions should be by the headlands rather than by the creeks and bays.

Very frequently the sermon will fall into three divisions. This is so frequently the case that it is often made the subject of jest. Some preachers avoid the threefold division on this account; but there is reason for it. It is often the natural thing, as it is generally the logical process, and no preacher should for one moment think of being debarred from having three divisions in his sermon because it has been made the occasion of so much foolish comment. He who thinks and acts independently in this matter will probably find after a number of years that he has more sermons in which there are three divisions than sermons in which there are any other number. But of one thing he should be particularly cautioned, not to have more divisions than are positively required by the treatment of his subject. It has been well said, "It is better to amplify than to multiply." And one should beware particularly of subdivisions. He might be cautioned to avoid them altogether, for they are generally unprofitable and productive of confused thought. An old Highland game-keeper said of his master that he was a good sportsman, but "he scatters terribly." So it may be with the preacher. This matter also has special reference to extemporaneous preaching, as we shall see in a subsequent portion of our book. He who preaches without notes will find it difficult to recall a number of subdivisions, and will preach better, more easily, and more effectively, when even his main divisions are not unduly multiplied. The only rule, however, which can be given is to permit the text or subject to govern. The divisions should be natural, not artificial. Whether they be few or many, they should be such as are virtually compelled in order to a complete exhibition of the truth which the preacher desires to unfold.

III. What should be the nature of these divisions? The sermonizer is quite likely to fall into fault in this matter if he does not exercise considerable care. He will make distinctions in his divisions which are not real, but imaginary or fictitious. He will make distinctions where none really exist in his text, or he will found his divisions upon the sound or meaning of certainly comparatively unimportant words or passages of his text, whose significance is not at all proportioned to that of other words or passages which he may be inclined to neglect. Dr. Watson says: "Whether a sermon ought to be parceled out into heads is an important question. Three detached sermonettes do not make one sermon, but on the other hand a handful of observations tied together by a text are not an organic whole. It all depends on whether the heads advance, ascend, accumulate, or are independent, disconnected, parallel. Heads are either watertight compartments, in which case you can not pass from one to the other and are exasperated by the iron door; or they are floors of a tower, in which case one will not halt till he reaches the top, because with every fresh ascent he gets a wider view." We suggest then that the following qualities should be found in such divisions as the preacher may find it necessary to make:

1. They should be comprehensive; giving, when all of them are taken together, a full exhibition of the sub-

ject, and each giving in itself a full exhibition of that portion of the subject which the preacher is engaged in discussing.

2. They should be co-ordinate. This relates both to their value and their character. The proposition which is set forth in the one should not be inferior in dignity and force to the proposition which is set forth in the other; nor should the observation which is made in one division be of a totally different character from that which is made in another, relating to some alien subject or one so far apart from the other divisions that they can not properly be joined together.

3. Divisions should be flowing; that is to say, one should pass easily and naturally from the first to the second; indeed, we may even say inevitably. The articulation should be complete. If the sermonizer finds that the transition from one division to another is abrupt or violent, he should so modify either the statement of his divisions, or the method whereby he passes from one to the other, as that the transition shall be readily accomplished. Some one has compared it to the rounds in a ladder; if one of them be taken out, the ascent is exceedingly awkward: or like missing a step in descending a flight of stairs, resulting in a violent jar.

4. The divisions should be distinct. There should be no invasion of the one by the other.

5. They should be unconventional. It is easy enough for a preacher to follow traditional models, and divide his sermons into parts upon that superficial plan which he has derived from insufficient analysis of such sermons as he has heard or read; but

6. The divisions should be the preacher's own. He should present his own view of the subject in his own order. Some of the best preachers which the Church has

ever known have refused for this very reason to consult commentaries of any kind until they had first formed their own plan of a sermon derived from a given passage. One of the worst things a preacher can do, particularly a young preacher, is to derive a plan from some homiletical commentary or similar work, rather than working the plan out for himself. It is the destruction of his originality, and seriously impairs his own logical faculty.

IV. What should be the order of statement in the divisions of a sermon? This question is not easily answered, because logical and rhetorical order do not always correspond, nor is the logical climax by any means the rhetorical climax of a discourse. It depends very much upon two things: first, the preacher's viewpoint; and, second, the object which he has in mind, the purpose which he wishes to accomplish. Sometimes the rhetorical order is the very reverse of the logical order, and the preacher finds it difficult to choose between them. Ordinarily, however, it is better to consult rhetoric than logic. This is because the sermon should be arranged with reference to the conclusion, with reference to the effect which the preacher hopes to produce. He wishes to encourage belief and promote conviction, and bring men to repentance and edify the people of God. He is not concerned for an argumentative triumph, but for a moral one; so his very logic is subjected to rules other than those which the forensic orator would adopt. The words of Henry Ward Beecher upon this subject are so full of good sense and wise suggestion that we may quote them in concluding this chapter. He says: "The greatest number of men, particularly uncultivated people, receive their truths by facts placed in juxtaposition rather than in philosophical sequence. Thus a line of fact or a series of parables will be better adapted to most audiences than a regular unfolding of a train of thought from the germinal point to the fruitful end. The more select portion of an intelligent congregation, on the other hand, sympathize with truth delivered in its higher philosophic forms. There is a distinct pleasure to them in the evolution of an argument. They rejoice to see the structure built up tower upon tower and story upon story. They glow with delight as the long chain is welded link by link, and if the preacher himself be of this mind, and if he receive the commendations of the most thoughtful and cultured of his people, it is quite natural that he should fall wholly under the influence of this style of sermonizing; but so he will feed one mouth and starve a hundred. It is this necessity of adaptation to the innumerable phases of human nature that reacts upon the sermon and determines the form which it shall take."

THE CONCLUSION.

THE CONCLUSION.

The conclusion too often neglected.

It should be in mind from the start.

It should be carefully prepared in advance.
    Impromptu appeals.
    "The corpse of an appeal."

A single conclusion.

Simple and modest.

Read Lyman's "Preaching in the New Age," V; Broadus "Preparation and Delivery of Sermons," Part II, Chap. II.

VIII.

THE CONCLUSION.

The conclusion of the sermon is often neglected. This sometimes results not so much from the preacher's desire or intention, but from his lack of time. He has perhaps done all that he should do by way of study, and the sermon has been well prepared up to a certain point; but beyond that point he either neglected his work trusting, it may be, to the inspiration of the moment, or he failed to find the necessary opportunity for its completion, and therefore the conclusion is crude and unworthy of his theme. It is not an uncommon thing indeed for preachers who are accustomed to speak from manuscript to carefully write out only the body of the discourse. The result in some cases is a lamentable failure. The audience can not fail to discern the point at which the preacher's careful preparation ended and his dependence upon the occasion began. Consequently they are neither pleased nor edified.

No preacher would be guilty of such a mistake, however little the time at his command, who realized that the conclusion was the most important part of the sermon so far as its final effectiveness is concerned. Its preparation may not require the same skill as that which must be exhibited in the introduction. It is always easier to get out of a subject than to get into one. Nevertheless the way in which one dismisses his subject, or seeks to bring it home to the hearts and consciences of a congregation, is the very last thing to be slighted.

Sometimes the preacher seems unable to adapt a conclusion to his sermon worthy the name. This may be because he has been engaged only in the discussion of a theme. He is not intent upon preaching in the full meaning of the word. But the two things are as far apart as the Antipodes. It is not the discussion of a theme in an intellectual fashion, however sacred or solemn the theme may be, which results in preaching, but the personal application of the truth of God. Therefore, the one consideration which must claim our particular attention relative to the conclusion is this very purpose of preaching. It is either the salvation or edification of men—such is its final object. After all, however, these two terms which we have employed may be resolved into one. Salvation may be construed as the single act of Almighty God whereby men are redeemed from sin and translated from the kingdom of darkness into the Kingdom of His dear Son; or it may be construed as a progressive work in which He who has begun it continues to carry it on unto perfection. The sermon, therefore, which is preached primarily to save those that hear must be invested with edifying features; and the sermon which is preached primarily for the edification of the hearers must possess saving features. If this be not so, the sermon in either case is so far forth defective.

The conclusion, therefore, should be in the mind of the preacher from the very beginning of his preparation. He should see it in his text when the text is chosen; and before he begins to arrange his thought. One of the first questions which he should ask himself is this: Why do I preach upon this text? What is my purpose in this discourse? And his answer should be found in some feature which looks toward the salvation or edification of his people. Then everything which he says throughout the discourse will be bent to that purpose. His very introduction will look to the conclusion: the various divisions of the sermon body will look to it also. Then, when the conclusion is reached, it is natural, logical, and we might almost say inevitable.

If this distinct purpose is not in the preacher's mind from the beginning he is like a traveler who packs his trunk to go nowhere in particular. He may store it with those articles which he thinks may be useful upon his journey, and yet if his determination is formed after his journey has been begun, he may find that he has included certain useless articles which are only *impedimenta,* and forgotten certain other articles which are absolutely essential to his trip. Perhaps he prepared as though he were going to the Tropics when his destination is the Pole. Where, then, are you going in this sermon? and whence are you going to conduct others? and by what means do you propose to get there? and are you traveling upon the right road? and is it likely that those whom you are conducting will follow you? A sermon should be constructed somewhat like those great stockades that are built by game-drivers in Africa and elsewhere, extending perhaps over several miles of country, but converging as they proceed, until they end in a death-trap. Those who drive the game begin at a distance with much noise and other means whereby to alarm the game and drive it between the stockades, and so they are forced onward until they fall inevitably into the trap.

The conclusion, therefore, should be most carefully prepared. Let no preacher imagine for a moment that because it is carefully prepared it may be lacking in feeling, vehemence, or moving power. This can not be so if the preacher's heart has been stirred as it should have been during the preparation of his sermon. There are some who virtually object to such a rule as this, and there are a few who habitually and consistently avoid the careful preparation of a conclusion, because, as they say, they do not wish to write down their closing words in "cold blood." But if there is any danger of one's writing a conclusion in cold blood it certainly arises out of the fact that the body of his sermon has been prepared in cold blood. The preacher who is stirred and moved with the great thoughts of God, which he is endeavoring to elaborate and so present to his congregation that they shall be led Godward, can not be cold in his preparation of the discourse, and it will be no more and no other than the indication of his own fervent desire, and his own scrupulous care for the effect of his utterances, that he prepares his final words with the most conscientious and painstaking attention.

Some of the greatest orators of modern times have illustrated this rule to the full, and spent more time upon the conclusion of their orations than upon any other part of it. Such was the case with John Bright. Lord Brougham revised the conclusion of his celebrated speech in defense of Queen Caroline twenty times. The peroration of Burke's arraignment of Warren Hastings was wrought over and over sixteen times. Yet no one would think of saying that these speeches were closed in cold blood.

But there is another consideration of value in this connection, that a preacher is not obliged to present exactly that conclusion which he has so carefully prepared. It may be that he will be prompted by the occasion or by his own passion to say something else than that which he has prepared, or to express his thought in somewhat different language. There is no reason why he should not do so, particularly if he is an experienced extempore preacher. In this case, so far from his preparation for his conclusion interfering with the flow of his passion, and the modification of its expression, it will be a positive help to it. It will temper it, control it, and direct it into proper channels.

At all events the preacher should never trust to the impromptu appeal after a carefully prepared sermon body. If one's conclusion is to be purely extemporaneous it should follow a sermon of like character, which sermon, however, we believe ought never to be presented. Our mental moods are altogether too uncertain to be relied upon. There may be that in ourselves, or in the attitude of the congregation, which will prevent the kind of an appeal which we anticipated, and seriously handicap us in the effort to close the sermon as we would have done. The preacher is only safe when his conclusion has been prepared. Therefore he should prepare some conclusion, even though he may modify it under the stress of circumstances.

Some particular forms of the conclusion will be treated hereafter in connection with the application, and yet another question which touches the application should be asked and answered here. Should the conclusion always take the form of an appeal? By this we mean a personal address to the hearers, urging them to specific action. The answer to this question is, "Not always," and it might be safe to say "Not generally," because if the sermon body has been what it should be, and the preacher has had that solemn purpose in mind in its preparation and delivery, of which we have spoken, then the whole sermon will be of the nature of an appeal, even though its closing portion be not cast in that exact form.

Dr. Watson says: "A striking and eloquent peroration (although this sounds cruel to a degree) ought to be suppressed. When the sermon has culminated after a natural fashion it ought to end, leaving its effect to rest not on rhetoric, but on truth. The sermon may cease suddenly because the audience has surrendered without terms, and the sermon has served its purpose. Speech can be too lengthy, too formal, too eloquent, and the preacher who says most sometimes sacrifices that upon which he might the most naturally depend. But in those sacrifices of self the preacher's strength lies. On them the blessing of God rests. Broken sentences when the speaker could not continue, unfinished sermons when the Spirit of God was working powerfully, have wrought marvels beyond all the wisdom of the schools." Dr. Lyman says: "When we are through let us stop. I know a minister of whom it was said that he lacked only one thing, and that was terminal facilities." Sometimes the preacher, out of his very enthusiasm, is tempted to make an appeal at the close of a sermon when people are not in a mood for it, and prolong it until it becomes tiresome. There are times when a ringing appeal is of the utmost value—when a congregation is deeply stirred, when consciences are manifestly reached, when men certainly appear upon the very border of the Kingdom, and only need a little urgency to force them in. Then it is not out of place for the preacher to prolong his appeal. Such is sometimes the case in great evangelistic meetings. But whether the sermon closes with an appeal—longer or shorter, or does not, the pastor-preacher must learn to depend more upon the inherent force and vitality of the truth of God than upon his own effort apart from it. President Faunce, speaking of what we call the "New Homiletics," says, "The old-fashioned 'application' and 'appeal' at the end of the sermon have now largely vanished. The application should come all the way through. The strongest possible appeal is a vivid perception and presentation of the truth."

It is a very noticeable thing that the Lord Jesus Christ Himself seldom enforced a formal application, either in his conversation with individuals or in his discourses to the multitude. His thoughts were so arranged that those who heard Him drew their own conclusions, and generally He Himself was content with a single sentence— "Go and do thou likewise."

One has well said that above all things the preacher should beware of "the corpse of an appeal." The conclusion of the sermon must not be a dead thing, and no appeal should be introduced by the preacher simply for the sake of good form. Let him say nothing that it is not in his heart to say. Let him manifest no urgency that does not come from his deepest soul. While the preacher is preparing his sermon, more particularly while he is preaching that which he has carefully prepared, everything within him becomes alive and energetic, and moves him on toward one final great impression. He has already felt it in the silence and solitude of his own study. The truth has found him and moved him, and it should be so when he comes before his congregation. This, as Dr. Lyman says, is the unique glory of our calling. He preaches to himself while he is preaching to others. The truth becomes mighty in him. He stands as in the very presence of Christ: he is an ambassador for Christ. He speaks in Christ's name from beginning to end. He is full of zeal for his Master. If such be his spirit, his method will not be seriously at fault. The Gospel of Christ will be in a sense incarnate in him, and men will be moved by his message.

The preacher should have only one conclusion. He should never reach a climax only to take a fresh start in order to reach a second. His conclusion should be single, set off by itself as distinctly as though it were cut out of marble. The preacher should not have the same conclusion to every sermon. It should be his earnest desire and his constant care to so vary his method in closing his sermons as to avoid monotony. This will be found not only the more interesting, but very much the more useful because no two parishioners are moved in the same way. If the preacher is a fisher of men he may learn from the expert angler to carry lures of different kinds, and to change his flies according to the kind of day, the waters in which he fishes, the season of the year, or those flies which he observes about him sporting over the stream.

As to the very last word. Luther is quoted as saying "When thou seest thy hearers most attentive then conclude, for so they will come again the more cheerfully the next time." But the preacher should so conclude in his very last words as to leave no impression upon the minds of his congregation that he is seeking any glory for himself, or making any attempt at any sort of display. Let him not go out "in a blaze of glory." Many earnest, conscientious preachers have destroyed the effect of sermons, prepared with great care and with the most sincere motive, by ending them thoughtlessly, perhaps, with some elaborate figure of speech, or certain sentences which they had purposely polished to the last degree. It should never be so. The preacher's last words should be exceedingly simple, modest, and plain—a verse of Scripture perhaps; the lines of some familiar hymn perhaps; a solemn question perhaps; or a simple, earnest statement of fundamental truth.

MATERIALS.

MATERIALS.

I. The best materials derived from general knowledge.

II. The best materials are found in observation and con-
    sation.
    1. Conversation with men.
    2. Conversation with specialists.

III. Special sources.
    1. The Scriptures.
    2. Exegesis.
    3. Theology.
    4. Church history.
    5. Philosophy.
    6. Sermons.
    7. All useful books.

IV. The use of materials.
    1. The correlation of studies.
    2. The utilization of learning.

V. The ministry of nature.

Read Brastow's "Modern Pulpit;" Slattery's "Present Day Preaching," II;
    Pattison's "Making of the Sermon," XIV; Van Dyke's "Days Off;"
    Johnson's "Ideal Ministry."

IX.

MATERIALS.

We proceed now to discuss the sources from which sermonic material is to be obtained. The source should be suited to the design of the worker as in all other kinds of work. The man who proposes to build a frame house does not expect to find it in a brick-yard; yet this is the sort of thing of which the preacher is sometimes guilty when he looks for sermon material from those sources which are not proper or adequate to its supply.

Yet this remark may carry with it a mechanical idea which is not intended. We must remember that sermons are not "built." The true sermon is an organism; and our illustration might be more in place, or be better understood, if it was derived from the growth of something which has life in it. The kind of soil, for example, which is best for the vegetable, or the kind of exposure which is best for the tree.

Before proceeding to discuss the special sources from which materials are obtained, let us consider two matters of a more inclusive character.

I. The best materials are derived from the preacher's general knowledge rather than from any special preparation with a view to a particular sermon. Of course, there must be both general and special preparation, but if we were shut up to one of the two we should very greatly prefer that preparation which comes from a preacher's general knowledge, to that special preparation which has been made with reference to the occasion only. Henry Ward Beecher, in his Yale Lectures, says, "Preaching will have to be your whole business. If you are going to be professional preachers, if you will make that your life calling, it is not probable that there is one of you who was built large enough to do anything more than that. It will take all that you have in you and all your time. I do not think a man could run a locomotive engine, paint pictures, keep school, and preach on Sundays to any very great edification. The man who is going to be a successful preacher should *make his whole life run toward the pulpit.*" This would imply that his time and thought are to be constantly given to those exercises and occupations in which he shall find preparation for his work, even though the particular subject which he proposes to discuss may not be in his mind. It is said of Mr. Spurgeon that in his later years his preparation for a sermon consisted of a few memoranda, the fruit of an hour or two's reflection on Saturday evening. Why was it that Mr. Spurgeon was able to preach as he did with so little special preparation? It was because of the materials which he had accumulated during a life spent in equipping himself for the pulpit. His whole life "ran toward the pulpit." His study, his private meditation, his fellowship with men, and everything else, were governed by this supreme purpose; and he had preached so long and after so much special preparation that it was easy for him to do, near the close of his life, what every preacher should prepare himself to do after the same fashion.

Very often the sermon which is not prepared out of one's general knowledge, but only out of that special reading and thought which may be given to the special sub-ject, does not accomplish its full purpose. It is academic, stilted, and formal; it is apt to be pretentious and pedantic. The preacher is always more fresh, interesting, and practical when his sermon is largely the outgrowth of accumulated scholarship and observation.

Professor James, in his "Talks to Teachers," has a paragraph which is fully applicable to preachers: "They talk much in pedagogic circles to-day about the duty of the teacher to prepare for every lesson in advance. To some extent this is useful. But the advice I should give to most teachers would be in the words of one who is herself an admirable teacher. 'Prepare yourself so well in the subject that it shall be always on tap: then in the class-room trust your spontaneity and fling away all further care."

This general preparation, as we shall see, should not be along any one particular line, but along many lines, all of them however converging upon the pulpit. Some preachers avoid certain studies and pursuits as secular. Certain books they will not read; certain diversions they will not practise; the company of certain men they will not seek, because they think these things are not in keeping with their high vocation. This is a grand mistake. There is nothing secular, which is done with a holy purpose, except that which is positively wicked. Everything should be grist which comes to the preacher's mill, if he has sought to find it in the right spirit and to employ it in the right way.

In order, however, to the use of this general knowl-edge the preacher must diligently cultivate his memory. Resources are of no value if they are not at command, and it should be the preacher's aim from first to last to have his acquisitions at his own disposal. This may be done in a measure in ways to be hereafter suggested, but it is well to emphasize it at this point.

II. The best sermonic materials are those of observation and conversation. The preacher should not be a mere doctrinaire, a mere theorist: his work must be vital, personal, helpful. There must be in it an adaptation to the real needs of men. Dr. Herrick Johnson, in his "Ideal Ministry," has a fine chapter upon this subject, "The Law of Adaptation." He defines the term as "saying the right thing at the right time in the right way." The sermon, therefore, should always answer some definite need, and have respect to men as they really are, and not as they might be and should be. Dr. Johnson proceeds to discuss the different minds and temperaments which the preacher finds in his congregation requiring treatment according to their respective individualities. He then considers the differing conditions under which sermons may be delivered, all of which require that the preacher should be many-sided, as he can only be by cultivating the habit of observation. The preacher should know how men, women, and children think, feel, and act. But this is not to be discovered by random observation, nor by indiscriminate conversation with all kinds of people. His method should be systematic, intelligent, and with conscious purpose. Some suggestions may be made with regard to the matter.

1. It will be well for the preacher to talk much with men—with *men* rather than with women. It is somewhat unfortunate for the ministerial profession that it is necessarily occupied so much with the gentler sex. This is because women are more generally at leisure than men, and when calls are made upon the households of his parishioners, the preacher is very apt to find the men absent. Oftentimes he makes no special effort to

find them in, as he might do by seeking opportunities of conversation with them and making appointments at their convenience. The result is that he may be led to look upon life from a viewpoint that is altogether too feminine, and fail to obtain that vigorous grasp upon the subjects with which the busy world is concerned, which would be gained if his conversation was more frequently with those of the sterner sex. This is no reflection upon the character of women, nor upon their intellectual attainments. Their views of life in its varied forms are frequently more just and even more comprehensive than those of men. They have loftier aspirations and more zeal for the Master; but even so it can not be denied that the preachr must needs put himself in the man's position more frequently than he does, and learn how men in the busy world think and reason. Henry Ward Beecher declared that he would have the theological school of the future very largely a "life school," which expression he borrows, of course, from the study of art. It is very suggestive, as it is very characteristic of its author. He defines it "as studies to understand men and deal with them face to face and heart to heart, and mold them as an artist molds his clay or carves his statue." And Mr. Beecher himself diligently followed the rule which he would have beginners in the work of preaching adopt. In his autobiography he tells us that he took great delight, whenever he could get the chance, of riding on the top of an omnibus with the driver and talking with him. In this way he said he gained sympathy for this class of men, and learned to recognize the brotherhood of men, so that when he saw one of them in his church he could preach to him and "hit him under the fifth rib" with an illustration very much better than if he had not been acquainted with him. Beecher knew every gatekeeper at the ferries on which he was accustomed to cross. He knew the engineers and the dock hands, all of them. He made it his practice to keep in touch with such people, and to become acquainted with their work and their ways, and he advised young ministers to "keep very close to plain folks." "Do n't get above the common people," was his advice. But it is just as important that the preacher should become acquainted with men in other callings than the omnibus or the engine may furnish. The more men the preacher becomes acquainted with for purposes of study the more effective he is likely to become. Therefore we advise further,

2. Talk with specialists; learn their secrets. We should discover if possible why they are interested in their work; what effect it has had upon their natures, and how we may derive illustrations from them for practical lessons which may be of service to men in like pursuits.

When we say "talk with specialists," we mean to let such do most of the talking. The preacher who would gather material should not introduce too much of his business in conversation with a man who is in a different one. Ask questions, draw him out, be a veritable pupil at his feet.

Talk with men and women who "do things." They may not have much time to give you; but what time they can give will be worth hours of vapid conversation with men that do no more or other than they are told to do.

Talk with men and women that employ and direct other men and women. Talk with the master-minds, the leaders of thought, the superintendents of great industries, activities, philanthropies, and missions. Talk with men and women that know more, see more, think more than you do. There are a hundred schools for every preacher to attend, without fees, that will furnish him with rich material in boundless measure.

The conversation, then, is to be a selective one; observation likewise. Do not be too careful about the subjects. They may not be in the exact line of the preacher's work. It may be all the better for him that they are out of his line, and he may find that they have extensions into the very sphere of thought in which he himself moves, and for which he is the most concerned. Let us be very teachable in the presence of all thinking men, however humble the thinker may be. So much in general.

III. There are some special sources of materials which demand our attention because it has been demonstrated over and over again that the man who relies almost, if not altogether, upon such matters as those just noted may be a shallow man after all. Self-made men are often very poorly made. Preachers who have no other resources than those which are derived from what may see and hear in the society that is about them are not likely to be of great service to the world. What they are able to see is not broad enough or big enough. To what else then shall we resort?

1. The most important special source of sermon material is of course the Holy Scriptures. These must be the constant study of the preacher if he is to fulfill his calling. Washington Gladden well says, "The Christian minister is first of all a student. He studies that he may teach. One reason why some preachers fail is unquestionably found in this that they are not students. Their time is taken up with a variety of matters whereby their own minds and hearts are not enriched. But how can

they teach who have not studied? If the minister is engaged all, or nearly all, of his time with that which does not prepare him for his pulpit work, he should seriously consider the case. The Bible above all other books will be the subject of his study. From it alone can we learn how the sinner may be saved and sanctified. From it alone can we learn about the Christ whose name we bear and confess, and whose Gospel it is the business of the minister to proclaim." Dr. Blaikie says, "To be able to grasp the great purposes of divine revelation as a whole; to see at the same time the drift and bearing of its several parts; to apprehend the great lessons of the various histories, biographies, epistles, and other matters contained in the Holy Scriptures; to make one part throw light on another, and bring out the chief lessons of the whole, are attainments of inestimable value to the preacher of the Word." And this knowledge of the Bible should be such that the preacher's acquaintance with it will enable him to carry his people into the deeper sense of it, into its wonderful movement and its distinct revelations, in order that they may not be disturbed by trifling questions with regard to certain details in the Scripture which are after all comparatively unimportant.

When once the preacher has obtained a comprehensive knowledge of the drift and purpose of the Word of God, he is able to lift his people up to so high a plane that those questions with which persons on the lower levels are engaged do not disturb them.

This implies to begin with a thorough knowledge of Bible history. Not that the preacher must know all about every person who is mentioned in the Bible, but that he should have sufficient information with regard to its principal characters. In a certain company of ministers, a remark was made with regard to "Jochebed's children."

One who was present, although he was a minister in charge of a very important pulpit, and preached to a most intelligent congregation, did not understand the reference. He did not know who Jochebed was. Now if she had been some very unimportant character it would not have been strange, but when it is remembered that she was the mother of Moses his ignorance appears inexcusable.

Another influential minister spoke to a large congregation of Paul's "sailing up the Tiber" when he came to Rome! And at another time he said that when Joshua and his host marched about Jericho the people on its walls remarked that it would all end in failure. "They were here forty years ago, and went back into the wilderness!" Such mistakes are worse than lamentable: they make the minister a laughing-stock, even to the intelligent laymen of his congregation.

The preacher must know his Bible. The very least that can be demanded of him is that he commit no mistakes in relating its historical incidents. The first source of sermonic material is the facts of Scripture. They take precedence of every other kind of Biblical knowledge. If the preacher does not have them all at command he should certainly have all those at command which are connected with any particular sermon. If it be not so the preacher is positively disqualified.

The preacher should also remember that he must study the very words of the passage from which he is to preach. He commits a serious error when he studies only about the passage with which he is engaged. This may be a very important process, but it is by no means so important as to study the passage itself. Many have done this who never discovered what the passage itself contained. The jewel is much more precious than the setting. The circumstances under which the passage was written, the people to whom it was addressed, and other matters of the like, may occupy the preacher's attention to the exclusion of the truth unto edification which the passage cotains. This implies, therefore,

2. That the second source of sermonic material is found in exegesis. The finest essay perhaps that Dr. Shedd ever penned is the first chapter in his Homiletical and Pastoral Theology entitled "Eloquence and Exegesis," from which we have already quoted. We would that every one in the ministry to whom these words may come might read it. We refer the reader also in this connection to what has been already said under "Textual Analysis."

3. The third source is systematic theology. Many a student, after he leaves the theological school, abandons his study of this subject. He supposes that it has done its work for him while he was still in the seminary, and can be no longer of any special service to him. It may be replaced by some other form of literature which he imagines will be of more practical use. By some ministers also it seems to be regarded merely as an academic science which has no positive hold upon the mind of thinking people, belongs only to the minister's study, and can not be practically employed with men and women of the world. And very considerable is said against it by those who have never studied it themselves. "Give us a quick lunch" cries the pew—as Dr. Jefferson puts it, and the pulpit all too often responds with alacrity. The parishioner frequently declaims against sermons which he supposes to be "theological;" and even the layman who betakes himself to preaching may declare that he "has no use for theology." Neverthless we counsel that the preacher should continue his theological

studies during his entire career, and he will find in them very much of positive and permanent value in his sermon work. Dr. Watson in his Cure of Souls remarks, "All this railing at doctrine is simply one of the innumerable forms of modern cant. Theology is an absolute intellectual necessity. No one can hope to teach religion in even its simplest form with permanent success without a competent knowledge of theology, any more than a physician can practise medicine without a knowledge of physiology, or an engineer can build a bridge who has not learned the higher mathematics. Without a system in the background of his mind the preacher's ideas will have no intellectual connection or artistic proportion. Without a system underlying his sermons he can not grip and impress his hearers. His own creed will be a chaos." But this does not mean that systematic theology in its formal theological form is preachable. This particular matter will be pursued hereafter when we come to consider the doctrinal sermon. Systematic theology is a source of material, but it is material, so to speak, in the rough. The preacher must continue to study it, but his knowledge of it must be recast when it appears in sermonic form. Otherwise preachers are not qualified for their work, and the thinking people among their hearers will soon discover that they know no more than themselves upon the highest subjects. Morever, this study of theology, instead of leading one into dogmatism, as is commonly supposed, has precisely the opposite effect; because the thorough student of theology has traversed the ground in connection with various theories advanced by different authors. He is acquainted with their writings, he knows their views and doubts and differences. He becomes not only modest in his declaration of truth, but learns to present that truth which has been thoroughly weighed and tested. In that case he is likely to speak with great influence and much authority.

This study of exegesis and theology gives to the preacher three advantages which should be noted in this connection.

(1) He is very bold in his statement of his convictions with regard to divine truth. This makes him a strong preacher. It clothes him with authority.

(2) He has somewhat to preach which has substance and depth to it. Dr. D. S. Schaff has well said in this connection: "If too much attention is given to mere preaching the preacher will soon have nothing to preach." If we mean to devote ourselves to "Applied Christianity" we must be very sure to start with that we have some positive and permanent Christianity to apply.

(3) It enables him to set truth in the proper perspective. The first things are first with him. Those which occupy the foreground are correctly placed. It is only when the preacher has thought the whole thing through as carefully as he can, and with such help as he has been able to command, that he is able to co-ordinate the doctrines of the word of God and show their proper relation the one to the other.

The preacher may be advised in this connection not only to keep up his studies in general theology, but also to read monographs on various theological subjects by those who are masters of their profession, and which appear from time to time.

4. The fourth special source of sermon material is Church History. This includes, of course, such a general survey of the history of the Church from the apostolic times as is included in the seminary curriculum, but in addition to this the student should acquire and diligently

read the most useful works which he can obtain upon special aspects of ecclesiastical history. While we do not live in the past but in the present, very much may be derived from the history of the early Church and of the mediaeval Church distinctly applicable to the times in which we live. Such works for example as Uhlhorn's "Conflict of Christianity with Heathenism," and De Pressense's "Ancient World and Christianity," are never out of date, and the author may be pardoned for also mentioning his own work, "The History of the Preparation of the World for Christ." The student should also be familiar with the history of his own denomination; the history of the Christian Church in the land in which he lives; and very particularly the history of Christian missions in their origin and their extension throughout the world. He will find in these studies very valuable material for the enrichment of his sermons upon a multitude of subjects derived from the word of God.

The old, familiar saying tells us that "history repeats itself;" but too few students, even if they really believe this statement, understand what it contains. Of course, it does not mean that men, events, customs, and the like are positively duplicated. It does not even mean that the situation is exactly reproduced. But it does mean that regarding character, motive, and habit *in the whole,* there is no radical change from age to age. Therefore our understanding of the past enables us to interpret the present, and fundamental principles derived from the study of what has been may be relied upon as applicable to what is and what is to be. Therefore old Thomas Fuller was right when he said: "Of all branches of learning history best becometh a gentleman—Church history a Christian." Professor James says: "The changing conditions of history touch only the surface of the show." History is the great interpreter of Providence, and of the Scriptures also. As such it is a fertile source of sermonic material.

So far, it will appear, we have alluded to those branches of learning which belong to the curriculum of the theological seminary. If this is noted by the reader let it be said that the writer is a thorough believer in them as the means of equipping the preacher for his work.

5. Ethics, philosophy, psychology. The same suggestion may be given with regard to these studies which has been given with regard to Church History—it is well for the preacher to read the best monographs upon these subjects. Let him consult the best books as they appear. It is sometimes objected to these studies that they tend to make a preacher too metaphysical, and accustom him to preach in language which his people can not understand, but it does not follow that because he himself is engaged with these studies that he should retail them to his hearers in technical terms. No man can become an arithmetician who has not studied algebra. No more can one preach the gospel as effectively as he might preach it who has not dealt somewhat with the profound. The advice which was given by an older preacher to a younger one, as quoted by Broadus, is most excellent: "Read Butler and preach to negroes." This is the very finest literary art, to simplify the profound; but one must be able to understand the profound, and understand it thoroughly, before he is qualified to simplify it. The best work which a preacher can do is to set his people to thinking deeply upon the most important subjects. This is to be done only when he starts upon their own level, and gradually conducts them to higher ground with which he has first made himself acquainted.

6. Sermons. Materials for our own sermons are very often secured from the sermons of others, and the student ought by no means to neglect them. Very frequently the minister has a positive distaste for other men's discourses, though sometimes he makes use of them to his own undoing. Bishop Quayle has a very suggestive section upon this subject. He says: "Every sermonizer should use every occasion possible to hear his brother ministers preach. He should listen to them in a respectful mood. If he comes with a critic's mien, then he had far better not come at all. No preaching will do a critic good. He is immune to the reception of good. If a preacher goes to hear another preacher preach so as to bolster up his own opinion of himself, and so minister to self-opinionation, then he is not only violating a Christian propriety, but he is distinctly crude." He testifies to his own delight in listening to his brother ministers, and to his own reading of their sermons at times when they could not be personally heard. One Sunday in New York he listened to Dr. Burrell, Dr. Jefferson, and Dr. Hillis, and he says with regard to that day's experience: "How spacious the habitation of that Lord's Day." Preachers should obtain volumes of the best sermons, particularly of those men whose preaching has formed a distinct epoch in the history of the pulpit, and marked a decided change in the method of presenting gospel truth. Among such may be mentioned St. Chrysostom, Savonarola, Canon Lyddon, Robertson, Chalmers, Bushnell, Spurgeon, Henry Ward Beecher, Phillips Brooks, D. L. Moody, and Watkinson. There are also volumes of sermons selected from different masters of the pulpit art which are accessible to the student. Such sermons should be carefully analyzed by him. He should seek the source of these preachers' power, and while imitating

none of them he should learn to govern himself accordingly. He will find also in some good history of preaching, such as Brastow's "Modern Pulpit," a survey of the characteristic methods of different periods, and a review of the work of different preachers in historical order, which will be of vast service to him in his own sermon work.

7. All kinds of useful books. And yet the preacher's use of books is to be exercised with very great care. One of the first things that the young preacher should learn is the absolute worthlessness for the preacher's purposes of the vast majority of books issued from the press. Many men, and they are not all preachers by any means, seem to imagine that it is a most commendable desire to accumulate a large library, and that their attainments are to be judged by the number of books that may be found upon their shelves. Young preachers particularly are often beguiled into buying books which will prove of no positive service to them. It is not the number which they possess, nor even the number which they have read, which furnishes them for their great work, but the positive adaptation of such books as they read to their high purpose, and their ability to command their contents. Dr. Shedd has well said: "The giants in theology have dared to let many books go unread that they might be profoundly versed in revelation."

Nevertheless the student is to be reminded that the reading of books is very greatly to be preferred to the reading of current ephemeral literature. Many a man gives altogether too much time to the perusal of his daily newspaper to the neglect of much more important and useful work. A minister would not be very sadly handicapped if he never saw a daily newspaper, provided he was the reader of some good weekly paper which would give him the news that was worth knowing in condensed form with suitable comment. This is not to disparage the daily newspaper. It certainly performs a very important service and meets a very manifest need of our civilization, but it is dreadfully abused both in its publication and in its perusal. Nor is the minister very specially assisted by the popular magazines of the day. At all events he should very carefully discriminate between them. Some of them are published for no other purpose than that of amusement; they furnish the reader with no valuable information and with no valuable motive. It would be better to dismiss most of them entirely from the home. Let the preacher confine himself to comparatively few weeklies and monthlies, and make a careful selection of those that will teach him the most, and the most help his spiritual life and his spiritual leadership.

The kind of books which a minister is to buy is not easily specified. We have said "all kinds of good books." It is even well for him to read the standard novels, because in this age in which we live the best novels are not mere romance fancifully constructed with a view to gaining the attention and exciting the curiosity, but they are representative of a serious purpose on the part of their authors; to set forth some great and salutary truth, to counteract some grievous error, to correct some malicious abuse, or in some other way to benefit society. Garvie says concerning this matter: "Surely the 'Scarlet Letter' helps us to realize more intensely and distinctly what remorse is. From Romola we may learn how suicidal is selfishness. In Silas Mariner we discover something of the laws of a soul's ruin and recovery." So it is with other more recent novels. The same may be said with regard to certain great dramas, and the work of certain great poets. If they do no more for the preacher than to stimulate his imagination they do much, but their service is by no means exhausted in this one particular. Many of them will show him the secret depths of the human heart and how they may be penetrated; the noblest aspirations of the human soul and how they may be evoked; the deepest despair of conscious guilt and how it may be escaped; the longing for salvation, of standing with God, and of eternal bliss, and how it may be satisfied. Books of science may also be read by the preacher and be of great service as material for his pulpit work; books of travel, and we believe beyond everything else, biography. The lives of the best men that the world has known should be read by the preacher, and he may draw from them needful inspiration for many a sermon upon the practical aspects of life.

Dr. Herrick Johnson has an admirable section upon the proper method of selecting books. It contains among others the following wise suggestions: "Do not buy a book simply because it is cheap. Do not buy a book upon a publisher's notice, no matter how flattering. Do not buy a book until the approving judgment of time has been waited for," and so on. One danger to the preacher in the selection of his books is found in the tendency to become semi-religious, from the attention given to books that are not wholly devoted to the best interests of mankind.

The man should buy no more books than he can make use of. As one has well said, he should be a "living catalogue of his own library." If he has read a book, however valuable, only to lay it aside and forget everything which it contains, he might far better have saved himself the time and the labor expended in reading it. It will be well for the student, therefore, to make notes of the best things in the books which he reads, and even to compile some sort of an index of his own to his library, so that that which he has upon its shelves may be at his command. In some way at least he should diligently cultivate his own memory of the contents of his books. If he can do nothing more he should run over the shelves quite frequently after they begin to be somewhat numerous, occasionally taking out this book and that which he read some time ago, and refreshing his mind with regard to its contents. He should so classify the books in his library that those on one subject should always be found together, whether they are of the same size and bound in the same way or not; and what is better than all else, he should seek occasion frequently to converse with others upon the books with which he is engaged. Nothing so aids the memory in this matter as the comparison of judgments. When one has talked over a book with another he is not likely to forget the more important things which are contained in it.

The preacher should also learn how to utilize certain valuable pamphlets that come to him from time to time. In most libraries they are nothing but rubbish, if indeed they are preserved at all; but a distinct place should be reserved for them in the minister's library. It is well after a number have been accumulated through a course of years to preserve the best and bind them in separate volumes, each under some general subject, and a separate blank book should be kept by the minister in which all those pamphlets which he has preserved are carefully indexed.

One thing more should be said before we leave this part of the subject. It is true that very many of our ministers, the majority of them indeed, are poor men and can not afford to buy many books, so that it might seem as though many of the suggestions which are offered in this connection are valueless to them. What shall be done in their case? Very much may be done to begin with by the circulating libraries of the day. Thanks to Mr. Carnegie and the multiplication of libraries which he has instigated, a good library is not very inaccessible to any minister. He may either visit it himself occasionally, or he may engage one of his brethren to visit it in his behalf, and obtain such books as he has seen noticed and which he desires to read. These libraries will generally obtain any book whose purchase is requested by a reputable patron, and there is really no difficulty in any aspiring minister obtaining such help as he may need in this way. Brother ministers also who are blessed with large libraries are always willing to lend their books to their less favored brethren. Again, the poor minister is to remember that he does not require very many books after all, as we have already noted. It is true in every branch of literature that one author borrows much from another, and one or two good books upon any given subject will often teach the minister all that he requires to know, and while good books furnish him with an immense amount of valuable sermonic material, yet he is to remember that the best material, as we have already noted, is to be derived from his own personal knowledge of the Holy Scriptures, using the few simple helps which he can certainly secure. Then, if his own heart and life be fed upon the living Word, he will be able to dispense it to others with no fear of falling short of their requirements and desires.

IV. After the preacher has once obtained his materials from such sources what is he going to do with them? One may be a great student and a great ignoramus at the same time. As those who possess a large amount of property yielding no income are called "land-poor," so it may be said with regard to certain students that they are "learning-poor." Their study does for them exactly what their property does for the others. It is a drain upon their time, their strength, and their effort, but contributes nothing to their usefulness. It is sometimes said with regard to one that "he has forgotten more than the other man knows." It is regarded as a compliment, but it is far otherwise; it is a positive reflection upon him. The man who has acquired much only to forget it, or to fail to make use of it, is not the better man of the two. The one who knows but little, if his knowledge is at command and is put to use, is by far his superior.

One may also be a great student and be a very poor teacher, and as preaching is first of all teaching, is in fact the very highest form of teaching, one may be a great student and a poor preacher. The old proverb reads: "Fear the man of one book." There is a vast amount of meaning in it, though it can not be pressed to its full conclusions. Yet it is manifestly true that those men, in professional life as well as those men in commercial life, who turn over their capital often are the men who are most speedily enriching themselves and benefiting those about them. In fact, there is a positive evil in too much study or too much reading. Oftentimes instead of contributing to one's self-confidence, it has the opposite effect. There have been those who have long delayed the publication of books for which they were well equipped because as they progressed in their studies they found more and more to be learned, and the publication of the book was indefinitely delayed. There have been those who sought to be teachers of others who, from the very studying which they had already done, became the more and more impressed with their own ignorance, and their teaching work was delayed until they were incompetent to teach by reason of their self-distrust. Another danger of too much reading is the tendency to become dependent upon the opinions and judgments of others, rather than to form our own independent judgment and minister to the strength of our own proper individuality. One may be "deep versed in books but shallow in himself." For some such source we imagine arises the predjudices which some ignorant people have against what they call "book-larnin'." It is supposed to be a very foolish prejudice, the result only of gross ignorance; but there may be reason for it, for sometimes those who are not themselves learned in books have natural talents, a keen observation, and a positively ripe judgment concerning the scholarship of others, and no prejudice is ever excited among ignorant people concerning learning when it is properly employed.

Some suggestions may therefore be offered in closing this part of the subject.

1. Let the student correlate his studies. Do not pass too quickly from one subject to another. Do not distract the mind with a variety of topics. Study for a time on one topic; pursue one general subject. View it first from this side and then from that side. Read what this author has to say concerning it, and what that author furnishes, and then endeavor to form your own judgment with regard to the matter.

2. Utilize your learning as soon as possible. Make use of it in the pulpit as soon as it has become assimilated. Do not do it too quickly; allow the matter to rest in the mind until the mind itself has become accustomed to it and has learned how to employ it, and yet let one determine within himself to put it to some good use as soon as it can well be done. By all means let the

preacher not study anything simply because he desires to study. This is the most foolish and useless thing that he can possibly do in this line. The man's learning must constantly be put into his capital, his working capital; it must not be like money in a stocking, hidden behind the baseboard. He must continue to accumulate it, but not to hoard it. It must be like his checking account in the bank, liable at any time to be called out: and this disposition on the part of the student will give him a certain reserve power which is of immense value to him. Broadus well says with regard to it: "When the preacher speaks from great fullness of thought, then what he says bears power from what is in reserve as the head of water gives force to that which strikes upon the wheel." More than this, he will have resources for emergencies. He will not likely be found upon any occasion barren of ideas and at a loss for something to say. He will know a hundred times more than he will ever get a chance to say; but his people will be influenced not so much by what he says as by what he evidently knows. No man ever has great influence who exhausts his entire stock at one session.

But the student must be careful not to husband this reserve, which is so valuable in itself, as *mere* reserve. He must spend his capital continually as if it were income, for there is no such thing as "invested funds" in scholarship which are not to be touched at any time, but sacredly preserved for the sake of that which they may yield. It is in this respect that young preachers particularly frequently fail. They are often disposed to give utterance to some thought or illustration which they know within themselves is valuable, but which they imagine they must withhold for a better opportunity. Spurgeon has confessed that he learned when he was quite a young man to give his people at all times the very best that there was in him, and there can be no doubt that the strict adherence to this principle had much to do with the making of Spurgeon, because the use of intellectual capital does not follow the same rules as the use of monetary capital. If our money capital be entirely spent we are ruined. If our intellectual capital be entirely spent we are enriched. The principle which is enunciated in the Book of Proverbs with regard to gold and silver is even more true when it is applied to the preacher's influence: "There is that scattereth, and increaseth yet more; and there is that withholdeth more than is meet, but it tendeth only to want." If the preacher acts upon such injunctions as these, he will find that his intellectual and spiritual capital is constantly upon the increase; his reserve becomes greater and greater, and more and more influential. His investments will be constantly changing for the better, and there will be with him no professional "dead-line" whatsoever.

V. One important source of sermon material remains—Nature. Though mentioned last it is very far from least. If the writer could have his way he would compel every minister—especially those who live in the cities, to spend a half day every week, from April to November, in the woods and fields.

The busy minister has no holidays, except those which are taken in bulk at his summer vacation. Perhaps he calls Monday his rest day; but this is often spent in writing up his correspondence, attending ministers' meeting, sitting on committees, or what not; and it furnishes him no relaxation whatsoever. And even when his summer vacation comes he may be so foolish as to spend it at some summer school or camp meeting, or in some other way that continues to work his fagged brain and deplete his physical resources. It is a very sad reflection that so few know what the gracious ministry of nature is, or how to utilize it. They think they need the instruction and stimulation which is to be obtained by attendance upon learned lectures and that they can not afford to miss such opportunities when they are off duty themselves. They do not know what instruction and stimulation they might receive in the forest and on the prairie and how much more profitable it would prove in view of all the circumstances. They are already stuffed with the theoretic and the abstract and they should seek a supply of the concrete and the sentimental.

It is not simply for purposes of relaxation that the minister should take his half day per week with nature. No doubt he needs the relaxation—he may need it sadly; and if he gets nothing more the change will be immensely profitable. But while he is getting his relaxation he may get something more. Mere relaxation will only enable him to use what sermonic material he has with better effect; but in addition to this he may get more material, of another kind.

Many have no other idea in this connection than that of exercise. It is by no means a bad idea. They need the exercise. They appreciate its importance. Therefore they play golf once a week or take a walk—just a walk, nothing more—anything to get exercise. But this adds no material.

The minister therefore should regularly take his half day—if he can—with some distinct intellectual purpose. He should pursue some subject entirely disconnected with his professional work. Let him botanize, or geologize, or photograph. Let him be an amateur ornithologist or entomologist. All the better if he specializes somewhat; studies mushrooms or butterflies or fossils or what not.

No harm if he combines several of these. But at all events let him turn his rambles to account. He will get all the more fun out of it; the relaxation will be more complete and he will get sermon material.

There are ministers who have done this sort of thing whose example should have more contagion in it. Here is Henry Van Dyke with his "Little Rivers," and H. C. McCook with his "Ant Communities." How very much and how very manifestly their preaching has been enriched by their "days off." And there are others, not so well-known to the reading public, who have shown a like profit from like pursuits.

It is not simply that the tangible results of the outdoor studies finds its way into their sermons, but that a certain breadth and freedom and freshness are communicated to them. They are ventilated as our bedrooms ought to be. The mustiness disappears. They possess a new, delightful flavor, they hint of the deep blue, and the stars, and the breeze, and the flowers.

There is no city poetry—except a few dreadfully melancholy rhymes like the "Song of the Shirt" or the "Raven." The poetry that helps the preacher and is quoted in his sermons is born of the woods or the sea, or of some of the scenes of nature. Jesus drew upon it all the time. So did prophets and apostles. So should we.

MINISTERIAL SENILITY

MINISTERIAL SENILITY.

How shall the sermonic product be kept fresh?
    The "dead line" in various professions.
    Achievments of old men.

Keeping the body young.

Keeping the mind young.
    The society of young people.
    Fresh books.
    The habit of the unhabitual.
    "Old Fogyism."

Read Dorland's "Age of Mental Virility:" Mrs. Bishop's "Seventy Years
    Young."

X.

MINISTERIAL SENILITY.

We come now to the question, How shall sermonic materials be so employed that the product shall be interesting, fresh, and up-to-date, and so far forth profitable? The answer to this question involves the consideration of a subject not usually embraced in homiletics, but which ought not to be neglected. This is the subject of ministerial senility. It is commonly supposed, by those who are accustomed to listen to preaching, that the minister as he grows old becomes more and more deficient in those intellectual and moral qualities which render him attractive, and to some extent it must be admitted that this reflection is just. It is the part, therefore, of wisdom not only in the minister who feels that he is already growing old, but also in him who expects to grow old some day, to guard against the incoming of those things which will render his preaching stale, dull, and unprofitable. How are we to escape ministerial senility? This question we shall attempt to answer. The dead-line of which we spoke in the last chapter is usually fixed at the age of fifty years. Is there any such dead-line? And if there is, is it a positive fixture, or does it vary with the physical and mental constitution of men? One would be disposed to answer this question in the affirmative upon a superficial view of the subject, because it can not be disputed that many ministers do pass such a dead-line, as evidenced in the fact that when they are thrown out of employment they find it difficult to become again settled, and even when they are settled their congregations often fall away from them. These facts can not be gainsaid, and it is not wise to attempt to do so. It is far better to look the facts in the face, and instead of disputing their existence rather to attempt to modify the circumstances which render them possible.

It may be said then to begin with that if there is a dead-line in the ministry, equally so there is a dead-line in all other professions. It may not be located at exactly the same point alike in all of them, but that it generally exists in all is indisputable. If there were no other proof of the fact, it may be found in the action of the directors of certain great corporations which provides for the enforced retirement of their employees at a certain age, the employees themselves having no voice in the matter. And if it be true of the professions it is very much more emphatically true in the trades and mechanical arts, where the older men are more rigorously ruled out than they are in the professions. Indeed it may safely be said that old ministers are as much in demand as old men in other callings.

But there is a deeper truth than this, and one which it were much better for us to consider; that there is not necessarily any dead-line at all in those avocations which call chiefly for intellectual activity rather than physical. This may be demonstrated by reference to many authorities who have given the most minute study to the subject, and collated a vast amount of testimony with regard to it. Dr. James Jackson, one of the most distinguished of American physicians, and who continued in his practice until he was nearly ninety, declared that a man at sixty-five years of age, provided he was in good health, was at the very prime of his life. This did not mean in Dr. Jackson's opinion that a man at sixty-five was capable of doing just the same work which a younger man might perform. He made use of this aphorism, "After a man is sixty-five he should not force himself to his duty," by which he meant that neither the mind nor the body could endure the same strain which might be put upon it at a younger age, but that the man's value to society ordinarily reached its climax at that age. One of the finest pieces of work which has ever been done in connection with this question is that of Dr. W. A. Newman Dorland in his little book upon the "Age of Mental Virility." He has collated in the opening of this book the records of four hundred men of acknowledged celebrity in various lines of intellectual activity, and from these has drawn certain conclusions which he has systematized and enumerated. One of his conclusions is this: that his records give the average age of fifty for the performance of the master-work of the worker. The age varies somewhat with workers of different classes, but the record of the clergymen, whose names he gives, puts their principal achievements at this age. If such be the case, as shown by unquestionable record, the age of fifty can not be a dead-line in the ministerial profession. But the author of this book goes on to show what the world would have lost had certain great workers died before the age of seventy. We can not mention all his illustrations; they occupy four pages of his book, in which the worker's name and his celebrated work are recorded without comment. We cite a few examples, namely: Spencer's "Inadequacy of Natural Selection," Darwin's "Power of Movement in Plants," Galileo's most valuable book "Dialogue on the New Science," Titian's great painting of the "Last Judgment," Benjamin West's masterpiece "Christ Rejected," Benjamin Franklin's inimitable "Autobiography," Disraeli's "Endymion," Milman's "History of St. Paul's," Tennyson's "Locksley Hall Sixty Years After," Washington Irving's "Wolfert's Roost." A great number of other important achievements might be added to these—all by men over seventy.

But it is not alone with men who have achieved celebrity that the dead-line of fifty frequently fails. It does so with many ministers whose reputation does not extend beyond the small circle, and whose names do not appear in "Who's Who." The author has been personally acquainted with such, ministers who have been called to new fields when they were past sixty, or even past seventy.

There is no reason, therefore, for any young man hesitating to enter the ministry imagining that his period of usefulness may be more brief than in some other profession; nor is there any reason for a minister who approaches the imaginary dead-line to suppose that his services will shortly cease to be in demand. The important question for both the young and the old to address to themselves is this, How may this ministerial senility be escaped?

In answering this question we must disassociate it in a large measure at least from things physical, by which we mean that it is not necessary for the minister to resort to any artificial expedients in order to preserve the appearance of youth. He will not remain young, for example, because he dyes his hair, or wears a wig, or trims his beard according to the fashion, or wears the clothes that are popular with the younger generation. Nevertheless it is of great importance that the minister give attention to those things which have to do with bodily vigor. There is no class of men who so generally neglect exercise, for example, as ministers, and yet there is no other way in which the muscles may be kept supple, the circulation brisk, and the complexion clear. And ministers can do many things in other lines, affecting their physical appearance, commonly neglected by them. The preceding chapter in division V bears upon this very matter.

There are certain physical signs of old age which, of course, it will be impossible for the minister or anyone else to escape. The eyes will begin to flatten, and the arteries will begin to harden in spite of all the care that the minister may exercise, but this will not interfere with the minister's preservation of his mental vision, and there is no reason why the *arcus senilis* of the mind should ever manifest itself.

The body may be kept young by proper attention to diet, as regulated by the advice of some competent physician, by a variety of occupations, and by the cultivation of that versatility in which some of us are sadly lacking. A minister past seventy years of age remarked to the writer that one thing which he very greatly deplored, as he was passing into old age, was the fact that he had never cultivated a hobby, and he went on to specify some such things as photography, carpentry, and other employments which would have given him more fresh air and exercise. Others have also made the same sad confession in their declining years. They were without resources; those very resources which would have contributed to the health of the body as well as the health of the mind. There are some familiar illustrations of the value of this sort of thing in men of high station and great influence, who preserve their bodily vigor in such ways. Gladstone is a notable example, and his favorite exercise of chopping is familiar to everyone who has ever read of him.

The care of the body, however, is by no means so important as the care of the mind. Ministerial senility is not a decrepitude of the muscles or of the arteries, but of the mind and heart. Theodore Parker, in his celebrated sermon upon old age, made the significant remark that the "aged scholar becomes an antiquary." The source of the whole difficulty is revealed in this one pregnant remark. It calls to mind the well-known picture in which an aged book-worm is represented as standing upon the top of a stepladder, apparently oblivious to everything which is transpiring about him. He has several books under each arm; he has more between his knees, and others are scattered on the steps of the ladder. Meanwhile he is evidently poring over the pages of one which he holds in his hands. He is an antiquary: he lives only with his books: he thinks not and cares not for the world beyond. Dr. Parker goes on to say: "This antiquary does not like young men unless he knew their grandfathers before them. He looks back upon the fields he has trod and looks in the newspaper only for the deaths." Oliver Wendell Holmes, who preserved his youthful spirits even to his old age, is the author of the words: "It is better to be seventy years young, than forty years old;" and Emily M. Bishop, taking these words for her text, has written an admirable book upon the subject, "The Road to Seventy Years Young." Oliver Wendell Holmes also has given us the following beautiful and suggestive verse:

> "At sixty-two life has begun;
>   At seventy-three begin once more;
> Fly swifter as thou near'st the sun,
>   And brighter shine at eighty-four.
>   At ninety-five
>   Shouldest thou arrive,
> Still wait on God, and work and thrive."

How is this condition of intellectual youth to be preserved by the minister? Edward Everett Hale went far towards answering this question in a few words when he narrated the story of a venerable lady of his own acquaintance who "at seventy years of age," he says, "was one of the youngest people in the circle of her friends." The young people were engaged, upon a certain occasion, playing an amusing game called moral photography. In this game the participants are asked to write promptly and without deliberation the answers to twenty questions respecting their tastes and preferences, as, for example, "What is your favorite flower?" "Who is your favorite poet?" and the like. Dr. Hale says that he gave this question to his venerable friend as he gave it to the younger ones: "What is your favorite amusement?" To which she replied immediately, writing down the words upon the slip of paper which had been handed to her: "Hearing young people talk." The very best way then in which to preserve the spirit of youth is to cultivate the acquaintance of youth, and to be interested so far as possible in that which interests youth. One reason why many become old is because their friends fall away from them and they form no new acquaintances. This renders them dreary, morose, and self-contained, to the very serious detriment of their influence. They take up the lamentation of Frederick William Faber:

> "Years fly, O Lord! and every year
> More desolate I grow;
> The world of friends thins round me fast,
> Love after love lies low."

The result of this breaking of earthly bonds need not produce a desolating effect upon the mind of the minister if he is diligently engaged in making new bonds.

He must seek the society of young people; he must live among them, and live with them, and live like them, and live in them. "Live" we say, which means something more than simply to be in their company. It is a most significant fact in this connection that many of the professors in our colleges and other institutions of learning retain to a most remarkable extent their fresh and youthful manners and sympathies. The reason is not far to seek.

More than this, it is not simply that we enjoy the association of young people, but that we cultivate the acquaintance of all sorts of young people, without confining ourselves to our own denomination, our own race, or our own class in society. It is that we open our mind to all those incoming things which are presented to us by those that are younger than ourselves; new theories, new causes, new needs, and new methods. This, and all which we may include in it, is comprised in what we have said with regard to association with young people. Beyond this the youthful spirit depends upon other intellectual pursuits, such, for example, as the books which the minister reads, the subjects which engage his thought, and the very diversions in which he seeks his recreation, and the social functions which he attends. Dr. Hale says, "Take care to keep up a line of reading or perhaps more than one which will interest your young companions. You will find very soon that you can not force them to read your favorite books by any expression of your admiration. Every generation writes its own books, and you and I must not struggle too hard against this law." He goes on to speak of the books which he and his companions were reading fifty and sixty years before, and which were then moving all the young life of the English speaking world. "But," he says, "they do not move it now. Do not try then to make the young people read your books, but loyally and sympathetically select certain lines in which you will read the books of to-day and keep more than even with your young friends."

The author of "The Way to Keep Young" even makes this suggestion among her fundamental maxims, "Learn a language every ten years if you want to keep the mind alert, bright, and ready." The writer has known those who adopted this suggestion. He has tried it himself. The effect produced upon the mind is a peculiar but most exhilarating one. The man who is master of two languages is twice a man, and the acquisition of a modern language at an advanced period in life goes far toward stimulating those peculiar mental activities which have to do with keeping young.

The minister must vary his own special work as he goes on, if he is to avoid ministerial senility. He must destroy very many of his old sermons. This does not necessarily mean that he is to commit them to the flames, but that he is not to continue to repeat them in the same form and with the same emphasis. If they are to be repeated by him at all they are to be used only as material for the production of something which will be as pertinent to-day as that sermon from which it was derived was pertinent at the time of its production.

And he is to do all kinds of work, specially the kinds of work which he does not like to do. Nothing so contributes to "old-fogyness" as dogged persistence in the line of one's personal tastes. Give others credit for their preferences, and sympathize with them. The author of "Seventy Years Young" tells of a certain physician who said, speaking of a neighbor, "He allowed himself to grow old. He has not walked down the hill and back in three years. For my own part I have made this rule about such things, which I commend to younger men—'As soon as you feel too old to do a thing, do it.'" The older one becomes, the more he must accustom himself to what has been called "energetic volition." "The habit of the unhabitual" must be formed with him. He must keep up the struggle of the mind to renovate its ideas and improve its habits. Mark Twain exclaimed upon his seventieth birthday that he had beaten the doctor for seventy years. He said, "Since forty I have been regular about going to bed and about getting up, and that is one of the main things. I have made it a rule to go to bed when there was not anybody left to sit up with, and I have made it a rule to get up when I had to. This has resulted in an unswerving regularity of irregularity."

Preachers might form to advantage some such rule. The whole thing may be summed up in a single word. To keep young, keep out of ruts; permit no habit to master you; let the rule obtain not only with things mental but with things material as well. Be not mastered by a habit relating to the food you eat, the chair you sit in, the bed on which you lie, the hours which you take for sleep, nor by any such mater. *Keep out of ruts.* Of course, this does not mean that we are not to subject ourselves to wholesome rules in all these matters, but that we are to strenuously avoid that monotony of taste and conduct which runs unavoidably into intellectual sterility.

Modern psychology has taught us much with regard to this matter—Prof. James says, "In all the apperceptive operations of the mind a certain general law makes itself felt—the law of economy. In admitting a new body of experience we instinctively seek to disturb as little as possible our preëxisting stock of ideas. We always try to name a new experience in some way which will assimilate it to what we already know. We hate anything *absolutely* new—anything without any name and for which a new name must be forced. So we take the nearest name, even though it be inappropriate. In later life this economical tendency to leave the old undisturbed leads to what we know as 'old fogyism.' A new idea or a fact which would entail extensive rearrangement of the previous system of beliefs is always ignored or extruded from the mind in case it can not be sophistically reinterpreted so as to tally harmoniously with the system. We have all conducted discussions with middle-aged people, overpowered them with our reasons, forced them to admit our contention and a week later found them back as secure and constant in their old opinion as if they had never conversed with us at all. We call them old fogies. But there are young fogies too. Old fogyism begins at a younger age than we think. I am almost afraid to say so, but I believe that in a majority of human beings it begins at about twenty-five."

On the margin of the book which the writer consulted in the Carnegie Library, some reader had written opposite this statement, in terms as emphatic as they were indecent *"That is a lie!"* The writer, however, believes it to be solid truth. He has seen old fogies in the seats of his very students. Some of them, too, men who criticised their professors for their antiquated views! In some the law of psychological economy is imperative before they begin to preach. So far from passing a "dead line" they never seem to get over the life line.

It is true that they continue to enlarge the field of intellectual vision; they add to their information; they accumulate ideas. But all they acquire is disposed in the mind according to unchangeable categories. They do not formulate any new law of thought, they make use of no new principles. In this work of homiletics they may learn much of the formal instruction and be able to recite upon it with ease. But they learn little or no homiletics for all that. They never will be fresh or interesting preachers. They will not meet the conditions of the age. Worst of all they will never be able to get a hold upon the young life which is the very hope of the Church.

But, on the other hand there are some who never grow old. One who knew Andrew Carnegie intimately well remarked that one reason of his great financial success was the fact that he would never consent to retain a piece of machinery in his mills when there was something else introduced into the market that would do the work better. The cost of the change was a minor consideration—the product was everything. This indicates a certain quality of mind in the great iron-master which is shown in many ways. He keeps close to youth. He gives millions for their education. He is still youthful in manner and spirit and the young love him.

Yes; and the young do not shun the old because of their years. This has been disproved in many instances. To be sure the illustrations are rare; but there are enough of them to establish the principle. There are a few old men and old women in every good-sized community whom the young admire and whose companionship they enjoy. When the writer was a college boy there was a man in his native city whose society he sought on his visits home more frequently than that of any one else; and he was just fifty years his senior!

May not ministers learn the lesson?

ORIGINALITY

ORIGINALITY

The preacher must be interesting.

I. What is Originality?

The Absolute and the Relative.

II. Obstacles.

1. Too much independence.
2. Too little independence.

III. Forms of Unworthy Originality.

1. Parade of Orthodoxy or Heterodoxy.
   "Great Sermons."
2. Affectation.

IV. How Originality may be Cultivated.

A hard lesson to learn.

1. Be Scriptural.
2. Preach the distinctive truth.
3. Use helpful literature.
   Dangers of mere scholarship.
4. Study men, life, occasions, etc.

Sensationalism.

Read Garvie's "Guide to Preachers," Part III; 9. Quayle's "Pastor-Preacher,"
p. 124 seq.; Broadus, Part I, Chap. V.

XI.

ORIGINALITY.

We recur again to the question with which we introduced the proceeding chapter, How shall the preacher's materials be so employed that the product shall be interesting and up-to-date? This question has not always received the attention which it deserves. The followers of the old homiletics were disposed to make light of it, and some even dismissed it as almost sacrilegious. With all such the question of interest had, at the best, a very small place. Was the subject important? Did it deserve attention? Were the hearers under a solemn obligation to listen? Such were the forms in which their meditations were usually cast. And even to-day there are those whose question is cast in a form which has become almost a vulgarism, "Is the subject worth while?"

But we are bound to remember that there are many subjects of great importance to which men would do well to listen, many subjects which are "worth while," whose discussion may be altogether dreary and stale. But in this age of the world people are not inclined to listen to such discussions. There are a vast multitude of people who are inclined to religion, and who are accustomed to attend divine worship, who will not go to church to be bored. Very often the most devoted Christians are found among this very class, and their motive is not an unworthy one. They desire to be instructed and refreshed, and they feel no compunctions of conscience in forsaking a preacher who does not command their attention and awaken their activities, for one by whom they may be taught and stimulated. We may set it down as one of the homiletical maxims of the present age that where one ceases to interest, he ceases to profit. Dr. Garvie, whose book entitled "A Guide to Preachers," from which we have already quoted, was written not for the ordained ministry, but as he himself tells us in his preface for lay preachers, devotes a whole chapter to the consideration of this subject. Perhaps it is just because his lectures were given before a class of laymen. But it is impossible to see how one who is to preach without ordination should devote himself to the interest of his congregation, while those who have been solemnly set apart to the sacred office may afford to dispense with it. Dr. Garvie gives some extended advice with regard to the way in which the art of interesting a congregation may be cultivated. The points which he makes are as follows:

(1) He should throw his material into such a shape that it will be easily remembered;

(2) He must stimulate the imagination;

(3) He should convey sympathy;

(4) He should take up such topics as move himself deeply.

He says, "In preparation the preacher ought always to consider whether what he intends to preach will set his own soul aglow or leave himself cold. For it is quite certain that the preacher will not move others unless he is himself moved. The complaint about dull sermons is often really a charge of coldness in the preacher."

Bishop Quayle should also be noted in this connection as illustrating the trend of the New Homiletics. In his book upon "The Pastor-Preacher" he also has a chapter

devoted to this matter entitled "The Sin of Being Uninteresting." He says, "The sin of being uninteresting in
a preacher is an exceedingly mortal sin. It has no forgiveness." This language is too strong, but it indicates
the trend of thought at the present time. The chapter
to which we have referred contains a number of epigrams in which the truth is expressed in a very happy
and forcible way. "We are not men of apathy. We are
men vigilant in intent, who have the sky upon our
shoulders and the round world in our hearts." "The
preacher must never drowse. His purpose is the changing
of the atoms of the soul so that it swings in a new circle.
Eternity is his tutor." "A sermon should be a fire, not
simply a smoke." "Nobody has to come to preaching.
Students have to come to class so as to get grades, but
the class-room method will not win a hearing." He has
also the following very fine illustration. "It is not meet
that such as dwell in lightnings work in the dark like
blind moles, and they do not. When the dynamo inveigles
lightning from the sky those workers have the lightning's torch to oil the machinery by. Even so the
preacher who has themes flaming bright beyond the lightnings must not walk by twilights. He must be fascinating in his recitation of facts which angels desire to look
into."

With all this we most heartily agree, but the question
is, How may one become interesting without resorting
to methods which are meretricious and undignified? and
which are incongruous with a solemn presentation of
the truth of God? The difficulty which an honest
preacher finds in attempting to interest an audience resides in his inability to direct his course between the
pretentious on the one hand, and the common-place upon
the other; and very many preachers in their attempt to

do what they feel that they should do in this regard have either run into a vulgar sensationalism or fallen into the prosaic and platitudinous.

The question which is involved in this whole matter is that of originality. It is only as the preacher succeeds in presenting truth in fresh form, and with timely application, that he engages the interest of those to whom he speaks. When he is successful in doing this he is pronounced an original thinker, and so indeed he may be, but some other preacher, (and young men are more apt to be led into the temptation than older ones,) looking upon his success and endeavoring to repeat it in his own experience, seeks to be original by methods which he can scarcely countenance himself, and which thoughtful people disapprove.

I. What then is originality? That is to say, What is that particular form of originality which is suited to the pulpit, and which engages the interest of a congregation? It has been well said by others that we must distinguish between that originality which is absolute and that which is relative. There is so little of the former that we might almost say that there is none at all. Broadus deals at some length with the distinction between these two terms. He quotes the Edinburg Review, "The ancients have stolen all our best ideas;" and Goethe, "Very little of me would be left if I could but say what I owe to my predecessors and my contemporaries;" and remarks that Confucius five centuries before the Christian era proclaimed himself only a student of antiquity. Nevertheless there is still left some room for absolute originality. Occasionally an idea is expressed or a theory propounded which is entirely new to the thinking world. Only it never comes by seeking it, and the preacher who supposes that this sort of originality can be cultivated will end in intellectual excesses and aberrations, because of which he may be relegated to the rank of cranks, if not of lunatics. The originality which is absolute is always, in the best sense of that term, a blunder. The men who are gifted with it are more surprised by its incoming than any one else. It is like the discovery of America. As one has said, Columbus found it "because he could not get by it," and we must remember that the discovery occurred because Columbus was not seeking a new world but an old one: he found America in searching for India.

So also it has been with many great inventions, as well as with many great discoveries: they have surprised their own authors.

But in order to such inventions one must not be given to sleep. His mind must be alert and active: he must be busily engaged with the nature and uses of old truth or he certainly will never discover the new.

And it should also be remembered that while there is little that is absolutely original, and while that little never comes to one who has given himself to the search for it, yet there is much which is absolutely original to the apprehension and the aspiration of many of the minister's parishioners, and it will not be amiss for him to seek for those principles and truths which will bring to his people thoughts which they have never framed, desires which they have never cherished, and services for Christ of which they had never dreamed.

The relative originality, however, is that to which the preacher should devote his particular attention, if he is to be interesting and fresh. This relative originality is that which, while it is not new in itself, is new in its relations and applications. The old truths bear to it the same relation that the old germs bear to what are called "seedling" products. There have been pears and apples in the world since the world began, and when their seeds are planted there is nothing more than pears and apples reproduced. But among the many reproductions which may follow the planting there will be found a few varieties of superior value, and in some respects very different from all which have preceeded them. No new fruit is produced, but that which is produced has all the value of new fruit. How very remarkably this is illustrated in the age in which we live, particularly in the work of Burbank, the great horticultural wizard. About twenty five years ago a farmer in North Carolina discovered among his tobacco plants one with a much lighter leaf than the rest, and possessing other peculiar qualities. He gave it great care and perpetuated its product. The result was a new kind of tobacco much more valuable than any other. It was still tobacco, but it had much of the advantage of a new creation.

Now when we come to apply this to the preacher's work we remark that the basis of preaching certainly is not original. As we have already seen, his theme is given to him: from this fundamental principle the preacher must never depart. He should not attempt to discover any new subjects of thought in the line of religious truth. He can not be original in this respect even if he would be, and yet this same basis of preaching becomes original in effect, with the preacher's experience and observation. The truths with which he deals are as old as the race, but as the race is renewed generation by generation, with its changing customs, its changing environment, and its changing conditions, the old truth is invested with new meaning and is put to new uses. Prof. James says, "It is an odd circumstance that neither the old nor the new by itself is interesting. The absolutely old is insipid; the absolutely new makes no appeal at all. The old in the new is what claims the attention. No one wants to hear a lecture on a subject completely disconnected with his previous knowledge; but we all like lectures on subjects of which we know a little already." The preaching of the old truth, therefore, issues in new interpretations, new combinations, new illustrations, and new applications, and that preacher who becomes the most expert relative to these things will so far forth be regarded as the most original thinker, and will prove the most interesting speaker. These things, therefore, the preacher should constantly cultivate, for it is in these things that his sermons will be found to possess their present-day value. The old truths are like old coins which have been reminted. Not a particle of the gold is lost, nor does it in any respect change its character, but it is cast in a new form, it is stamped with a new design, it bears a fresh inscription; and on this account—not because it is a new metal, but because it is a new issue, it may properly bear the initial of the mint from which it is sent. The preacher may say "It is mine."

It is in this way that the old truth actually becomes the preacher's own. It is his very truth and there is no reason why he may not cherish a paternal pride in it; and likewise because it has become his own he secures for it the interest of those to whom it is presented.

II. Such being, as we understand it, the nature of originality, we pass to consider some of the common obstacles to its acquisition. We need but mention to begin with those erroneous views concerning its character to which we have already referred. There are others in addition to these.

1. The disposition upon the part of the preacher to

depend too largely upon his own self. One may be an original thinker, but there is nothing which will so quickly destroy his originality as for him to be made in any way aware of the fact. Self-consciousness is more destructive of originality perhaps than any other one thing. It is said that even Wellington lost power and influence after the battle of Waterloo. It was for this very reason.

And there are some who, because they speak readily, finding no difficulty in filling up the time with such thoughts as they have, and with thoughts which appear to them to be somewhat out of the ordinary, believe they are sufficient of themselves. But the soil of the mind is very much like the soil of the fields. It will certainly be exhausted in time except it be frequently fertilized. More than that, nothing is more exhausting to the soil than the constant production of the same crop. Every farmer knows that rotation is the rule of fertility, but with the preacher who depends largely upon his own resources, there is neither fertilization nor rotation. His intellectual soil will be sure to run out. He must not only give himself to such study as he may derive from intercourse with his fellow men, and from books of various kinds, as we have already noted; but he must be particularly alert to the reception of suggestions of new and strange truth. One mind often acts upon another mind as a charge of electricity passing over one wire acts upon another which is parallel to it. A current is induced in the second conductor of equal power with that which is shown in the first.

One reason why many preachers who would be original are not so, is found in simple indolence. Men fail in the pulpit sometimes for the same reason that they fail in other walks of life. The plain truth is that they are too lazy; they are not willing to work for results. They have not the patience to investigate, and reason, and study. They imagine that genius is a spontaneous product, and that its accomplishments are not the result of conscious effort. They ought to know the truth with regard to this matter, that the vast majority of those whom the world has pronounced geniuses were men of indefatigable toil. The illustrations are too numerous and too familiar to require any citation.

2. The second obstacle to the cultivation of originality is found at the very extreme from that at which the first is found. There is not sufficient dependence upon one's self. As there are in commercial life what are called the "get-rich-quick" plans, so there is in the intellectual life what may be called the "get-wise-quick" plan, and the preacher sometimes falls before the temptation. There are very few who are guilty of using other men's sermons, although even this is sometimes done in countries other than our own; but while the preacher may hesitate to do quite so much as this, he is sometimes not averse to using another's plan, or following the exact outline of a sermon which he has heard or read. He resorts for example to what are known as homiletical commentaries, and searches diligently for such subjects and divisions of subjects as may suit his purpose. If he does not go so far as this, he will at least not hesitate to employ the very argument which another has presented, or the very illustration which another has used.

Everything of this sort is absolutely destructive of the preacher's originality. It has the same effect upon the mind which so-called prepared foods have upon the stomach: it unfits it in the course of time to receive and assimilate any strong or wholesome mental pabulum. We have already indicated what one is to do with other men's sermons, and with literature of a like kind. They are to be studied and analyzed, the hiding of the preacher's power is to be discovered, and more particularly in this connection the secret of his fresh and original utterances. But the thing itself is never to be employed at second-hand.

III. What are some of the unworthy forms of attempted originality? There are a number of them, the most conspicuous of which we may mention.

1. The parade of one's devotion to a certain kind of doctrine: it makes comparatively little difference what kind of doctrine it may be. It may be heterodoxy; it may be orthodoxy. There are some who seem to imagine that they will appear the more original in departing from the faith, but there are others with an almost equal self-deception who appear to think that they will be the more original by keeping to the old faith in the old form. But originality is not exhibited in the studied parade of any form of faith. It is absolutely inconsistent with dishonesty of any kind. If one is tempted to become heterodox that his utterances may be the more fresh, he will only make his attempts the more laughable. But the same may happen in the other case. The parade of scholarship, the use of unusual terms, particularly technical terms, the reference to abstruse subjects and unfamiliar objects, to which the preacher is sometimes inclined with the mistaken idea that it will make capital for him, should be expressly avoided by him who would be strictly up-to-date. Henry Ward Beecher said with regard to this matter, in his Yale Lectures: "There is one temptation concerning which I must be allowed to give you a special and earnest caution. It is on the subject of 'great' sermons. The themes you will handle are often of transcendent greatness. There will be times

continually recurring in which you will feel earnestly the need of great power, but the ambition of constructing great sermons is guilty and foolish in no ordinary degree. I do not believe that any man ever made a great sermon who set out to do that thing. Sermons that are truly great come of themselves: they spring from sources deeper than vanity or ambition. Perhaps I should have said 'show' sermons rather than 'great' sermons, sermons adapted to create surprise, admiration, and praise; sermons as full of curiosities as a pedlar's pack. Such discourses are relied upon to give men their reputation. To construct such sermons men oftentimes labor night and day, and gather into them all the scraps, ingenuities, and glittering illustrations of a lifetime. They are the pride and the joy of the preacher's heart, but they bear the same relation to a truly great sermon as a kaleidoscope full of glittering beads of glass bears to the telescope which unveils the glory of the stellar universe. These are Nebuchadnezzar sermons over which the vain preacher stands saying, 'Is not this great Babylon which I have built for the royal dwelling-place, by the might of my power and for the glory of my majesty.' Would to God that these preachers, like Nebuchadnezzar, might go to grass for a time, if like him they would return sane and humble." Dr. Lyman Abbott gives the same caution. He says: "Preachers should be afraid of great sermons: their congregations are. The minister may perhaps preach one occasionally by accident, but it always ought to be an accident."

2. The second unworthy form of attempted originality is affectation. The preacher seems to imagine that to be odd is to be original. Therefore, he does not dress like other men; he cultivates a peculiar delivery; or his affectation may be in his pulpit manners. He gives him-

self to paradox, epigram, sententious sayings of various kinds, for which there is a continual and very apparent strife. Little more needs to be said upon this matter except to remember the words of Phillips Brooks that "it would be very easy to be a John the Baptist if it resided in nothing more than a garment of camel's hair and a diet of locusts and wild honey."

IV. We come now to a most important question, How shall originality be cultivated? Prior to this, however, there is another question which may need an answer, Can originality really be cultivated at all? To this latter question we reply with an emphatic affirmative; it certainly can be cultivated. Herein is a paradox—originality to be cultivated! Strange indeed that such matters as naturalness and simplicity must be acquired; but so it is. Why is not one original without effort and without practice? Simply because we are ruled by conventional customs. It is not only the bane of the pulpit, but of many other aspects of thought and work. The old proverb has it that we "cannot teach an old dog new tricks." But in a certain sense we are all "old dogs," in that we inherit the principles and practices of our predecessors. We follow example. As James and John would have called down fire from heaven upon the inhospitable Samaritans because Elijah did, so we, also. But Jesus taught them that even the example of a prophet is not always a proper precedent, and displayed His own divine originality in taking another course.

It is this slavish adherence to precedent which stands in the way of our originality. The child becomes formal and stilted before he has reached his "teens." He has already learned to wear a mask to conceal his true self and to hide his own impressions. So we have to learn the hard lesson of a return to the normal. Yes, it is indeed hard! It is the more hard sometimes because when one attempts to be himself the very attempt renders him most unlike himself. It is like sitting for a portrait; the expression of the countenance is not that to which friends are accustomed. Yet one should strive to be himself in all honesty. As before the eye of the All-seeing God, the preacher may continually say to himself, "Let me preserve my intellectual and spiritual integrity; let me say what I really believe; let me not tie my conscience to any one's dictum;" and God will help such an honest soul.

Let the preacher remember that even if he is not himself he can not be anyone else, nor can he successfully adopt the methods of anyone else. Chancellor Day remarks: "Every man has a right to be original. He will be if he is himself. In a sleigh factory one day I saw a shaft-bending machine. A row of ash sticks were placed in it after having been steamed, and the power was applied, and they all bent over beautifully alike. But I thought that if some had been white wood, some pine, and some birch, it would not have been so. The machine would have broken some of the sticks, and some of the sticks would have broken the machine. It is not best to put one's self into the common mold."

If one really succeeds in being himself, as we believe any man may, he will certainly be original, and this just because no man is like any other man in all respects. And probably after all has been said with regard to the matter, and we review all our considerations with regard to it, we shall find that the great hindrance to originality is simply this, that one tries to be something or somebody else than that which God intened him to be. If it were only possible for us to throw off the clamps that bind our intellectual processes, and let our minds work willingly and freely, we should be very much more useful to the world in which we live.

The fact is that everyone is original to a certain extent. The old lady stated the exact truth when she said that either everybody was peculiar or nobody was peculiar. We are all peculiar in certain ways, and in the proper government of our very peculiarities we find our largest field for action and our greatest power for good.

How then shall we learn to be fresh and original?

1. No better rule can be given to begin with, for the preacher who would be fresh and original, than that he should be Scriptural—truly Scriptural, breathing its atmosphere, emitting its fragrance, and thereby conveying to others its deeper spirit.

The reason why the Bible ministers to originality is this—that it sets forth the absolute form of thought and conduct. There is nothing fictitious or factitious in it. It lays bare the unchanging heart of man. Its careful student therefore learns to know himself and to be himself; and learning this, he learns to teach others the fundamental and the normal.

Old as the Bible is, it still remains the very freshest book that is ever placed upon our shelves, and a most significant thing with regard to its study is this, that those very ministers who are the best exponents of the New Homiletics insist the most emphatically upon Scriptural preaching.

There are some who suppose that in order to be fresh, even when they preach from Scriptural texts, they must depart from their plain teaching and introduce material derived from what they regard as advanced thought. Certainly this is the very best way in which not to be fresh and original. If any one is in doubt with regard to it, let him consult the sermons of those who preach to the largest audiences or have the largest following. Let him consider the work of the great modern evangelists and others, who stir the heart of the people, and conduct the great agencies for the good of mankind. D. L. Moody was an unlettered man, and had very few scholarly sources from which to draw, and yet no preacher for several generations has displayed a finer originality than he. Consult his "Notes from My Bible." In preparing this chapter, the book was opened at random, as it has often been before, without any attempt to find particular illustrations of our position. The place found was page 136, containing his notes upon certain verses in the fourth and fifth chapters of the Gospel by John. The text is so familiar that we need not refer to the particular verses. The following are some of his notes. Speaking of the woman of Samaria, he says: "Twice on earth our Lord asked a favor, and twice was he refused. Here, when He asked for a drink, and on the cross, when He asked for water and they gave Him vinegar." Speaking of the well of water he says: "God does not want a dam but a canal to carry the gospel. Dam up a spring and you get a frog-pond." And again: "Water rises to its level, and the water of life that comes from the throne of God will carry one into the presence of God." Concerning the Savior's remark to His disciples with regard to the fields white to the harvest, he says: "Any farm-laborer is called to reap, but it takes a skillful man to sow." Again: "John the Baptist was a burning and shining light. To burn is not enough; a fire-brand does that. To shine is not enough; a glow-worm does that." These are illustrations from a single page of those very fresh remarks with which the sermons of Mr. Moody abound. Spurgeon might also be quoted to show how exceedingly fruitful Scriptural preaching is in the cultivation of originality. His "Feathers for Arrows" have suggested the way to use the Scripture by illustration and application to very many teachable ministers.

Brastow says, in his "Modern Pulpit:" "There is a demand for preaching that is more distinctly textual and expository, or at least that avails itself more freely of Biblical material." He has certainly read correctly the signs of the times. S. Edward Young, who was accustomed to preach to large congregations in the theatres and in the public parks of Pittsburg, remarked to the writer that after he had begun to expound the Scripture to these people they were not content with any other kind of preaching. Brastow continues: "A pulpit use of the Bible commensurate with the popular interest in it, with our better knowledge of it, with our more concrete illustrative method of preaching, and with men's religious needs, is in process of development. This use of the Bible will make the work of preaching more suggestive, more living, more real and cogent."

We can scarcely estimate how the dominant note of the Holy Scriptures, as it is set forth in the Gospel of Jesus Christ, is being sounded in every department of thought and work to-day, and therefore we can scarcely estimate the importance of the preacher emitting the call of the day by the clear and true sounding of this Biblical note. The age in which we live has come to possess an intense realization of the claim which human life has upon it. Art, science, and philosophy are being driven resistlessly towards reality. All are calling for that which is vital and for that which is eternal, and from no source can the preacher derive his adaptation to this dominant factor in the life of to-day more than from the study of the Scriptures. When he attempts to do this he finds himself becoming adapted to the most characteristic phases of modern life; he actually acquires a new and better dialect in which to state the old but ever living truth. His mind becomes alert; his intellect is reawakened; he meets the end of the age in which he lives.

2. When the preacher endeavors to work in the spirit which has been thus indicated, and proceeds to discuss a particular passage of Scripture, he will minister to his originality in the attempt to find its distinctive truth. We mean by this, the truth which is contained in this passage that is not contained in other passages, though they may deal with the same general subject. Do not preach a sermon upon any text that might just as well be preached on a dozen others. No two passages of Scripture convey exactly the same lesson, or minister to exactly the same grace, except those which are positive repetitions. Take, for example, two of the miracles, or two of the parables of the Savior, which to the superficial reader seem so much alike as to convey exactly the same truth. A closer examination will reveal the fact that the one has something in it which the other lacks. Let us recur again, for example, to the miracle of the miraculous draught of fishes in Luke 5, and what might seem to be the repetition of the miracle in John 21. Let the preacher ask himself, Why did the Savior perform two such miracles, apparently so very much alike? Let him proceed to lay the one down beside the other, and note the respects wherein they differ. Let him ask himself if he finds anything in the one which was adapted to the beginning of the disciples' training, and anything in the other which was adapted to the close of that training, and their entrance upon their apostolic work. Let him note what might at first seem mere incidentals, the fact that in the first miracle the nets were breaking, but not

so in the second. Let him compare the effect upon Peter's mind in the first miracle with the effect upon the minds of all the disciples, including Peter, in connection with the second. Then let him ask himself whether he can preach the same sermon upon both miracles. The two passages of Scripture are no more alike than two gravel beds may be, in one of which gold may be found, and in the other of which it is absent.

The preacher should not begin to write until he has found this truth—the distinctive truth of the passage. Oftentimes it furnishes the very largest element in a discourse which is truly fresh and inspiring.

3. The preacher need not imagine that in order to be fresh and original he must derive all his comments upon the passage in hand from his own rumination upon the subject. Neither must he imagine that he can import into his sermon the fresh and original comments which others have made upon it. But this he may do, he may read any literature connected with the subject with which he is engaged, containing thought parallel to that which he derives from the passage, and read it in order to the stimulation of his own mind. This is what Broadus calls "water in a dry pump." Many times it will avail to draw forth that which is sweet and refreshing. This is particularly true of the use of poetry.

The product of this literature, therefore, is to be carefully considered and thoroughly assimilated before it is employed by the preacher. He makes use of none of it thereafter in the very form in which it is conveyed to him, but he has fed upon it, digested it, and derived strength therefrom. The exertion that follows is his own. The sermon product that is begotten of such work is original, but the preacher must be careful that he is not led by another in any way.

It can not be denied that there are certain dangers to originality in scholarship. If a man has not become enough of a scholar to engage in original research, and has gone no further than compilation, never reaching the stage of assimilation and appropriation, his originality will be very seriously impaired.

If the preacher is to be fresh and original he must shun this sort of thing. It is not that he is not to be a reader and a student, but that he must not suffer himself to become pedantic. He should present to his people from the pulpit only that which is fully and truly his own.

4. Let the preacher apply all his labor and study to the actual thought and life of men. If he is to be fresh he must reach that thought and that life as they really are, and as they are manifested in the rank and file of those that are about him. He must very seldom if ever preach to exceptional people. He must very seldom deal with exceptional sins or unusual sorrows. The subjects with which he is to be engaged are to be those with which his own people are engaged every day in the week, if not indeed every hour in the day. The Scripture which he has studied, the distinctive truths which he has found, the books which he has read, the observation he has had, are all to be material from which he may derive that which shall refresh and edify the souls to whom he ministers as they go about their daily work, and are burdened with their daily cares, and lead them in the way of salvation. One of the best things that Vinet ever said in discussing homiletics is this: "The basis of eloquence is the commonplace." It deserves to be written in letters of gold. It is worth being burned into the minds and consciences of every one who ministers in the name of Christ. Originality is not

to be found in the heights above or in the depths beneath, but right on this common level whereon we and
the people about us move. McKay Smith, in a brilliant
article upon this subject, says that what the people need
is "not simple remarks upon profound subjects, but profound remarks upon simple subjects." The import of
his words may not be at once apparent. What he means
is this, that many ministers think that their reputations
will be enhanced and their originality will be displayed
in discussing some very abstruse theme, which they are
really incompetent to handle; but they seem to imagine
that because the theme is so profound they will be regarded as profound themselves. The fact is they do
neither themselves nor their people any good. What the
people wish is instruction concerning the simple matters
of life, and they wish these subjects discussed, not in
words which they can not understand, nor in reference
to principles which they have not mastered, but in language which nevertheless goes down to the very roots
of things and conveys the undermost and final truth upon
the subject.

In order that we may have this eloquence of the commonplace, and make these profound remarks upon simple subjects, we must study not only the people that are
about us, but we must study occasions. Every day will
furnish us with something new; every week will bring
us opportunity for timely utterances. We must study the
age in which we live. We must not only be in it, but we
must be of it. We must know its current thought and
its characteristic life; its particular dangers; its special
promises, and all other things found in this age which
have not been found in the ages which preceded, at least
in the form in which they now appear.

This does not mean that we are to commit the folly

of composing whole sermons whose themes shall be derived from the occasion; it does not mean that we are to indulge in wholesale criticism of the age; or that we attempt to furnish a universal panacea for its ills. But the occasion and the age should be taken into account in every sermon that is delivered, and there may be frequent reference to the incidental things as the best taste and the most need will suggest.

And the preacher is to study himself. This study of himself will take with him a peculiar form: he will not use anything in the pulpit, by way of argument or illustration, that would not appeal to himself if it were presented by another preacher. Likewise he will not attempt to inflict upon the people that which he would consider stale and unprofitable if it were inflicted upon himself. In this sense he is to study himself, for he is not very unlike the people to whom he ministers.

V. A word may be said in concluding this subject concerning sensational preaching. It may be well to define it to begin with, because there is much preaching which is called sensational by those who are humdrum and conventional in their methods, without any good reason. Many a preacher who makes an honest attempt to be fresh is regarded with some suspicion by certain of his fellows, and does not receive fair treatment at their hands. It is far better, at all events, that a preacher should run to sensation than to stagnation.

And yet that which is really sensational should be condemned. What is sensationalism? Wherein does it differ from freshness and originality? The answer may be given in a word: sensationalism exalts the incidentals, while the proper originality exalts the essentials. Two ministers in the same city, occupying pulpits in churches on opposite corners of the street, were preaching during the same winter courses of sermons which were illustrated by charts and pictures. They were both ministering to large and attentive audiences, but during the winter a certain family left the one Church displeased with the exercises, and connected themselves with the other. When asked why this was so, by one who was anxious to discover the essential difference in the method of the two men, the head of the family replied: "The one uses his sermon for the sake of his pictures: the other uses his pictures for the sake of the sermon." The discrimination was just; it explains the whole matter. Bishop Quayle remarks, speaking upon this subject: "Only weak men are sensational. The preacher who knows the art of preaching will never need to be sensational; he will be inspirational." And Brastow says: "Sensational preaching is a concession to vulgarity that is intolerable." Oftentimes the preacher who has been given to sensational methods abandons them. One such has said: "I turned my pulpit into a lecture platform for the discussion of religious themes from a scientific view-point, but I have decided I will stop this. It does not pay; it brings in the end no permanent results. I can not see where any lasting good has come to my Master from such a course." Another has said: "If I preach popular sermons at night, along lines literary and historic, I pack my house to the doors, but when I begin to preach gospel sermons the crowds melt away, and the more gospel I get into the sermon the less of crowds I have left; but I have resolved what to do, to quit all this." With regard to this last preacher, we should remark that undoubtedly the reason why the crowds melted away under his honest endeavor to preach the gospel was because he had been preaching popular sermons so long that he had forgotten how to preach the gospel attractively. A cer-

tain daily paper, in one of its leading editorials, remarked: "Popular preaching has been tried without
success. Pulpit orations seem somehow to lose their
charm, and it no longer pays to cater to the secular tastes
of the multitude. It is very generally the case that the
preachers who lay the gospel on the shelf, and undertake
to enlist interest by theatrical methods, achieve a temporary success, but find in the long run that they are on
the wrong track. The crowds attracted at first by spectacular inducements soon fall away, and at the same time
the sternly orthodox element, which is the backbone of
Church membership, is apt to be alienated and to seek
elsewhere opportunities for worshipping in the old fashion, plain and unadorned."

How then may one who earnestly desires to be fresh
and original safeguard himself against sensationalism?
The answer is in three parts:

1. Let him cultivate good taste. This will largely
depend upon the community in which he lives, and the
character of the congregation to which he ministers. If
he is in doubt about his own judgment in the matter, let
him take advice and seek counsel.

2. Let him be thoroughly Scriptural in his preaching,
and let it be the whole design of his preaching to set
forth the message of the Word of God. It was just here
that Moody and Spurgeon saved themselves from the
charge of sensationalism. Their methods often aroused
enthusiasm, and sometimes provoked laughter, but they
were not charged with sensationalism.

3. Let him earnestly desire to save and help others.
Let him not think of his own reputation and his own
glory, but of the good of his fellow men and the glory
of his Master. Let it be his earnest prayer "Lord help
me to preach the saving word to those to whom I minister, and thus to glorify thy great and gracious name."

INSTRUCTION.

INSTRUCTION.

Instruction the first element of sermonizing.
    Neglected in the past generation.
    Necessity of its revival.

I. What shall the preacher teach?
    1. Fundamental truth.
    2. Doctrine.
    3. Ordinances.
    4. Christian activities.
    5. Christian morality.
    6. Source of comfort.

II. How shall instruction be given?
    1. Not in offensive particulars.
      Example of the prophets, John, Jesus.
    2. By the exposition of Scripture.

Read Faunce's "The Educational Ideal in the Ministry;" Forsyth's "Postive Preaching and the Modern Mind;" Jefferson's "Minister as Prophet," Chap. V.

XII.

INSTRUCTION.

The first element of sermonizing is Instruction. There is absolutely nothing which takes precedence of it. The preacher should be a teacher before all things else. The sermon from which the hearer learns nothing is a failure. The apostles were sent forth by the Savior to teach as well as to preach, and Jesus Himself was emphatically a teacher. He was so regarded by His contemporaries, and has been so regarded ever since. All the great leaders of religious thought from the beginning have excelled in the teaching function, and it is highly important that the teaching faculty should be developed by every one who attempts to proclaim the gospel.

The past generation did not attach the proper value to the educational feature of preaching, and it fell very largely into disuse. Altogether too much emphasis was placed upon the fact that the preacher is called a "herald" in the New Testament, and it was commonly supposed that exhortation should be the chief feature in pulpit utterances. This lack of instruction was defended with some show of justice upon the consideration that religious education was largely conveyed through other channels than the pulpit, notably by means of the Sunday school, the Young Men's Christian Association, and other similar agencies. It was held that people who were accustomed to attend Church were already indoctrinated and familiarized with the characters and facts of the

Scripture. The result was a notable decline in church attendance and in pulpit power; but there was no attempt to correct it. Henry Ward Beecher, in his first series of Yale Lectures, delivered in the winter of 1871-2, emphatically belittled the teaching element in sermonizing. He said: "A preacher is a teacher, but he is more. The teacher brings before men a given view or a department of truth. He expends his force upon facts or ideas. But the preacher assumes or approves facts and truths as a vehicle through which he may bring his spirit to bear upon men. A preacher looks upon truth from the constructive point of view. It is not enough that men shall know; they must be." This quotation indicates Mr. Beecher's idea of the scope of preaching, and he pursues it through a number of paragraphs. The preacher, he declared, is an artist, a master-builder, a reproduction of the truth in personal form, but not in any distinctive sense a teacher. Ten years later, in 1881, Professor Phelps, of the Andover Theological Seminary, published his lectures on preaching. It is apparent to one who reads the book that there is promise of a turn in the tide, but it has not really turned as yet. Professor Phelps, however, notes the defect in sermonizing occasioned by the omission of the teaching element, and says: "We need to reinstate the Biblical instruction of our churches and of our youth in the pulpit and in the hands of pastors. This, it seems to me, is the vital point to be carried. The fatal evil is that preaching should be isolated from the work of Scriptural teaching." And again: "One of the most vital changes which our present system of Christian work needs is to reinstate in the pulpit the work of Biblical teaching and restore the leadership in it to the pulpit. I say 'restore' because the pulpit once had that leadership, for it had the whole of the work.

It is no innovation to devise methods for setting the pulpit again at the head of all expedients and of all training for the Scriptural education of the people." Professor Phelps gives, in the same connection, a chapter from his own experience in which he was led to modify his pulpit methods, and instead of searching for unique texts, to make use of the results of his Scriptural studies in his pulpit. This course of Biblical sermons which he prepared, and which ran through four months during his experiment with the system, was renewed after a time and continued for six years. He says with regard to the experience: "My success was not brilliant, but I am confident that my Biblical course saved my pulpit."

At the present time, however, there is a very decided attempt to restore to the pulpit that element which Professor Phelps discovered that it lacked. President McClure, of McCormick Seminary, delivered an address before the Presbyterian Social Union of Pittsburg, in the fall of 1910, on the subject: "A Teaching Church the Need of the Age." His ideas seemed to strike many who heard him with all the force of novelty; but they were most significant as proceeding from such a source. One of the exponents of the New Homiletics is found in the Yale Lectures for 1908 by President Faunce of Brown University. It will be observed that these lectures were delivered thirty-seven years after those of Henry Ward Beecher, to which we have referred. This course of lectures is entirely occupied with the teaching function of the pulpit, the subject being "The Educational Ideal in the Ministry." The title to the first chapter is "The Place of the Minister in Modern Life." It gives the cue for all the chapters that are to follow, and under the title are two quotations, the first from the prophecy of Daniel 12: 3, and the other from Luther's

"Table Talk." "The teachers (marg.) shall shine as the brightness of the firmament, and they that turn many to righteousness as the stars for ever and ever." "The good preacher should have these properties and virtues, first to teach systematically." It is hard to select from such a book, so full of suggestion upon this subject, but the following may serve as illustrations of the good things which it contains: "Every civilized community is to-day throbbing with educational activity. The impulse to gain new knowledge and apply that knowledge to life is clearly the dominant impulse of our time. The whole world is going to school. Instruction has gotten far outside the school-house and the college. Public libraries have sprung up in every village. The university extension has spread out its tendrils until a single university now enrolls three thousand students in extension courses. Public lectures are usually no longer of the old lyceum order, heterogeneous and aimless, but are definite courses of lectures by experts in some one field of knowledge. Correspondence schools have multiplied until a single school now enrolls 350,000 pupils. A new reading public has been developed. Hundreds of thousands of people are eagerly scanning the papers and frequenting libraries. Hundreds of thousands of parents are making heroic sacrifices to give their children the best possible mental training," and much more of the same nature. After considering all this he proceeds to discuss our great national peril, which he says is this, "that the supremely important task of our generation will fall between the Church and State and be ignored by both." This important task is religious training. To this, therefore, he argues that the pulpit must devote itself. He declares that no strong or enduring people ever yet existed without definite and continuous work in religious education, and that "without it the nation is palsied at its very heart."

The writer has been devoted to these principles ever since he became a teacher of Practical Theology, and one of his homiletical maxims from the start has been cast in the form of the opening sentence of this chapter, "The first element of sermonizing is Instruction."

There are two questions, then, to be answered in this connection, first, What shall the preacher teach? and second, How shall he teach it? We proceed to consider them.

I. What shall the preacher teach? We might answer in general terms, everything that has to do with the spiritual good of his people, but this answer is both too broad and too indefinite.

There are a large number of things which some people in this age seem to think the preacher ought to teach for which he has no call whatsoever, and it is very important that he should safeguard himself at this point. A vast variety of schemes and projects are anxious to get into the pulpit and obtain the prestige of the preacher's position and influence. Sometimes the preacher is very seriously tempted to turn aside from his proper calling to discuss such matters, and some occasionally do so, but it is generally done with a loss of capacity to undertake those specifically spiritual duties which devolve upon the holy calling.

The preacher is not to teach those things upon which adequate instruction is provided in other ways. The Church was not instituted to teach farming, finance, or athletics. Men are not trained for its ministry that they may enlighten their fellows upon art, science, philosophy, commerce, political economy, and many other subjects. The preacher must stick to the spiritual. When his advice is sought upon any subject in public or private, in the pulpit or out of it, it will be better for him to confine himself to those aspects of the question which touch man's relation to God. When this is not done, and either the Church or the preacher departs from its proper teaching function, a certain secularization of sacred things is accomplished which reacts upon the Church in its higher and holier ministries.

While it is impossible to specify all the subjects upon which the minister should give instruction to his people, and while one preacher may not find it necessary to discourse upon the same subjects which another may be called to discuss, it may be well to indicate some of the more important.

1. The first subject is fundamental truth. We mean by this term that truth has to do with the salvation of the soul. It may well be doubted if the majority of those who attend Church in the present age have any clear notions with regard to this. But even though the older portion of the congregation may have intelligent ideas with regard to it, there is a succession of hearers attendant upon our ministry, and a succession of generations growing up in the Church who need to be enlightened with regard to the principles of the doctrine of Christ year by year. In this respect the pulpit stands in the same relation to such as the secular school, and it would be just as foolish for the pulpit to dispense with primary instruction as for the school to do so. Nor can this work be relegated to the Sunday school, or even to the home. Whatever may be done in this regard in such quarters it does not relieve the preacher from his solemn responsibility.

This teaching of fundamental truth includes instruction with regard to the nature, guilt, and consequences of sin, and with regard to the nature of the justification which is in Christ, and of the way in which it may be imputed to the penitent and believing soul.

A number of years ago a certain young minister inquired of his companion, who like himself had just been settled in his first charge: "Have you ever thought of selecting from the Scripture the very simplest gospel text which you could find, and of preparing upon it the simplest possible sermon which you could prepare, showing the way of salvation in as plain terms as possible, such as even a child could comprehend?" Neither of them had done so, but they agreed to do it. It is not known what became of the sermon of the first, but that of the second was repeated many times through a number of years. It was always received with much interest, and was never delivered without conversions following it. Out of that sermon a simple tract was prepared in the same sort of language and for the same purpose. It was entitled "More Light." It was privately published at the first for use only in the preacher's congregation. It was brought to the notice of the American Tract Society; it was published by them in a variety of editions; it was subsequently translated into many languages and hundreds of thousands of copies have gone over the world. Many have been converted by the reading of the tract who never knew its author. These influences for good were the product of instruction of the simplest kind in fundamental truth. The preacher who devotes himself to this sort of work will be amply repaid.

Closely connected with this is instruction with regard to the nature of the change which takes place in one when he believes on the Lord Jesus Christ. This change is known as regeneration, or the new birth. It is not only a doctrine of the Scriptures, but it finds a place in modern psychology; for while this science is much devoted to those laws of intellectual growth whereby accumulations are slowly made, and changes in the mental constitution are slowly wrought, yet it is frequently confessed by the best authorities upon this subject that such sudden changes as occur in conversion must be recognized and confessed, and that there is no incompatibility between the general laws laid down by psychology and the most startling alterations in the way of character. It is the preacher's duty to teach men how these alterations are brought about; how the positive change in character may be determined; and how it is to be so effected that there shall not be a return to the former conditions. The preacher should teach the necessity of the converted man's making as decided an initiative in his Christian life as possible, throwing about his resolution every possible safeguard, taking a public pledge, making a formal confession of his faith, and determining by divine help not to suffer any lapse in character through the recurrence of his evil habits. If what is called "continuity of training" is taught by psychologists to be the only proper means of making the nervous system act invariably right, it may be well for the preacher to show how this principle is fully borne out by the teachings of the Scripture. The new life may be launched in such a way that all the old bonds will be broken, the old motives blasted, and new desires and new affections will be formed. Science has come to the aid of religion in this respect. Nevertheless the preacher may teach that regeneration is a supernatural work, accomplished only by the aid of the Holy Spirit, and is in this respect one of the most forceful arguments for the divine origin of the gospel which can be placed before men. Other fundamental truths allied to those which we have mentioned should be carefully taught from the pulpit. It is impossible to mention all of them.

2. The preacher should teach doctrine. In this term we refer to something of a more advanced character than those fundamental principles with which we have been engaged; we mean the deep things of God, the mysteries of the kingdom of heaven. The fundamental principles which we have reviewed are the milk to which the apostle referred, and doctrine the strong meat.

In every congregation there are a large number of thinking men and women who read religious literature, who are familiar with the latest thought upon religious subjects, and who are very much more anxious to be settled in the truth with regard to all these things than the preacher himself may suppose. Many of them will talk much more freely with each other than they will with the minister himself. Many of them hesitate to confide to him their intellectual difficulties, but they are profoundly desirous to obtain light which they may follow with no uncertainty. Such men and women look to the man in the pulpit for guidance, and they have a right to expect it from him. They welcome anything which he may say upon these questions, provided he appears capable of discussing them, and absolutely honest in the views which he advances.

A great deal is said with regard to "practical preaching." The spirit of the age is such that nothing is considered as of great value unless it can be put to use, and therefore it is supposed by some that there is no practical preaching in the proper sense of the term except that which refers to external duty, Christian activity, works of benevolence, or something of the kind. But to limit the term "practical" to preaching of this character renders it a positive misnomer. That preaching is practical not alone which results in external action, but which accomplishes a distinct purpose. Preaching is practical when it confirms faith, inspires hope, ministers courage, or in any other way assists in settling the minds of those to whom it is addressed. In this view of the matter no preaching is more practical than doctrinal preaching, if we understand by this not the mere exhibition of dogma for dogma's sake, but the clear and helpful exhibition of the great truths which are contained in the word of God for the sake of the edification of those to whom they are communicated.

These thinking men and women, to whom we have referred, need instruction more than they need anything else. Very few of them are in a combative frame of mind; very few, indeed, are violently arrayed against the Bible or the Church; and therefore the preacher should not undertake anything which would antagonize them. He must not ridicule their positions, or make light of their doubts, or think it necessary to produce labored arguments in order to convince them. The first element of sermonizing, in this respect, and to this end, is instruction. These people want to know more about God, His nature, the administration of His government, His providential dealings with mankind, His provisions for their well-being here and hereafter, and more than all else how one can be on terms with Him. These men and women long to know more about Jesus Christ. Who was He? Wherein did He differ from mere men? What was the burden of His teaching? What did He do for the world on Calvary? What is the deeper meaning of His resurrection and ascension? Thousands of people are hungry to-day for positive instruction with regard to such matters—instruction which they should not fail to receive.

It was not so, as we have already observed, in a

former age. In the early period of Protestantism, and just because the Reformers had broken with the Mother Church, it became necessary for the preacher to teach his people the views of truth which were held by the Protestant bodies. The Puritans who came to New England were doctrinal preachers. The Puritan ministry observed with great diligence the teaching function. Perhaps their discourses would be tiresome in this age, and perhaps their methods of presenting truth would not secure that attention from modern congregations which was given by those whom they addressed; but their ministry was suited to the age and, their people were thoroughly instructed. This method was perpetuated through several generations until we come to the beginning of the age of the so-called "pulpit orators," the age of the last generation. There were a number of these distinguished in their way, and followed by a vast number of people. Most of the preachers of the Protestant Church emulated their example, and endeavored to become pulpit orators themselves. All these drew upon the accumulated resources of instruction which their predecessors had furnished. They assumed the religious knowledge upon the part of their congregations, and they did so very properly; but inasmuch as they largely failed in exercising the teaching function themselves their capital was after a time expended. A generation was born without the knowledge of Scripture truth which their parents had had. The attempt was made to supply it chiefly through the work of the Sunday school, but with indifferent success. It was really not supplied at all. It now devolves upon the preacher of the present age to restore this capital, and to set forth without delay the teaching of the Bible with regard to the deep questions that agitate the minds of men.

3. Ordinances. By this we mean those institutions

of divine origin for which it is the special duty of the
Church to provide, and whose sacredness the Church
must maintain. The first and chief of these ordinances
is the family. There is crying need for instruction on
the part of the pulpit with regard to this holy ordinance.
The original meaning of marriage has been almost forgotten: the divine constitution of the family is not understood, and there is no one thing in American life, or
for that matter in the life of the whole world, which
stands so much in need of reorganization as the family.
Marriage is the organization of a household with a view
to the propagation of a Godly seed. The marriage bond
is absolutely indissoluble except by adultery or death.
In the case of adultery the offending party has no right
before God to ever marry again. The family is the unit
of society; it comprises three elements—the man, the
woman, and the child, in the order which has been stated.
It has but one representative before the state—the man,
the head of the house, the exponent of its family life;
and it may be seriously questioned whether it ought to
have more than the one representative before the Church
also. If the preacher will give solid instruction with regard to the divine ordinance of marriage, and the divine
institution of the family, he will perform a vast service
for his people, settling their minds with regard to certain questions which are rife at the present day, divorce,
voluntary childlessness, suffrage, and the like.

Preachers should also give instruction with regard
to those ordinances which belong peculiarly to the
Church; the meaning of worship, its different elements,
prayer, praise, and the proclamation of the gospel. He
should teach his people the proper attitude of their minds
during worship and how they may secure the greatest
good from its observance.

The preacher should give particular instruction with regard to the sacraments of the Church, Baptism and the Lord's Supper. It should be remembered that the sacramental system of any Church is its central and dominating feature. It controls its worship, its polity, and its theology. It makes the Church of God what it is, and it makes any particular form of Christianity what it is as distinguished from other forms. In former generations preachers were accustomed to give minute instruction with regard to the sacraments. The older men of to-day can remember when the occasion of every Lord's Supper was improved as an opportunity for teaching those truths of Scripture which are symbolized in the sacramental elements. But during the generation which is just passing Protestant preachers departed almost entirely from these practices. Their preparatory addresses and their sacramental sermons were almost entirely devoted to sentimental and pathetic meditation upon the sufferings of Christ, or to earnest exhortation to consecrated lives. Those who comprise the membership of our Churches to-day have largely grown up without understanding why the Lord's Supper is observed, how it should be sanctified, or what it signifies.

4. Christian activities. The preacher should give his people particular instruction with regard to the large organized endeavors of the Christian Church at the present time, more particularly its missionary operations. He will find not only that his people are very ignorant with regard to what is going on in the world to-day in the course of its enlightenment, but that they will listen with interest, even with eagerness, to the information which he may bring to them. He should also carefully direct those activities that are prosecuted in his own congregation, and be himself a very part of them. There

should be a Sunday school normal class in every Church which the preacher himself should conduct, because he is the arch-teacher of the congregation, and this work should not be committed to the hands of any one else. It is of the utmost importance that the preacher know what is being taught in his Sunday school, and he can not know in any other way so well as by himself telling his Sunday school teachers what to teach. In many Churches also certain societies undertake systematic training, the Young People's Society, and the Women's Missionary Society, for example. There may also be a Temperance Society in the Church, or other organizations which endeavor after a fashion to instruct their members in some particular line of work. The preacher should see to all this: his pulpit work should have reference to it. Occasionally he should pass these different organizations in review, and call the attention of his entire congregation to that which they are doing. Beyond this, he should not fail to have in mind some distinct Christian work to which he can refer the members of his congregation, and in which he shall counsel them to be engaged.

5. Christian morality. We should use the term "ethics," but that we think it might be misunderstood. It is not simple ethics which the preacher is to bring to his congregation, but that sort of ethics which is tied to the throne of God, and finds its expression in the Gospel of Jesus Christ. We call this Christian morality. There is very much need for instruction along this line because, owing to the general dissemination of Christian principles and the general conformity to Christian standards, a very large number exist who do not confess the Lord Christ, and who do not claim to be Christians, who yet wish to be regarded as moral men. Christian morality is in the air: it is one of the assets of modern civili-

zation. The Christian minister must recognize the fact, and so teach his people as that Christianity shall not only get credit for that which it does outside the Christian communion, but also that those who value morality shall find their motive for it, and their explanation of it, in the gospel of our Lord and Savior.

This Christian morality has its extension out into all the fields of thought and effort. It touches politics, commerce, and the social life; and the preacher should instruct his people with regard to its application to all these things.

6. One more subject of instruction should be mentioned. Those which we have already discussed touch the mental and actual life of the congregation—their thoughts and their efforts. But the preacher has also a very large field for instruction in another department. He has to deal not only with the motives and efforts of men and women, but with their joys and sorrows, their disappointments and heartaches; and considerable of his thought should be given to the matter of consolation. It is not enough for him that he should express his sympathy from the pulpit. He should teach his people where comfort and strength are to be found, and how they may be secured. He is not to lead them along the line of mere sentimental consideration, and dwell upon the mercy of God, or the compassion of the Savior without showing upon what they rest. The slipping feet of his parishioners will stand much more securely when he leads them beneath and behind all this to the fundamental elements of consolation, and their throbbing hearts will be set to rest much more effectually when he is able to unveil for them the purpose of God and the work of the Redeemer.

A certain Christian lady, who was deeply bereaved, was visited by her friends who, in order to her consolation, enquired if they should sing for her. She gladly answered, "Yes," and they inquired what should they sing. She answered:

> "Not all the blood of beasts
> On Jewish altars slain,
> Could give the guilty conscience peace,
> Or take away the stain."

Such an answer might seem very strange to some, especially to a young and inexperienced preacher. But the old saint fully understood the source of all true comfort. It is found only in the provisions of the divine grace as exhibited upon Calvary. Slattery says with regard to this matter, and most appropriately, "The preacher must preach doctrinal sermons. He must preach the most divine things of God which he can grasp. For comfort to be comfort must be more than sweet words and flowing assurances. It must be based on the firmest, deepest facts of life. There must be reasons, reasons so good that the mind will be convinced. The doctrinal sermon stands for comfort because it is constructive. It never tears down; it always builds up. Men need comfort; they therefore need faith, all they can get of it."

It would be well, therefore, for the preacher to lay out for himself a definite course of instruction, which may be modified, of course, by circumstances, but so arranged as that such subjects as we have indicated, with others that it may seem well to him to cover, may be embraced in it.

II. How is this instruction to be given?

1. It is not to be given by entering at any time into the offensive particulars of human life and conduct. This refers more especially to those subjects which have to do with the public life of a community. There was a time not very long ago when some preachers supposed that, in order to preach successfully with regard to vice, it was

necessary for them to fully inform themselves with regard to conditions in what is called the "red-light" districts of the cities. They went "slumming," protected by a police escort. They visited the gambling houses and brothels, and brought to their people an account of their visits. This horrible infection even invaded some of the theological seminaries, and young men preparing for the ministry were persuaded to do this awful thing. The sort of instruction that comes out of such experience is worse than worthless. So far from doing good, it does only harm to the preacher himself and to those who listen to him. An array of evil conditions, the details of sinful practices, are not edifying. Likewise there have been those who have supposed that the man who has himself experienced the effects of a vicious life was the best one to warn the people with regard to it, or to instruct them with regard to the way of escape from it, and such men are sometimes eagerly sought after. Their descriptions of their own degradation have proved attractive to a certain class of minds, and have been supposed to be stimulating to their morality. The same false principle has obtained in various ways. A certain very commendable effort to reclaim fallen women was largely sustained through the sale of a book which described the methods by which young girls were lured to their ruin. But all such methods are to be deplored, and the preacher is not called upon to follow any of them in his methods of instruction. The principle upon which they rest is altogether mistaken. The best teachers of purity are those who have always been pure themselves. We may "set a thief to catch a thief," but we may not commission one to reclaim him. It is not the preacher's business to set forth the details of any sinful course of life in order to remedy it.

No more is it his business to instruct those who are

not conducting their affairs according to the principles of the gospel with regard to particulars—such as the making of contracts, the engaging of employees, and other matters as belong to their own personal supervision. It is not for him to instruct his congregation at length with regard to the various duties of Christian citizenship, nor to give particular advice to those who direct the affairs of the political world. He is not to catalogue the sins of polite society, or hold them up to the ridicule or scorn of his congregation. The preacher may not legitimately pursue any such course in order to instruct his people with regard to the matters which have been already set forth.

The preacher will do well to make a careful study of the method of the inspired preachers as it is set forth in the Old and the New Testaments. The prophets of ancient Israel gave very particular attention to such matters as have been mentioned. In a certain sense they were political and social reformers, but they were not reformers in the sense in which that word is ordinarily used, in that they did not attempt to right the wrongs and correct the abuses of society by instituting a distinct regime in the place of that which already existed. Take the prophecy of Amos for example. We learn very much more of the internal condition of the kingdom of Israel under Jeroboam II. from this prophecy than we do from the contemporaneous historical books. Its actual state is very plainly set before us. We perceive the effect of the financial prosperity which the people enjoyed in consequence of the extension of their territory and the increase of their trade. We see their splendid summer houses and winter palaces, many of them adorned with marble and ivory, and furnished with splendid hangings, and articles of beauty. The luxury of the

people is set before us in their beds of ivory, their sump-
tuous couches, their elaborate banquets, their merry music, their splendid drinking vessels, and their costly
anointing oils. In the meantime we observe their devotion to the externals forms of religious service—their
daily sacrifices, their tithes every three days, their abundant free will offerings and the like, and yet there is no
minute discription of any of these things, but only those
graphic references which are found here and there in
the prophet's arraignment. There is no attempt upon
his part to paint a picture of the times, and yet his
preaching is as timely as possible. He condemns them
for their injustice, their oppression of the poor, their
many immoralities, even those of their aristocratic women. He pronounces the judgment of God upon them
in no unmeasured terms, and tells them plainly why they
have been already cursed with drought and mildew and
the blasting of their vineyards and olive-yards. Amos is
faithful to his commission. He holds the plumb-line of
Jehovah before the eyes of Jehovah's recreant people, and
when he is counseled to take refuge in flight lest he pay
the penalty of his boldness and his fidelity by his death,
he refuses to be turned aside. His preaching is full of
illustration, argument, exhortation, and gentle pleading
with the people. He uses one of the most remarkable
figures of speech in order to describe the condition which
is coming upon Israel which is to be found anywhere
in sacred literature. It is that of the "Famine of the
word of God" found in the eighth chapter of his book,
beginning with the eleventh verse. And his other figure
of the pursuing sword, found in the ninth chapter, is
equally expressive. Though these sinners of Israel were
to dig into Sheol, thence would the hand of Jehovah take
them. Though they were to climb up into heaven He

would bring them down. Though they should hide themselves in the top of Carmel, Jehovah woul search them out. Though they should cover themselves in the bottom of the sea, even there He would find them. Captivity would not conceal them from the Almighty. Jehovah would follow them to the end. And yet, for all this terrible warning and proclamation of severe judgment, the preaching of Amos contains some of the sweetest promises which are to be found in all Old Testament prophecy, expressed also in a figure of speech. The house of Israel would be sifted among all the nations as grain is sifted in a sieve, but the least kernel should not fall upon the earth. The tabernacle of David which was fallen down was to be rebuilt and its breaches repaired. The blessing of God was to return upon the land, its barrenness was to be healed. The days would come when the plowman should overtake the reaper, and the treader of grapes him that sowed the seed, and the mountains should drop sweet wine and all the hills should melt. Jehovah would bring back the captivity of His people Israel. They would again be planted in their own land, and would no more be plucked up out of their land for ever.

The preacher who desires to know how he is to give instruction to his people can not do better than to make a careful study of such preaching as that of Amos. But the other inspired preachers proceeded upon the same method. Consult, for example, the preaching of John the Baptist. Jesus declared that he was the greatest man that ever lived. Certainly he was the greatest preacher who ever preached, Jesus Himself alone excepted. No man has ever enjoyed such popularity, using that word in its best sense, as John the Baptist. Evidently his preaching was attractive and original, or he would not have commanded such a following. He emptied the cities, he populated the wildernesses, he threw society into a ferment. All classes came into the wildernesses to hear him, soldiers and civilians, Pharisees and publicans, merchants and mechanics, and they were swayed beneath his oratory as reeds before the wind. They heeded his calls to repentance and multitudes were baptized by him, confessing their sins. But John the Baptist, like Amos, was not a reformer in the technical sense of that word, nor did he preach a reform as the term is generally understood. The student may learn for himself just how he preached. Consult, for example, the account given by Luke—his answer to the question of the multitudes, to that of the publicans, and to that of the soldiers on service. He gives us no photographic picture of the evil life of the age. We do not learn from him the character of the extortions of the publicans, or the cruelty of the soldiers! but we do see from his answers to their questions that they knew that he understood all the conditions of their lives and was capable of advising them with regard to their correction.

But above all, the preacher will learn from the method of the Savior Himself, for Jesus is Himself the supreme example of the way in which instruction is to be brought to the people with regard to moral and spiritual subjects. Is it not a most remarkable thing that He who came to be the Savior of the world, to turn it upside down, to reverse the very principles by which it had been governed, and to reorganize society so completely that many of those things which were uppermost were henceforth to be undermost, and many of those things which were undermost were henceforth to be uppermost, yet does not enter into any formal description of the evils which He will Himself correct? Jesus has not given us a single discourse such as are demanded many times by the people of to-day of the preachers of to-day. When the Pharisees conspire with the Herodians to entrap Him into a sermon whose text they would themselves furnish Him, He refuses to be drawn into the controversy. His answer is as skillful as it is profound. "Show me the tribute money. Render unto Cæsar the things that are Cæsar's and unto God the things that are God's." No wonder that they marvelled. When the young man comes to Him, beseeching Him to become himself a civil judge, and thus sit in judgment not only upon his own brother, but upon the very jurisprudence of the age, Jesus Himself declines to render a verdict. He was not sent to be a judge in such affairs, but He improves the occasion to preach a far better sermon than would have been given had he entered into a discussion of current jurisprudence, and warns His followers against that wretched covetousness which gives occasion for so many law-suits. And so in a vast variety of incidents, into which we can not enter, the Savior is the supreme example of proper pulpit instruction.

2. Proceeding then to answer in more explicit terms the question, How is this instruction to be given, we note that it is to be given by the exposition of the Scripture and in no other way. In order to do this work the preacher does not depart from the word of God, its explanation, and its application. He does not seek for subjects of instruction by themselves upon which he may discourse when he enters the pulpit. He does not say, for example, "Now, I shall preach to my people to-day a sermon upon the political situation, upon the vicious amusements to which they are given, upon the dishonesty which is invading business life," and so on. But while he is himself engaged in the reading of the Word

of God he finds a passage containing some abiding principle which he perceives to be particularly applicable to political conditions, forms of amusement, or the conduct of worldly business. It may be that this passage is set forth in connection with some historical incident or other illustration of its character and power. He preaches that passage of Scripture. While he does not depart from it, and while he is chiefly occupied in making its meaning clear, he shows its timeliness, its pertinency to the peculiar juncture, and its application to affairs as they are at the time. So he preaches; and sermon is full of such instruction as he should convey. A fine illustration of the method is found in the story of a great teacher of history who was accustomed to say to his class, "I expect you to get your facts out of books. In my classroom you will get only their interpretation." So the preacher should expect his people to get their own facts. If he undertakes to furnish them he may involve himself in serious error if not in positive disgrace. He is not an expert in such things. Politicians know far more than he with regard to the corruption in public life. Business men know far more than he with regard to the evils of speculation and what not; and so with much else upon which he may be tempted to preach. The people then may get the facts for themselves, but they will look to him for the interpretation, and in order that he may interpret them as he should it is not necessary that he should know all the facts, but only that he should know, and know certainly, and know well, their positive bearing, as he has learned it from Scripture.

This is particularly true when some great event occupies the attention of his people. The event may be some catastrophe, the revelation of some deep iniquity, or something of a different character, which promotes careful and serious thinking upon the part of his people. They come to Church expecting to hear something from the man in the pulpit with regard to that which has so startled them, and the man in the pulpit should have something to say with regard to it. He will have something to say, but it will be said in connection with some Scripture which has come into his mind in this very connection, and which shows its relation to the will of God, the judgment of sin, or human responsibility.

If the preacher proceeds upon this principle he will show men how to estimate in life what artists in their own profession call "values." He will show them those things that bulk large in human influence and human action. He will teach them, as an old philosopher said centuries ago, to "see life whole." He will set life for them in the light of eternity. To use an old but most significant theological expression it will all be *sub specie eternitatis.*

Education is defined by psychologists as the organization of acquired habits of conduct and tendencies to behavior. We accept this definition for sermonic purposes, and declare that this is exactly the education which the pulpit is to communicate. The preacher is to seek above all things else in his education to organize the capacities of his people for conduct. First of all, these habits are to receive from him an initial organization in connection with the education of that fundamental truth of which we have spoken. He is to endeavor in his pulpit work to have them launch new habits and new influences, in consequence of a new impulse which has been given to their minds with tremendous initial force under the power of the Spirit of God, so that their old order of habits shall be broken up, new motives introduced and new habits engendered, and all his educational work in the pulpit is to be along the same line, no matter what special subject he may pursue. He is to buttress and reinforce the consciences of the men who sit in the pews, so that they may do the particular work of reformation which he himself is not called upon to do. It is his business to reorganize society, but only by giving power to its leaders. It is not his place to reorganize business, so that dishonest practices shall be broken up and fair play shall be the rule, and right understanding shall exist between those that serve and those that are served. This duty devolves upon Christian business men, not upon the preacher, but it does devolve upon the preacher to give to those Christian business men their initial impulse and to support them from the pulpit in all their holy endeavors. So likewise it is the part of Christian citizens to interest themselves in political questions: Christian lawyers must detect political corruption and pursue those methods in detail which look to its removal; but the minister is to be behind these Christian lawyers and Christian citizens and support them by those divine principles which he expounds from the Word of God. It is the duty of Christian physicians to instruct the people with regard to certain forms of vice which prey upon the health and morals of young people, corrupt their physical natures, and render them unfit for marriage and a burden to themselves. It is for the Christian physician to correct those evil practices whereby marriage itself becomes only a legitimate concubinage and the evils of divorce are increased. But it is for the Christian minister to stand behind the Christian physicians of his congregation and encourage them to do that work in detail which devolves upon them.

So it is that the minister's work of education proceeds. From first to last he must have before him the example and teaching of the Lord Jesus Christ, and all his instruction is to be given in His spirit and lead to His cross. He must set forth in the plainest terms the nature of that sin, and the guilt of that sin which brought the Lord of Glory to earth that He might overcome its effects and save its subjects. He must be given to no tawdry philosophy by which indifference to sin is cultivated, and the effects of sin obscured. He must not hide from his people its hideous drift and its awful end. It is said of Thomas Arnold of Rugby that one reason why he inspired the boys of England by the brilliancy of his own ideals was that he also made their teeth chatter before the hideous power of sin. He hated it himself so cordially that when his boys were detected in some offense, the master snatched their hands as from scorching flame, and his noble face looked down upon them with contempt and scorn. The pupil saw his sin and was thereby saved from its power, and there was nothing that those young lads in Rugby so much dreaded as the condemnation of their master. It must be somewhat so with the preacher, and with his relations to his people.

ARGUMENTATION.

ARGUMENTATION.

This is not an argumentative age.
Instruction has precedence.
Method of the apostles and of Jesus.

I. Uses of Argument.
1. To confirm believers.
2. To win the undecided.
3. To silence scoffers.
The preacher to:—
(1) Bear in mind that he is not replied to.
(2) To give special care to definition.
(3) To be modest.

II. Method of presentation.
1. The "Burden of Proof."
2. Presumption.

III. The best argument.

IV. Order of arguments.

Read Broadus, Part I, Chap. VII; Bond's "Master Preacher," Chap. X Jevon's "Logic;" Crother's "Gentle Reader," III; Denny, Duncan, and McKinney's "Argumentation and Debate."

XIII.

ARGUMENTATION.

There is not the same need for argumentation in sermonizing which there once was. The age in which we live is not in any large sense an argumentative age. There are, indeed, very few departments of thought in which there is any loud call for argument. It seems to be confined almost altogether to politics, but even in politics it has very largely decreased, and in many important respects it has been largely modified. There are no longer the acrimonious debates of a past generation, and there are few public questions which are calculated to provoke them; so that in the administration of civil affairs, as in much else, the "campaign of education" has become the popular thing.

It is even so in the pulpit. There was a time when all the various Christian denominations seemed to feel the importance of educating their young preachers in the art of debate. Sermonizers were expected to be finished logicians. Many of these denominations were struggling for their very existence; their peculiar doctrines were to be defended, and their peculiar views of truth and duty were to be urgently advanced. Common Christianity, indeed, has at times seemed to be threatened with serious calamity, and the common faith had need of trained and capable defenders. In these denominations, and in such days, polemical theology was a very important part of the curriculum of the theological seminaries, and students were much devoted to it. But those days have virtually passed, and the need of argumentation is felt to-day only among a few bodies of Christians which depend for their growth upon the vindication of certain peculiar ceremonies or theories whereby they are differentiated from the rest of Christendom.

This change in the character of the age has produced a very manifest change in the peculiar zeal of the most acceptable and influential preachers. The defense of the truth of God is just as important as it ever was. It is still assailed, and it must be still defended; but the truth of God is held in common—at least in its fundamental elements, by such a multitude of people, and by the ministers of so many different religious bodies, that the zeal for those subordinate respects, wherein the views of the members of one denomination differ from the views of those in another, has largely disappeared. Orthodoxy has become to some as offensive a term as heterodoxy has been to others. This is not because those who are offended by it are not orthodox, but because the word carries with it a certain sense of partisanship which is not in keeping with the spirit of the age. Zeal for the truth is one thing; but zeal for orthodoxy is altogether another thing; because while in the minds of some orthodoxy can not be distinguished from truth, the clear and practical thinkers will maintain that while the truth which lies in the Word of God is in every sense divine, the form of expression in theological formulas is in a very large sense human. So, in connection with the passing of the argumentative spirit, a certain belligerent and rancorous zeal even for orthodoxy, such as characterized many good men in the past, has been relegated to oblivion. The old "war horses," as they were called, of a past generation have well-nigh disappeared. The few that still remain find their occupation gone, and when one of them still persists in blowing the trumpet he is very apt to find himself without an audience.

Instruction, as we have considered, is taking the place of argumentation in the Christian pulpit. The campaign of education is on with the ministry, as with many another class which seeks the good of society.

The older books upon homiletics gave a very large place to the consideration of argumentation; some of them devoted chapter after chapter to the subject. Various forms of argument were considered, one after another, with minute care and large emphasis, but it is a most significant fact that the books upon preaching in its various forms which have appeared within the past few years contain scarcely a reference to the subject. The writer has examined many of them with a view to determining the exact condition of the case, and in only one has he found a separate chapter devoted to the subject—that chapter containing less than five pages, and reviewing very briefly but four of the ordinary forms of argument.

He, therefore, who would be a true prophet of the age must take this characteristic of the age into due consideration.

And yet, notwithstanding all that has been said, it still remains that argumentation has its uses, and that the study of argument should by no means be omitted. It is only that we cast that which may be called argument into the form adapted to present conditions, and employ it for those purposes to which it is properly directed. The argumentation of the pulpit to-day should follow more closely the apostolic example, and be of the form which is best indicated by the English word "reasoning," by which word the peculiar term of the New Testament is translated.* It is used in a number of places in the New Testament, of which the following are good examples: "Paul, as his custom was, went in unto them, and for three Sabbath days reasoned with them from the Scriptures, opening and alleging that it behooved the Christ to suffer, and to rise again from the dead: and that this Jesus, whom, said he, I proclaim unto you, is the Christ. And some of them were pursuaded." Acts 17: 2-4. It appears from this quotation that such was the custom of the Apostle Paul. He "reasoned" with those whom he addressed. We have in some cases his discourses in full which show the form of his argument. We are told that in this particular case he reasoned from the Scriptures, explaining them, and showing that the Christ, according to the Scriptures, must suffer, and after his suffering be raised again from the dead. Such was the teaching of the Old Testament fulfilled in Jesus Christ, whom he accordingly proclaimed to be the very Christ. It will be seen that while this is of the form of argument it is not syllogistic argument, but argument that leans to instruction. Again: "Felix . . . . sent for Paul, and heard him concerning the faith in Christ Jesus. And as he reasoned of righteousness, and self-control, and the judgment to come, Felix was terrified." Acts 24: 24, 25. In this case Paul was engaged with the three great subjects of Christian preaching inclusive of all which is properly proclaimed from the pulpit—the justification of the sinner in the sight of God; his government of himself and his strife after holiness; and the coming judgment of all men. Paul's method in this case seems to have been similar to that which he adopted in the former one. It is this sort of reasoning

---

*This term is διαλέγομαι—a very different thing from συζητέω, which is translated "question"—with angry and virulent import.

which the preacher of the present age should strive to cultivate. The prophets of old addressed the Jewish people in much the same way. When Isaiah, speaking in the name of God, calls upon the recreant people of Israel, "Come now, and let us reason together, saith Jehovah," he proceeds very much as the Apostle Paul did long after him. "Though your sins be as scarlet, they shall be as white as snow; though they be red like crimson, they shall be as wool." The Savior Himself argued after very much the same fashion, but there was reason why His preaching should have been more emphatically argumentative than the apostles' who preceded Him or the apostles' who followed Him. His unique character and His manifest purpose brought Him into conflict with the religious teachers of the day, and it became necessary for Him to be polemical. We may observe in His preaching a large number of examples of formal argument, but to these we shall refer further on. Jesus was a master of dialetics: His arguments were correct and convincing, and they richly repay distinct study.

Let us proceed to note some particulars with regard to argumentation.

I. What are the uses of argument? Let it be remembered that suitable argumentation is no more or other than the art of persuasion. He who adopts it, particularly in the pulpit, for any other purpose, has misused it. Dr. Willis G. Craig, among the many aphorisms which he has given to his students, has said: "The whole object of debate is to change the minority into the majority." It is a wise and weighty remark, and should be borne in mind by the preacher. It is similarly expressed in the opening sentence of "Argumentation and Debate;" "The problem of argumentation is to make use of the best means of bringing others to believe or to act as we wish them to believe or act." Consider how much such a principle involves. It rules out of argument everything calculated to arouse the antagonism of the opponent; everything that reflects on his motives; everything that ministers to pride or prejudice; everything that is associated with ridicule and sarcasm; everything that looks for personal victory and the glory of conquest. The principle confines the debater to those arguments and considerations which are likely to please and win our adversaries. We seek for votes. As O'Connell says, "The matter of primary and sole importance is the verdict," so that St. Augustine, centuries ago, set forth the exact qualities of suitable pulpit argumentation when he declared that it should be "plain, pleasing, and persuasive." The preacher must "carry his point," and everything which he can bring to his aid that will make his subject the more engaging should be employed for the purpose.

The uses of argumentation generally speaking are three, as follows:

1. Its most important use is to strengthen the faith of those who already believe. There are very many whose faith is of such a character that they cry in their deepest souls, if not in the hearing of others, "Lord, I believe: help thou mine unbelief." Their faith is oftentimes strengthened by the form of argumentation which we have counseled, in which there is no argument at all of a formal character. It is only that their ignorance is instructed, reasons are given for the positions which they ought to hold, or their activities are stimulated, so that in their own exertions they become established in the faith.

2. Argumentation has its uses in the convicting and convincing of unbelievers. But the unbelievers who are

won by argument of a formal kind are not generally those who are decidedly hostile to the truth, so that we do not mean by the term those who are arrayed against Christianity, but rather those who yet lack the decision to accept and serve the Lord Christ. They are on the border line; they are "not far from the Kingdom of God." With these the preacher reasons as the Apostle Paul with Felix. It will be well for any one who is interested in this matter to carefully examine the sermons of the most successful revivalists. Consider the form which their reasoning takes, and the methods which they employ to bring the undecided to a stand.

3. But argumentation has a third use: it may silence those whom it may not convince. The Apostle himself wrote of some whom even he was unable to win, "whose mouths must be stopped." This process requires special skill, but skill that may be acquired by diligent preparation.

A missionary upon his return from India was much annoyed with the conversation of a young Englishman who had been spending some months in the country. He improved every opportunity to cast suspicion upon the missionaries' work. He declared that he did not believe that the Hindus could be won to Christ, and that during his sojourn in the country he had not seen a single native Christian. After a few days the young scoffer was describing his experience in hunting tigers, and entered into a minute description of the sport. As he was concluding, the missionary remarked that he had been in India for many years and had never seen a tiger; that he doubted the young man's stories and did not believe that there were any tigers in the land. "Ah," the young man remarked, "but you, sir, never went where the tigers were." "No," said the missionary, "and you never went where the Christians were." The missionary had bided his time, used his argument at the proper moment, and silenced the young skeptic for the remainder of the voyage.

For such uses as the above the minister may properly employ argument. But let him bear in mind certain things while he proceeds with the work.

(1) Let him very particularly remember that the preacher is never replied to; no one is given an opportunity to answer him. Therefore he must be absolutely fair with his congregation: he must use no argument with others that he would not like to have used with himself in a similar situation. Let him remember that only the very best reasons should be employed for his purpose; and let him remember that he is not to seek his own victory, but that of the Master whom he serves. It will be well therefore for him ordinarily to plainly state his own position, or the proposition which he proposes to discuss. There is probably nothing which more readily defeats the purpose of argument than the appearance of indirection or trickery. The preacher should never take his audience at a disadvantge or unawares. He should never indulge in a course of reasoning whereby they may feel that they have been trapped. Moreover, when the preacher has freely stated his position at the outset, he will be the more likely to proceed carefully with a reasoning that is wise and sound, simply because he knows that his congregation is aware of the proposition which he proposes to publish. His honesty will disarm their antagonism and allay their prejudices.

(2) The first and chief attention in argumentation must be given to definition. A definition has this very special importance—it is the beginning of proof. Often it is the very gist of explanation and argument. Some-

times it removes the need of argument, because it prevents ambiguity and consequent confusion and misunderstanding.

But it must be a true definition—not a mere "judgment." A judgment is only the expression of some relation which one term bears to another term. "Hypocrisy is the homage which vice pays to virtue," is a judgment. It does not definite the term "hypocrisy."

The definition must be acceptable to the people and not to the preacher alone. And the definition must be simple and intelligible and not run into abstractions and subtleties which the congregation will neither appreciate nor follow.

(3) The next matter of importance is modesty. The preacher must not indulge in too many superlatives. He must beware of extravagant statements. Let him adopt for his wares the rule of the best commercial houses and "not price his goods beyond what the market will bear." Let him not overstate values, or claim too much for any argument which may be advanced. And let him use only those arguments which he himself can handle; and if he is not well versed in certain branches of learning, to which greater men perhaps than he have given attention, let him make no excursion into their fields, nor rely upon their weapons. And let him be prepared for rigid cross-examination. None may be had at the time, but he may find after he has left the pulpit, and fallen in with his parishioners by the way, that they will have questions to put to him for which he will find himself altogether unprepared.

II. The method of presentation.

1. When argumentation is adopted by the preacher, an important question for him to settle is, How shall it be best presented? The answer is found where it has

usually been located by the best authorities upon this subject; it should be so stated as to throw the burden of proof upon the adversary. This term "the burden of proof" refers to one's obligation of proving an assertion. It usually falls upon him who affirms, because he who makes the affirmation is bound to sustain his position. Until that appears to have been done the adversary has nothing to do. He is not bound to disprove a mere assertion: no more is the preacher bound to disprove the assertions of those who array themselves against Christianity. This is not because the burden of proof has actually been shifted from him who affirms the truth of Christianity; but because the duty of presenting evidence has fallen upon his opponent. The evidences of Christianity are so many and so convincing that their denial must be upheld by evidences of equal force or the cause of the unbeliever is lost. The preacher of the truth in the present age possesses a very great advantage who clearly apprehends this principle and acts upon it. There are very many to-day who, in the presence of truth, content themselves with mere denials, or challenge the preacher to make good his position. They virtually say to him, "You say that the case is thus and so. You declare that this or that is true. Prove it: show us your illustrations of it. By what arguments do you uphold it?" The preacher is not to be led astray by any such opposition, and unguardedly attempt to do a work to which he is not called. The great preachers whose words are contained in the Scripture are fine illustrations of the proper method to be pursued by the preacher of to-day. The prophets did not undertake to defend Jehovah against the many who arrayed themselves against him, but they called upon those who departed from God to make good *their* position. Listen, for example, to

Isaiah and note his location of the burden of proof. "Produce your cause, saith Jehovah; bring forth your strong reasons, saith the King of Jacob. Let them bring them forth, and declare unto us what shall happen: declare ye the former things, what they are, that we may consider them, and know the latter end of them; or show us things to come. Declare the things that are to come hereafter, that we may know that ye are gods: yea, do good, or do evil, that we may be dismayed, and behold it together." And upon their failure to make good their position, Isaiah continues, "Behold, ye are of nothing, and your work is of nought; an abomination is he that chooseth you." Note also the method of Elijah upon Mt. Carmel, in the deepest decline of the kingdom of Israel. He said that the prophets of Baal were many and strongly entrenched in the very court of Ahab. Therefore he called upon them to justify their faith and prove the power of their god. Elijah said, "Choose you one bullock for yourselves, and dress it first; for ye are many; and call on the name of your god." He guarded himself against any possible deception, saying, "but put no fire under." The Savior himself was given to this same method. He frequently cast the burden of proof upon those who opposed him. "I also will ask you one question." "What is written in the law? How readest thou?" "What think ye of Christ? Whose son is He?" The preacher who can employ such a method as this in the presentation of the truth will exert unusual power. The question which he proposes to those who hear him is, *Can the unbeliever make good?*

2. Argumentation is properly presented by setting due value upon presumption. This term is used in three senses: (1) The inclination to accept a proposition before it is argued; (2) Legal presumption, in which

one is supposed to be innocent until he is proved guilty; and (3) Preoccupation, the general acceptance of a position or proposition with the favorable opinions of those who have considered it. The presumption which we consider is that inference which has been so long accepted that it rises in the minds of its adherents to the level of fact. It should be said with regard to this that presumption does not lie simply with age, long use, or general acceptance upon the part of a people, as many suppose that it does. It is no sure sign that anything is good and desirable because men have for ages been devoted to it. If such were the case then Confucianism is the best religion for the Chinese. And so also with regard to many hoary superstitions and practices. In the preacher's mind age and character must go together. He can make use of the principle only when long use has been attended by the judgment of the best of men and has contributed to the best of ends. When there is such presumption, it is solid ground upon which to rest a proposition. A long established custom or creed, however, should not be attacked by denying its virtues or its benefits. If such appear, they should be recognized and acknowledged, and it should be shown, on the other hand, that there is more virtue and larger benefits in that wherewith we should displace them. It will thus be seen that the principle of the burden of proof and the principle of presumption act upon each other and support each other.

III. The best argument.

We do not consider the various forms of argument which may be employed in the pulpit. They may be readily ascertained by one who desires to cultivate the art of debate. It is well, however, to emphasize the argument from testimony as generally the best for the preacher's use.

Testimony is involved in every other form of argumentation. It is virtually inseparable from it. There can be no proof without evidence.

Testimony is witness borne to a fact. The religion of Jesus is preëminently a religion of fact—historical fact to begin with and after that the fact of personal experience and action.

This argument is, therefore, more frequently employed in the Scripture than any other, as much perhaps as all other forms of argument put together, both in the Old Testament and in the New. The God of the Scripture appeals to his witnesses and calls upon them for their testimony. The Savior himself made use of this argument very frequently. He appealed to the testimony of the Old Testament Scriptures, to the witness which his Father had borne concerning Him, to the testimony of his fore-runner John the Baptist, and to the report of His own disciples concerning his words and works. When John the Baptist in prison sent to him to enquire whether He were the Christ or not, he relied entirely upon this form of argument in his answer, and John's own disciples were to report to John the events which they had seen and heard. Again and again he told his apostles that they were to be his witnesses after his resurrection, and again and again do they refer to themselves as such. The argument from testimony, however, has much more value in our own day than in any which has preceded it. It is not only satisfactory, but it is in the highest degree cumulative. Multitudes of the best of men and of the most blessed institutions have contributed to it. In volume, character and persistence it is unrivaled.

Not only so, but in the affairs of our common life, in business, politics, medicine, and law, immense importance is attached to this form of argument. The entire legal profession rests upon it, and for this reason perhaps a large proportion of lawyers are believing men. Simon Greenleaf, the great authority upon evidence, has written one of the best books in confirmation of the Gospel story to be found in the English language, "The Testimony of the Four Evangelists Examined by the Rules of Evidence that obtain in Law-Courts." A recent work in the same line, also by a distinguished lawyer, Frances J. Lamb, is entitled "Bible Miracles Examined by the Rules of Jurisprudence as administered in Courts of Justice."

But the argument from testimony is not only of great value in itself, it is also a very great support to other forms of argument. For example, the argument from prophecy relative to the resurrection of Jesus Christ from the dead gains immense force when it is corroborated by the testimony of witnesses with regard to the fact.

Still more the preacher himself is a witness. If he is not, he is scarcely entitled to preach. He can and must bear frequent testimony to the work of grace which has been wrought in his own soul. James Martineau was a frequent attendant upon the preaching of Mr. Spurgeon, and when he was asked by one of his friends why it was so, "Because," as his friend said to him, "you do not believe all he says," Martineau answered, "No, but *he* does." And so it should be with every preacher. And still further, all Christians who have experienced the grace of Christ Jesus are themselves witnesses, and their testimony may be employed by the preacher in frequent connections with great power. This argument from testimony, therefore, is the one which preachers may be counseled to use the most persistently, and from it they may expect to secure the largest and best results.

IV. The order of the presentation of arguments. Generally in preaching the strongest argument should be the first presented, and because the strongest argument is always the Scriptural argument, it should be given the precedence of all others.

The best debaters have ever been not those who reserved their fire, or waited for an undue length of time to hear the arguments of others, but who occupied the floor as soon as they could obtain it, who put forth their strong reason at the opening of the debate, and who kept their opponents so busy answering their arguments and defending their own positions against attack that the arguments of these opponents could secure little place and have but little weight.

Take, for example, such a subject as the immortality of the soul. If the preacher is to discourse concerning it, he will make a great mistake if he begins, let us say, with such meagre suggestions of a resurrection as are to be found in the natural world,—the revival of plants in the spring, the butterfly emerging from the cocoon, and other trivial matters of the like—then proceeding perhaps to the speculations of heathen philosophers and their uncertain groping after the light; then, let us say, to such suggestions as may be found in other religions or concessions contained in various philosophic writings; then perhaps to the fore-shadowings of the Old Testament and its incomplete revelations concerning the future life; reaching finally the declarations of the Lord Jesus Christ and His resurrection from the dead. This certainly is no way in which to present argument from the pulpit. The resurrection of Jesus Christ should have the very first place in the discussion of this subject. The Savior's teachings with regard to immortality should precede all other teaching and all other suggestion whatsoever, and very little need be added if this has once been done.

The preacher is to remember what we have already noted, that in sermonic work the climax is not ordinarily logical but rhetorical. A preacher may not be a fine logician, but he may have and should try to form a sound judgment with regard to his own gifts ond powers in this respect. His arguments may not be syllogistic in character, but they may be presented with such sincerity, such earnestness, and such urgency that a better effect may be produced than if he had given himself with all diligence to the forging of a complete chain of argument. Let him not undertake to do too much. Let him start from common ground. Let him so speak that the most difficult subjects with which he deals shall be made plain to the common people, and let him appeal with all confidence at any time to these three things: the Scriptures, the human conscience, and common sense.

ILLUSTRATION.

ILLUSTRATION.

Illustration must add something to the truth.
    It is not for purposes of mere ornamentation.
    It is allied to argument.

I. Rules for use of illustration.
    1. Positive relation between the illustration and the thought.
       The growth of language.
    2. The point of resemblance must be kept prominent.
       Humor in the pulpit.
    3. It should not be prolonged.
    4. Two illustrations should seldom be used at once.
    5. The thought must be prepared for the illustration.
    6. There should be no introduction.
    7. Should not be below the grade of the subject.
    8. Variety.

II. Some sources of illustration.
    1. Original.
    2. Familiar.
    3. Special sources.

Read Bond's "Master Preacher," VI; Freeman's "Use of Illustration;" Jeff's "Art of Sermon Illustration;" "Preachers and Preaching," VIII.

XIV.

ILLUSTRATION.

The term "illustration" includes all the figurative forms of speech. There is sometimes a fine illustration in the use of a single word, and the study of this one branch of the subject might profitably be considered. Indeed, it should be considered by every one who desires to become proficient in the use of language. We shall employ the term, however, with reference only to those extended illustrations for which a number of words are required.

It is scarcely necessary to define the term: but this should be said with regard to it, that illustration, in any proper sense, must convey more truth than may be expressed with out it. An illustration should add somewhat to the abstract term. Indeed there is scarcely use for illustration if this be not done. ' But whether the addition be apparent or not, the illustration must at the very least clarify the truth, and this very clarification is in a sense an addition.

The principal use, therefore, of illustration is found in this addition. An illustration is not to be used for its own sake, no matter how fine it may appear in itself, and it is exceeding doubtful if it is ever to be used for the purpose of ornamentation. This is contrary to the rules of some rhetoricians, who insist that ornamentation is a very proper use of illustration. We quote from a recent writer upon the subject: "It is sometimes legitimate to use an illustration largely for the sake of ornament. The preacher thereby introduces a bit of color on a surface that would otherwise be too much of a monotone." But this is scarcely permissible. The proper use of illustration for the sake of making the truth more ample, more forcible, or more clear, gives it a certain dignity which it ought to possess, but which it will not otherwise possess. More than this, it removes illustration out of the domain of the mere story-teller. Thought is the all important thing in every form of discourse, and the preacher can not afford to neglect it or forsake it at any point in his sermon. There is a great temptation here to those who are gifted in anecdote and can tell a story well, but the preacher must be careful that he is not beguiled into it. The book from which we have quoted begins with the following sentences: " 'Please tell me a story,' says the child. And the child is father of the man. It is a common remark of preachers that nobody listens more eagerly to the children's address, with its anecdotes, than the grown-up people." The author proceeds to say, "the books that are most circulated from the free liberaries are novels. The magazines that circulate the most are story magazines." And he refers back to the great antiquity of the custom as found in the Oriental story-tellers from time immemorial. We believe that such considerations as these lead the preacher positively astray.

Dr. Jefferson says very truly and impressively, "There are two kinds of preachers—men of thoughts and men of thought. The man of thoughts keeps all sorts of books of illustrations, drawers filled with clippings and envelopes stuffed with bright ideas, and when the time comes for the making of the sermon, he places the thoughts in a certain sequence, like so many beads on

ILLUSTRATION 237

a string. He brings his beads before his congregation, counts them over, spends thirty minutes in doing it and the people go home thinking they have been listening to a sermon. But in a deep sense that performance is not a sermon at all. Reciting a string of thoughts is not, strictly speaking, preaching. Preaching is the unfolding of truth. One idea is sufficient to make a powerful sermon. A man who can take a great idea and by sheer force of brain unfold it until it glows and hangs glorious before the eyes of men and so burns that hard hearts melt and consciences awake and begin to tremble, is a preacher indeed and actually performs the work of the Lord. But the little dabbler in other men's thoughts who fills up his time with second-hand anecdotes and stale stories and tales intended to make people cry never gets down to the place where the soul lives and does not know either the preacher's agony or his reward."

The author from whom we quoted above seems, in another paragraph to reconsider his commendation of the story-teller and remarks: "Let no idle reader imagine that this is a plea for anecdotal preaching, the stringing together of ear-tickling stories for their own sake," and yet he says that the illustration will be remembered with the point illustrated for years perhaps, whereas the thoughtful sermon without it will scarcely survive the following week. But this is not a fair comparison. Illustrations are not remembered unless they are good illustrations. Good illustrations are those which are associated with thoughtful discourse. The thought survives. The illustration certainly helps to keep it alive, but the thought and the illustration act each upon the other, and it is their happy combination which promotes their continued life and influence.

Illustration is very closely allied to argument: indeed, it often is a form of argument. Argument may sometimes be turned into illustration by a single change in the phraseology, or illustration changed into argument by the same method. This is particularly true of the argument from analogy. Recall the argument of the Savior, "If God doth so clothe the grass of the field, which to-day is, and to-morrow is cast into the oven, shall he not much more clothe you, O ye of little faith?" These words of the Savior are an argument. But had He said, "God will certainly clothe you because you are dependent upon Him. Just as He clothes the grass of the field, though it flourishes to-day and to-morrow is consumed,"—this would be illustration.

Illustration is not really proof, but it often has the value of proof. It illuminates the argument and emphasizes it, and if it be what it should be it carries conviction with it. If it does not do this it is of little use, and should ordinarily be discarded.

I. Let us consider some of the rules for the use of illustration.

1. It is of the first importance that there be positive relation between the thought and the illustration. It should be something more than mere resemblance, and we are sometimes led astray because there is resemblance and nothing more. There should be some distinct ratio in the thought and the illustration which is intended to illuminate it. A teacher of rhetoric frequently has occasion to point out to his students the lack of true resemblance in the figures of speech which they employ. There should be a positive identity in the thought and the illustration. The one should match the other as the casting matches the mold. It is only that the thought is conveyed in two different forms, but it must be exactly the same thought still. In the one form it may

ILLUSTRATION   239

be called the obverse and in the other form the reverse.
A student was preparing a sermon for childern on the
text, "My son, if sinners entice thee, consent thou not."
(Prov. 1:10.) He proposed to illustrate by a rat-trap.
But his teacher pointed out to him that there was no
true resemblance between a good man trapping vermin
and a bad man catching innocent souls. The illustration
was abandoned.

Very little may be lacking in order to complete the resemblance yet the little lack is sufficient to mar the illustration. In this case the thought and the illustration
may be brought together by modifying either the one
or the other. It is like that retouching of a portrait
which suggests the countenance that it is intended to
represent but does not truly reflect it. It may be that
the addition of a simple line, or the removal of a certain
shadow, is sufficient to so modify the portrait as that it
shall become a true likeness.

The illustration must be such that the hearer is able
to recognize the relation at once. If it becomes necessary
for the preacher to explain it, or to show at length
wherein it applies, the illustration should never have been
used to begin with. It is as bad to explain an illustration as it is to explain a joke. The rule which obtains
in art that the true picture needs no title ought to obtain
also in rhetoric. An illustration is a sort of picture:
all that it ever ought to need is its exhibition in order
to its own explanation.

This matter of true resemblance is itself illustrated
in the very origin of illustration. In the dawn of civilization illustration occupies a very much more important
position, and is much more frequently employed, than
subsequently. Language in its beginning is figurative.
The alphabets of the most primitive nations are expressed

by pictures: the words are composed of such pictures, and sentences are but a series of such word pictures added together. But spiritual truths from the very beginning have required very much more illustration than truths of any other character, and, therefore, when God began to teach His people the great truths concerning Himself and His salvation He was obliged to communicate His ideas in connection with a series of figures of speech. This is well set forth in Walker's "Philosophy of the Plan of Salvation." The very etymology of the Hebrew which was chosen by the Almighty as the vehicle of His religion is a very interesting study in this connection. Originally there were very few abstract terms to be found in it, and even now those which are regarded as expressive of abstract ideas contain a figure by means of which they may be traced back to the original object whence they originated. For example, the Hebrew idea of power was derived from the horn of an animal, and so it came about that after a time the very word which signified "a horn" signified also "power." The human hand was also used as an illustration of the same idea because it was through the hand that the man exerted his strength, so that in the Hebrew the words "hand" and "power" are often interchangeable. "The power of the tongue" reads literally "the hand of the tongue." Just so "sunshine" in Hebrew is synonymous with "happiness." The idea of justice or judgment is derived from the word which means "to cut" or "divide," referring back to the division of the spoil among those who were engaged in war or in the more harmless occupation of the chase. So it came about that when the Almighty desired to convey to these same Hebrews a sense of His goodness, His purity, and His will, He made use of terms derived from the material world, figurative

ILLUSTRATION 241

terms, illustrations. The Jews were taught purity by means of outward symbols, washing, and bathing; or by means of their discrimination between animals, some of which were imperfect and others without blemish. Very much of the Old Testament system was built up upon this same illustrative method, and it was not until the New Covenant was declared that the full meaning of the illustrations appears. So the author of the Book of Hebrews, referring to that old system of purification, says (9:23), "It was necessary therefore that the copies of the things in the heavens should be cleansed with these: but the heavenly things themselves with better sacrifices than these. For Christ entered not into a holy place made with hands, like in pattern to the true; but into heaven itself, now to appear before the face of God for us." Indeed, the Savior Himself, after introducing the New Covenant, made use of illustration to an extent and with an effect in which He has never been equaled. His illustrations are found not only in the parables, but in those figures of speech which we find upon almost every page of the gospel story. In the Sermon on the Mount we may count sixty-two of them. The list of His word pictures is very large; the familiar ones will be recalled by the reader, such as salt, light, bread, treasure, gates, trees, harvests, leaven, keys, tombs, lightning, winds, shepherds, wheat, vine, sheep, and goats.

The preacher, therefore, who would employ illustration must bear such things as the above in mind. He must do for those to whom he ministers, who are still uninstructed in heavenly things, very much the same thing which the Old Testaments prophets did for their people, and which Jesus did for those who heard Him. Oftentimes the truth can not be conveyed to the mind without an illustration in which there is thought which

reflects it. The story is told of a missionary to Africa,
who had spent years among the negroes without learning the word, for which he was earnestly seeking,
whereby the relation of Jesus Christ to men might be
set forth. He listened to every conversation with anxious
attention, hoping to hear the word which he had not yet
heard, but which he believed must be found somewhere
in their vocabulary. Finally upon one occasion, when
his men had returned from a lion hunt in which one of
them had been attacked by the beast and almost slain,
and another had come to his relief, he heard that wel-
comed word. He sprang to his feet: he called upon the
man again to speak it. Translated into English it was
this, "He was my savior." The negro up to this time
had had no sense of the relation which that word bore
to sacred things, but the very word itself was not only
transfigured but it became the channel through which the
saving knowledge of Jesus Christ was more distinctly
communicated to his mind; and this, as the missionary
well understood, and as he himself came to understand,
because the resemblance was distinctly apprehended.

2. The particular point of resemblance must always
be kept prominent. This is more important when the
illustration is of some length. It must not be obscured
by any minor detail, nor overlaid with any sort of elaboration. Just here many go astray. They think that it
is the part of good rhetoric to "work up" the illustration, to polish it, to overlay it with fine words and attractive phraseology. They remind one of the well-
known story of the artist who painted a picture of the
Last Supper. He called in his friends for their criticism,
and the first to speak remarked upon the wonderful skill
which he had displayed in painting the cups upon the
table. At once the artist seized his brush and painted

ILLUSTRATION 243

out those cups. He declared that he would have nothing in his picture that should obscure the face of his Redeemer. Following the same line there is that in art to which we have already referred which is called "values." To these the artist gives his very particular attention. The important feature in the picture must be given the most value; otherwise the picture is a failure. And it is exactly so with illustration. The point of resemblance gives it all its value: it must not be obscured. Sometimes it is positively forgotten by the preacher. It is told of one who had heard a very affecting story of a father who with great difficulty had rescued his son from a burning house. The details of the story were of the most interesting and pathetic character, and the preacher, feeling that it was a fine illustration, determined to use it in his next sermon. He did use it. He told the story with a great deal of feeling, but, much to his surprise, his congregation did not seem to be moved by it. Worse than that, he observed that they looked one at another in blank surprise. His illustration was for some strange reason a failure; he could not account for it. After the service he spoke to his wife about it, and asked her how it was that the illustration had failed. She said to him: "You told the story with a great deal of feeling, but you forgot to say that the house was on fire."

In this connection a word ought to be added with regard to humorous illustrations; because sometimes the preacher has such a mistaken sense of the dignity of the pulpit, that no matter how fine an illustration may be, if it is calculated to produce a smile he feels that he has no right to use it. Now, while that preacher is very much to be blamed who seeks only to gratify his personal pleasure or his personal vanity by the use of humor in the pulpit, he is almost equally to blame to whom the Lord has given wit, but who fails properly to employ it. There are some illustrations of very great force and value which have their humorous side. They are not to be neglected on that account. There are touches of humor in the Bible itself. Paul is positively witty in some of his expressions. Garvie well remarks with regard to the matter, "Humor is one of the great endowments of man. Not a few preachers would be saved from absurdity by the touch of humor. Worse things may be heard in a church than a laugh. If humor is spontaneous and natural to a man it must be carefully restrained so that it shall not detract from the solemnity and sanctity of the message. Humor for its own sake, or to advertize the preacher, or to attract hearers, is a grievous offense. But the humor that conveys truth more vividly and interprets life more genially need not be altogether banished from preaching."

The connection between the use of humor and the particular matter with which we are now engaged is this, that the point of resemblance is often made the more sharp and effective thereby than it could be made in any other way. Sam Jones, the Georgian evangelist, was an adept in its use, and it was not generally any blemish upon his preaching. Speaking of those whose emotions form too conspicuous an element in their religion, he told of a little steamboat in his own state, whose whistle was too big for its boiler. It could not run and whistle at the same time, so that when the engineer blew the whistle the paddle-wheels ceased to revolve. Such illustrations are truly powerful. Their very humor helps them to be so. Many of the great evangelists, who are most intent upon leading men in the way of salvation, are given to frequent humor in the

ILLUSTRATION 245

pulpit. Moody often raised a laugh in his congregation; so did Spurgeon; but they were none the less earnest on that account. Those who attack Christianity in public always make use of humor. They know its power and use it with great effect. With them it often degenerates into ridicule, which has no proper place in the pulpit, and to which the preacher should never be given. But the defenders of the gospel certainly ought not to relegate a faculty of such immense service to the opponents of Christianity. Only, if it be employed, it should always be with dignity and with good taste, and it should always be kept subservient to the highest and holiest purposes. If such be the spirit and intention of the preacher, he may not hesitate to employ a humorous illustration. It will prove at times a most effective method of clarifying the truth, or of conveying its lessons.

3. The illustration should be as brief as possible in justice to its full value. It must not outrun its use, because it is not the illustration in itself which is the valuable thing, but the truth which it is intended to illuminate. The danger in a lengthy illustration is that it is apt to engage the thought of the people for itself, and to lead them away from the truth for whose sake it is introduced. Sometimes the preacher himself becomes so enamored of his illustration that it carries him away from his subject, and occasionally he even forgets the truth with which he was engaged. He may even say to his congregation something of this sort, "Let me see, what was it that I was talking about?" But even if he does not say so, the people will say so to themselves. The truth must permeate the illustration. In one sense the truth must irradiate the illustration as truly as the illustration the truth.

Occasionally the preacher exalts his illustrative material so that it forms the body of his discourse. Perhaps he chooses for his purpose some text of Scripture which is itself figurative in expression. He makes it the business of his sermon to expand the figure, to illustrate it with additional figures, to look at it from all sides and in all relations; so that his sermon is nothing less than an extended illustration. This ministers weakness to his discourse. It is very seldom productive of the best effects.

4. For the same reason two illustrations should seldom be used in immediate succession. The preacher should ask himself why he desires to use two in succession. Is the first illustration somewhat obscure, incomplete? Then it were better not to use it at all. Are both illustrations so fine in his judgment that he does not think he can afford to part with either? Then it were better to save one of these fine illustrations for some other occasion and some other subject when he will be in need of it. Is he intent upon the rhetorical effect which he supposes may be produced by the multiplication of his figures? He may indeed succeed in getting it, but it will be at the sacrifice of the truth itself. One illustration is always sufficient for any single point. If it is a good illustration the preacher will not only make his point thereby, but he will run no risk of diverting the attention of his congregation.

There are, however, some occasions upon which two illustrations may be used in very close proximity. This is when two aspects of the truth have been presented, each aspect requiring special illumination; but even in such a case the illustrations will be better if separated by a sentence or two, in which the second aspect of the thought will be reiterated, or presented in special form. We frequently find in the Scripture these double illus-

ILLUSTRATION 247

trations, and observe the reason for them in the connection in which they are used. For example, upon the great Day of Atonement two goats were employed because it was impossible to represent the whole truth of the atonement in one alone. The same goat could not both be sacrificed upon the altar and sent away into the wilderness. The Savior also sometimes employed two or more parables for the same purpose, as, for example, when He spake the parables of the Lost Sheep, the Lost piece of Money, and the Prodigal Son. These three parables are not repetitions, but set forth three entirely different aspects of the mercy of God in the reclamation of His penitent children.

5. The thought must be prepared for the illustration as carefully as the illustration is prepared for the thought. This is one of the most important rules which may be given for the use of illustration. In its observance, indeed, resides the very art of illustrative address. The selection of a suitable illustration is, of course, the first consideration, but once the illustration has been selected it must be so used as that its correspondence with the thought shall be absolutely clear.

It is just here that very many fail who might otherwise excel. Their minds are very fertile in the invention of illustration. Their language falls into figurative form without an effort, and material throngs upon their mind, but it is misused only because it is not well fitted to the discussion of the subject.

This is the chief difficulty in the use of such illustrations as are furnished ready made in certain books and magazines which deal with the subject. The illustrations are given, but detached from any thought whatsoever. The authors take it for granted that those who use them will be able to form the connection, but such

is not always the case. Sometimes the preacher does
not say a word which suggests the illustration which he
is about to employ. He makes ready for its coming with
no care and with no deliberation, and when it comes it
does not fit its place. It has no place. If, on the other
hand, the very language of the thought has been arranged
with reference to the illustration which is to follow, it
becomes its very matrix. The reason for its use is at
once apparent, and the truth is marvellously emphasized
and clarified.

Very great care must therefore be taken with the
statement which is preliminary to the illustration, with
the progress of the thought in view of it, and with precise words which are employed. No better author can
be studied with reference to this particular matter than
Watkinson. Let us observe an example taken from one
of his sermons. The subject of this sermon is "Revised
Estimates:" his text is taken from Gen. 42:11, "We are
true men." He is engaged with his third point in this
sermon—"They rested in their present goodness, and
forgot their past wickedness, declaring, 'We are no
spies.'" "They were right," says Watkinson, "in that
particular matter, but what of the past?" As the preacher
goes on to enlarge upon this he quotes the words, "God
requireth that which is past," and says: "There is no
statute of limitations in the moral universe; and however
blameless we may be to-day, the past clings to us, condemns us, calls for blood. We shall never be 'true men'
until purged from our old sins." Now he is about to
introduce a fine illustration from the life of Sir William
Herschel. He has prepared for its coming in the words
which have beeen quoted concerning the "statute of limitations," and the clinging past. He proceeds with his
story. After Herschel had constructed his large tele-

ILLUSTRATION 249

scope and discovered the planet Uranus, he was directed to appear at Windsor so that George III. might hear of the wonderful discovery from the lips of the discoverer himself. The astronomer came at the time appointed, bringing with him his telescope and a map of the solar system, but as Watkinson says, the last thing he thought of was his personal delinquency. Herschel, while a youth, many years previously deserted from the army. The fact had been brought to the knowledge of the King, and when the astronomer was ushered into his presence the King remarked that before they could talk about science an imperative matter of business must be transacted. "Whereupon he handed to the astonished astronomer a paper, written by the royal hand and bearing the royal signature, pardoning the deserter. The monarch's instinct was correct; the royal pardon must cancel the old sin, and enable the King on a proper footing to show favor to the quondam offender."

For this reason it is apparent that there can be scarcely an exception to the rule that the thought must precede the illustration, and that no illustration may be introduced without foregoing thought. Sometimes the preacher begins his sermon with an illustration, an anecdote, or something of the sort, before anything has been said except the mere quotation of the text. Those who fall into such a habit as this are very apt to exhibit it frequently. The reason for it is this, the thought lies in their own minds although they have not yet given expression to it. They use the illustration as though they had. It is, therefore, a form of anticipation, and a very vicious form. It is itself a signal illustration of "putting the cart before the horse." There should always be something to illustrate before the illustration is introduced. State the thought; cast it in proper form for the illustration that is to follow; fit the illustration to the impression of the thought which has preceded it; and conclude with a distinct statement of its particular application. In this way the "ground joint" is made which provides for the proper flow of the preacher's ideas.

6. Do not have any introduction to the illustration; do not talk about it in advance. One is not to preface it with such a remark as this, "Now, I am about to use an illustration of this truth which is derived from such and such a quarter, or which I find to have such and such a use." Do nothing of this sort. Introduce the illustration in its proper place—that is all.

7. Do not use illustrations which are below the grade of the subject. A dignified thought must not suffer from the vulgarity of the illustration. The preacher must not suppose that when he passes from thought to illustration he is descending to a lower level in which he may permit himself certain liberties of address, in which he would not indulge in the more prosaic portions of his sermon. He is sometimes disposed to be altogether too familiar with his congregation when he passes to an illustration; to use vulgarism which he himself would consider otherwise out of place; or to speak of certain experiences by way of illustration to which he would not otherwise refer. It is true, as we shall presently see, that illustrations may be derived from very familiar objects, and furnish the pulpit with its best material, but because these illustrations are derived from common things they are not to be used in a common way. That is to say, as Dean Howe has well expressed it, that the preacher must always "discriminate between the common and the commonplace, the familiar and the vulgar, and not render the sermon insipid by the meas-

ILLUSTRATION 251

ures introduced to adorn and commend it." The elevated thought which is demanded by the discussion of spiritual subjects should not be vitiated in any way.

8. Seek variety in illustrative material. The preacher, when once this rule is suggested to him, may recall that most of his illustrations are taken from some one particular field: it may be science, it may be biography, it may even be personal experience. Joseph Cook, the great Boston lecturer, although he was singularly gifted in the use of illustration, yet referred to Lady Macbeth so frequently and in so many connections that he wore his illustration pitiably threadbare. It was said of another preacher of considerable prominence that every sermon "took him to China" because he had friends who were missionaries in China, and most of his illustrations were derived from missionary fields. The preacher who would both interest and instruct his congregation must beware of this fault, and select his illustrations from various sources.

II. We now consider the sources of illustration. Before passing then in review, a word should be said with regard to that point in sermon construction in which the illustrations may be expected to appear, because sometimes the preacher, particularly the young preacher, seeks his illustrations when his sermon is but begun. He may even seek them so soon as the subject itself is presented to his mind, or at least before there has been much elaboration of it. It will be well for him, however, not to consider the matter of illustration at all until his sermon, or at least its separate parts, has been substantially finished. Jeffs, in his book upon the "Art of Sermon Illustration," remarks that "the sermons of the average preacher will be bare and bald of illustration unless he has had his text ready and his line of though in mind for a reasonable time." He refers to Henry Ward Beecher as saying, "that he had many sermons in various stages of preparation, like apples ripening in a drawer, and he never preached a sermon until it was ripe." So the author says, "The illustrations do not appear, as a rule, until the ripening stage has arrived, but then no preacher ought to enter the pulpit to feed the congregation with green fruit. He will be always on the lookout for suitable illustrations, and if he realizes the value of the imaginative element in preaching, and subjects his imagination to intensive cultivation, he will not be likely to complain. There is much more latent imagination in the average preacher than he himself suspects." The preacher, therefore, should not despair because illustrations do not present themselves as readily or as quickly as he might desire. They will be very sure to come, even to the most prosaic man, who subjects his thought to the ripening process.

1. The sources from which illustrations are derived should be chiefly original. This simply means that the preacher is not to make use of other men's illustrations, particularly so in other men's ways. Many a man paralyzes his imagination by his constant dependence upon the imagination of others. For this reason such works as we have referred to, in which illustrations are furnished to the preacher ready made, should never be employed by him. He must find his own illustrations.

How is this to be done? The answer is very simple; it has already been foreshadowed in what we have said upon the subject of originality. He is to provoke his own thought by dealing with subjects which are out of his ordinary line, reading books which do not strictly belong to his own profession, talking with men in other pursuits, and the like. Indeed, it will be well for the

ILLUSTRATION 253

preacher if he occasionally does something else than preach; engages in work other than that which is supposed to be distinctly religious, attends the gathering of men for other purposes than those for pure worship. His own thought must be enriched and stimulated by very novelty. The preacher who found that his sermon last Sunday was barren of illustration may do nothing more this week in order to correct the matter than to read some fresh book or magazine article upon some recent discovery in science, or upon the work and influence of some distinguished man in some other line of work than his own. His own mind will be an abnormal one if original illustrations are not furnished to him by some such method. But whether his illustrations are wholly original or not, let him by all means avoid those illustrations which have been used from time immemorial, "frayed lace" as someone has called them—"The pebble thrown into the water," "The boat in the rapids of Niagara," and others of this character.

2. Make much of familiar objects. Do not derive illustrations from sources with which the congregation are absolutely unacquainted, or if for any reason there seems to be a special call for them, the audience must be made acquainted with the subject sufficiently to understand the illustration when it is introduced. It were better, however, to follow the example of the sacred writers, particularly of the Savior Himself, to whose illustrations we have already referred.

This caution, however, must be observed with regard to those illustrations which are derived from familiar things, that it is not the familiar relation of such things which is to be employed; otherwise the illustration will be stale and uninteresting. It is the unfamiliar relation in the familiar object which gives it its special power.

So, indeed, it was with the Savior Himself, and so it has been with all masters of rhetoric from His day to this.

3. When it comes to the particular sources from which illustrations are to be derived it may only be said that they are too numerous to be catalogued. The Scriptures, of course, occupy the first place. Most of the preacher's illustrations should be derived from Scripture. Then there are science and history, including current events; and literature, including poetry; and art, pictorial, architectural, and musical; and best of all perhaps the preacher's own experience and observation.

This one thing should receive special emphasis in concluding our study of this particular subject. All the illustrations which are contained in the sermon should be related to its general scheme. While they have particular reference to the special thought with which they are connected, they must follow in the line of the dominating thought or principle on which the sermon is organized. It will be well for the preacher to have somewhere in the course of his sermon, preferably near its conclusion, one comprehensive illustration which shall be the whole sermon in concrete. Such an illustration when found is a blessed discovery. It often makes the sermon what it is. Illustrations have often been likened to windows because they let in the light. But the leading illustration of the sermon should be something more than a window. It should have an outlook not merely in one direction. The light which enters should never be in danger of interception by a passing object, and more than all it should not look downward or merely outward. The leading illustration should be a great skylight, open to the very heavens and flooding that which it is intended to illuminate in its every part.

IMAGINATION.

IMAGINATION.

Imagination and fancy.
  The great source of power in all callings.
I. Imagination and illustration.
  1. Invents illustration.
  2. Clothes and colors it.
  3. Gives prosaic material illustrative value.
II. The operation of the Imagination.
  "Stereoscopic" views.
  Abstract becomes concrete.
  Historical Imagination.
III. The preacher's greatest power.
  The realization of the possible.
IV. The cultivation of the Imagination.
  1. The perceptions.
    Nature—Art.
  2. Poetry.

Read Broadus, Part III, Chap. V; Poe's Essay on "The Poetic Principle;"
Crother's "Gentle Reader," II.

XV.

IMAGINATION.

We have already spoken of the imagination in the previous chapter as an aid to the production of illustration. The subject, however, requires separate and special treatment. The imagination is the faculty of the mind which is most engaged in this work, and it is to the imagination of his hearer that the preacher appeals.

The imagination must be carefully distinguished from the fancy. Both belong to the creative power of the mind, are often employed for the same purposes, and their exercise produces similar results; but they are by no means the same faculty. Imagination is more profound and more logical. Fancy is more superficial and more capricious. Yet even so they may not ordinarily be distinguished. For homiletical purposes it may be well to state the difference in the following terms: Fancy creates its own material; the imagination deals with material which is furnished to it. The material upon which the fancy works is unreal; that upon which the imagination works is real. The imagination adopts this material, sets it in new and brighter light, multiplies its relations and suggestions, and so substantially changes its very structure. As the word itself implies it is the image-making faculty. It produces a picture of that which may be in concrete form. It is therefore the great source of power to men in all the walks of life. The inventor and the discoverer are particularly indebted to it, and to some extent all who become successful in their avocations—the statesman, the merchant, the artist, and the soldier. Napoleon Bonaparte possessed a more vivid imagination than any man in Europe, and through it often inspired his soldiers to deeds of utmost valor, as, for example, at the Battle of the Pyramids, when he exclaimed, "Soldiers, from yonder heights forty centuries look down upon you!"

I. It will be seen, therefore, how intimately the imagination is connected with the production of striking and useful illustrations. It is, indeed, of the very essence of illustration. This may be shown in three different ways.

1. It often invents illustration, in case there is none forthcoming from any other quarter. This is a form of fiction, but its use is entirely legitimate within certain bounds. The Savior Himself frequently employed it. His parables were all of them works of fiction, and the imagination may do for the preacher, in a limited way, what it did for the Lord Jesus Christ in a supreme way, as when he introduces an illustration with the remark, "Let us now suppose" or something of the kind.

2. The imagination clothes the prosaic with brilliant colors. Indeed, it bears the same relation to thought which color bears to monotone in pictorial art. The picture may be the same in form and structure, and yet it is transformed into a new thing by the colors which the painter employs. The colorist may not be a good draftsman, in which case his work will not be specially effective, but when the drawing is good the coloring is a mighty help to it. So it is with the imagination. The most prosaic thought may be set forth in language which renders it much more attractive and adds greatly to its beauty and its power.

3. Even when this is not done, the imagination may invest the material with a character which serves all the purpose of illustration. There may be nothing added to it in the way of color, so to speak, but it is set in a better light; it is held before the mind of the hearer in various positions; it is turned this way and that, as the jeweler turns the precious gem that its facets may catch the light from all directions and reflect its dazzling beauty. It elaborates details, it uses points, resemblances, and relations which would be lost to view without its aid.

The imagination, therefore, is of great importance to the preacher if it be properly held in check. The rule which he must constantly observe is this—*keep within the limit of fact*. Do not permit the imagination to run beyond the real. That which the imagination uses or presents must be at least the possible. It must never seem to the hearer that that preacher has gone beyond such limits and introduced that for which his material furnished him no warrant. It is not at all unusual for a preacher to import into Bible scenes description or narration which is absolutely fanciful. There is not the least warrant for his additions. Therefore, however graphic they may be they are simply playing false with Scripture. The imagination should never be suffered to enter the realm of the improbable, otherwise the preacher will be led into vain and foolish speculation, possibly into fanaticism.

II. How does the imagination actually operate? The simplest form in which to express its operation is this, it transforms the abstract into the concrete. The abstract still remains, the concrete is the clothing or the coloring. Broadus, in attempting to set forth this idea, uses the word "stereoscopic," a word very happily chosen to express his idea, but he fails to note that the stereoscopic requires two view-points. Two photographs taken from exactly the same place and laid side by side, although they may be viewed through the proper glass, will be as flat as either single picture of the composite. A stereoscopic view becomes what it is because it simulates the vision which is obtained through the two eyes. The lenses are placed some distance apart. So in illustration. The abstract is the one view-point, the concrete is the other view-point, the stereoscopic effect is the result.

Many examples might be given of this operation of the imagination from the best literature. Nothing can be better, however, than the language of the Savior Himself. If we confine ourselves to His Sermon on the Mount we shall find a number of examples. This sermon abounds in illustrative material. Dr. Bond, in his "Master Preacher," has well spoken of the power of the imagination as exhibited in Jesus Christ. He says: "It was highly sensitized and developed. His imagination was dramatic in its concepts and manifestations. The dramatic moment, when the interest of the occasion culminated, never failed to appear to Him. He saw the multitude as sheep without a shepherd. When the seventy brought to Him the glad report of their successful mission, even the demons being subject to their commands, Jesus said unto them 'I beheld Satan fallen as lightning from heaven.' This was the gift of His grand imagination. It was also pictorial. With Jesus this quality was more than ordinarily pronounced and cultivated. His imagination was eminently practical. He could gather up the images of the everyday commonplaces because He saw how to transfuse and transform them." Turning then to the Sermon on the Mount, observe how particularly rich it is in these imaginative expressions. "Ye are the salt of the earth," "Ye are the light of the world." "Where thy treasure is, there will thy heart be also." "The lamp of the body is the eye." "Enter ye in by the narrow gate." "Beware of false prophets, who come to you in sheep's clothing." And yet in the same sermon the Savior uttered many truths in abstract which His imagination immediately translated into the concrete. We place a few of them in parallel columns that they may be carefully observed, and their relation to the particular subject noted.

"Resist not him that is evil."	"Whosoever smiteth thee on thy right cheek, turn to him the other also."
"Take heed that ye do not your righteousness before men, to be seen of them."	"Sound not a trumpet before thee."
"Be not anxious for your life, what ye shall eat, or what ye shall drink," etc.	"Behold the birds of the heaven," "Consider the lilies of the field."
"Judge not, that ye be not judged."	"Why beholdest thou the mote that is in thy brother's eye, etc.

This particular operation of the imagination whereby the abstract is transfigured into the concrete is particularly useful in realizing and depicting the scenes of the Bible. This is because the Bible is an Oriental book written in ancient times. Customs have not only changed in the course of the centuries, but the customs of the East are very different from our own. How much there is in the Bible which can not be made plain to the reader or hearer of the gospel to-day but by the aid of the imagination—tents, turbans, camels, caravans, and much else of the same character, Roman arms, Greek games, and the like, and in addition to these physical things the forms of speech that are associated with them.

Therefore, the first thing for the preacher to cultivate in this line is a historical imagination. In a certain sense he must transport himself to the time and place in which the words were spoken. He must realize the condition of the man who spoke them, and of those whom he addressed. He must live with Moses in Egypt in the days of the Pharoahs. He must be saturated with the spirit of the great temples, sphinxes, pyramids. He must travel with the Israelites through the wilderness of Sinai. He must be awed by the tremendous heights that hang over the valleys through which the little streams are flowing that bring fertility and beauty. He must walk with the prophets through the land of Canaan from the time of Abraham to the time of Christ. He must know something of the great armies that swept over it, the famines that afflicted it, the vineyards with which its hills were adorned, and the flocks that were shepherded in its pastures. He must travel with the Apostle Paul in the Roman days, know something of the Greek civilization which he encountered and the Roman laws to which he was subject. Very much of Bible history is nothing but an outline, and he must fill it up by such knowledge as he may acquire from sources outside the Bible, and for which his imagination will prepare an embellishment and and an addition. If he deals with the mere language of historical Scripture and does no more, his preaching will be prosaic, literal, formal, lifeless. Take, for example, the miracle of the Feeding of the Five Thousand. It was at Bethsaida. The Savior instructed His apostles to have the multitude sit down: He then blessed the bread and multiplied it for their use. But let the imagination run: picture the scene. It is not necessary to go outside the sacred story in order to find material, for one of the evangelists tells us that the multitude was made to sit down upon the *green* grass, and another says that there was *much* grass in the place. The Savior made a happy choice, therefore, of the location in which His miracle was to be performed. As old Matthew Henry says: "He had respect to the furniture of his dining-room." That is imaginative! But Mark also informs us that they reclined by companies upon the green grass, and the word for company is literally a "flower-bed." If the preacher has it in mind and remembers the soft and beautiful coloring of the fabrics of the East—scarf, burnoose, and girdle—and can describe these people in their picturesque garb gathered in their little circles, he may furnish to his congregation an idea of the scene which will be beautiful and helpful beyond measure. Flower-beds in the green grass!

Take another example, the visit of Nicodemus to the Savior at Bethany: the close of the conference. Is there nothing more to be said about it than that the Savior concluded His discourse and Nicodemus departed? The closing words are as follows: "He that doeth the truth cometh to the light, that his works may be made manifest, that they have been wrought in God." No doubt it was the house of Martha. Why not imagine the Savior as escorting Nicodemus to the door? Why not picture Him as taking the Jewish ruler by the hand, and under the starlit dome making a courteous but emphatic reference to his coming by night, and dismissing him with the suggestion that he come by day upon his next visit? "Good-bye, Nicodemus, but remember he that doeth the truth cometh to the light. Good-bye, Nicodemus," and the ruler disappears into the darkness.

It is this realization of that which is associated with

the Bible history, that which is contained in the original meaning of its words, that which is suggested by its situation, that gives the preacher a peculiar power with those to whom he preaches.

But this historical imagination has its use in depicting the scenes of the future as well as of the past: the future on earth when the gospel shall have won its way among all nations and every knee shall bow to Christ: the future in the heavenly state, the eternal city with its golden streets, and its trees of life, and its pearly gates—each separate one a single, glowing monolith!

III. The greatest power that the preacher can ever possess or ever use is derived from his realization of the possible; not the mere realization of the probable, for that may be achieved by the ordinary mind; but the realization of the possible, that which many perhaps esteem impossible, that which is to be achieved through much toil and many sacrifices, and bitter tears and the surrender of precious lives. But the preacher who can foresee the coming of that which can not come except in such a way, and by the gracious and multiplied blessing of Almighty God, will inspire his people to action, and minister to their faith, and confirm their hope as the unimaginative preacher will never be able to do.

This hope of attaining the possible has sometimes been called a "castle in Spain." Verily, it is a good thing for the preacher to have. Paul had his "castle in Spain." Had it not been so he would not have been the successful preacher that he was. He was intent on preaching the gospel not only to those who lived in countries contiguous to Jerusalem, but those who were distant and ignorant. After he had preached from Jerusalem and round about even unto Illyricum, he still declared that it was his aim to preach the gospel where

Christ was not already named, and not to build upon another man's foundation, "but as it is written, They shall see, to whom no tidings of Him came, and they who have not heard shall understand." Paul ended his career at Rome, but if he had not had his castle in Spain he might never have been brought even so far as Rome. In writing to the Church at that place he indicated to them that even the Imperial City was, in his mind, only a way-station on the road to Spain. He said, "Whensoever I go unto Spain . . . . I hope to see you in my journey." and again he said that after he had gone to Jerusalem to carry the contribution for its poor, he would return again and "I will go on by you unto Spain." He was not to be satisfied until he had reached the *Ultima Thule*. He was *"going by them"* to the end of the earth!

In this sense the preacher is a seer, as we have indicated, and it is only when one has such an imagination as Paul's, or as that of the Lord Jesus Christ Himself, that he will project great enterprises for which, though small and unpromising in their beginnings, he sees a blessed growth and a glorious outcome.

IV. How then may the imagination be cultivated?

1. First of all through the perceptions. We must learn to see, to hear, to feel. We must learn to see in things physical that which is hidden to the ordinary eye, to hear in audible sounds a music that does not enter the dull ears. Like Michael Angelo, before his uncut marble, we must say, "There is an angel in that block of stone." Every preacher, indeed, should be to some extent a student of art. He should be fond of pictures and he should know how to judge a picture. He should visit art galleries, and, if possible, try to do some artistic work himself, because art is simply a representation of the unseen in the visible. A teacher of art once had a student who

gave unusual promise, but who had been engaged only with such study as could be taken up in the artist's studio in the city. He found it impossible to make his pupil believe that there were certain colors and forms in nature. His admonitions with regard to such matters, and his corrections of imperfect work were received with considerable suspicion and incredulity. But the summer came; the pupil was taken with the master into the woods, among the hills, beside the waters, and was taught to see. It was enough, and if the education of the imagination proceeds no further than this, it goes a long ways. Let the preacher live close to nature and seek every occasion to learn its higher ministry. Those who have done so have universally been imaginative. "The children of nature," as we call them, are peculiarly gifted in this respect—the Indians and the Arabs for example. And it was because the authors of the Bible lived so close to nature that the Bible itself has in it so much that ministers to the imagination. Take, for example, the description of a thunderstorm which is found in the 29th Psalm. Read it, study it, learn something from it. The cloud rises out of the Mediterranean Sea, "The voice of Jehovah is upon the waters." It passes over the mountains, "Jehovah breaketh in pieces the cedars of Lebanon." It moves off into the Eastern desert, "The voice of Jehovah shaketh the wilderness." The calm succeeds the storm, "Jehovah will bless His people with peace."

The perceptions are cultivated by a number of studies which whet the imagination, particularly those that deal with distant things or ancient things, and which can not be mastered without the aid of the imagination—astronomy, for example, geology, and others.

2. Imagination may be cultivated by the study of

suitable literature—poetry first of all, because poetry, if it be true poetry, is the product of the imagination. It can not be defined. Every attempt to do so has been a failure, but we all know what is meant by true poetry. The poetry of the Scripture is particularly rich in its imaginative features. Consider the 23rd Psalm. How much is expressed by the author which would have been lacking in a prosaic, matter of fact recitation of the same truths which it contains. He might have said, "The Lord is my Shepherd, He cares for me, He takes me where there is food and water." This is the same thought as that of the original, but what a contrast! The Psalmist's thought outran the food and water; his perceptions had been cultivated by his contact with nature. He saw the pasture and the stream; his mind dwelt on the color of the grass, and the quiet of the meadow brook. He thought of satisfaction, of security, of serenity. He wrote, "Jehovah is my Shepherd; I shall not want. He maketh me to lie down in green pastures; He leadeth me beside the still waters!" The Hebrew original is even more beautiful and expressive. Literally it is "pastures of tender grass" and "waters of quietness." What has the poet done for us by such expressions? He has done in marked degree what all poetry does for those who are susceptible to its influence. Poetry gives us:—

(1) *The penetrating vision;* an oblique view of truth, its unusual aspects, its special relations. It unveils its hidden beauties, connects it with analogies, and sets forth its symbolism.

(2) *Lofty aspiration.* It appeals to the highest motives; sets forth the best uses; deals with supreme services. It emphasizes the nobility of manhood, and commends fellowship with God.

(3) *Dramatic intuitions;* the play of the passions;

the deeper meaning of words and actions; the significance of movement; the revelation of the inwardness of things; above all the inner heart of man.

(4) *Quick sympathies;* sensitiveness to pain and grief and joy and happiness; a fellow feeling with all mankind; sympathy with Jesus Christ in His work of redemption.

(5) *Concreteness of thought;* not abstract philosophy; not unsubstantial theorizing, but form and shape even to the most shadowy of our conceptions.

(6) *Choice diction.*

It would seem as though too much study could not be given to poetry, and yet there are those who derive harm from an undue attention to it. But this is only when the habit of allegorizing is formed, and a certain use of language is adopted which is ill adapted to prose, a kind of transcendental style which never touches the earth, but lingers forever in the air. The preachers who display this style remind us of a remark which Webster once made concerning his opponent in a law case; "Gentleman of the jury, this man neither alights or flies forward. He hovers." Some preachers are nothing but poets; their sermons are altogether sentimental and imaginative. They conduct their audience, as it were, into a beautiful piece of woods, vocal with the songs of birds, adorned with wild flowers, fascinating in its play of light and shadow, but suddenly the guide disappears and the followers are left—*"in the woods!"*

Perhaps the simplest and easiest way to show the influence of poetry upon the imagination is to choose some subject with which some poem deals, and make the attempt to write a sermon in the spirit of the poem, not repeating any of it, not employing perhaps any of its language, but adopting its style, its view-point, and its method with practical and positive additions. Suppose the preacher were to do this with the subject of prayer. Suppose he were to employ for his purpose only certain well known hymns such as "Prayer is the soul's sincere desire," "Jesus, where'er Thy people meet," "Inspirer and hearer of prayer." Let him make use of the suggestions which are found in these hymns, the aspect in which prayer is regarded in them. Let him endeavor to carry his imagination along the same lines and see what the outcome may be. Or if the preacher does not produce a whole sermon in such a way, suppose he makes the poetry a guide for a portion of the sermon; or suppose he quotes poetry in connection with the thought to which he has given utterance.

This suggestion applies not only to poetry in meter. There are certain prose writers whose style is decidedly poetic and imaginative. The preacher may give attention to these, also.

The practical outcome of all this will be that the preacher, having cultivated his own imagination and employed it for illustrative purposes, will appeal to the imagination of his hearers. He will enable them to see that in truth which has been concealed from them. He will enable them to appreciate the lessons of the past. He will carry them into that future into which he has been able to peer, and they with him will have a foreglimpse of the new heavens and the new earth wherein dwelleth righteousness. He will stir their deepest emotions; he will excite their best sentiments. He will move them as they are never moved by barren thought or cold logic.

APPLICATION.

APPLICATION.

Distinguished from the "Conclusion."
I. It is in the text and the subject.
II. It is in the man.
III. Various forms.
 "Means and methods."
IV. Use of the emotions.
V. The place for the application.

Read Kennard's "Psychic Power in Preaching;" Kern's "Ministry to the Congregation," XIX; James' "Talks to Teachers," VIII.

XVII.

APPLICATION.

We have already referred to the application in connection with the conclusion. The two terms, however, are not synonymous: the conclusion is a rhetorical term denoting the closing portion of an address; the application is a moral or spiritual term denoting the use which is to be made of the address—perhaps in the conclusion; perhaps elsewhere. Spurgeon expresses the proper sense of the term when he says, "Where the application begins the sermon begins," that is to say, the sermon is the application, and conversely the application is the sermon. In this connection a fine anecdote is related of Spurgeon, as quoted by Kern. He says, "A young man preached one Sunday morning in London, taking as his theme the Great Day of Atonement (Lev. 16:34), and thirty years after, one of his hearers wrote to him, "I distinctly remember carrying away the inerasable impression of power that could not be explained and refused to be measured, power shown in lucid statement vivid picturing, pungent appeal, and red-hot earnestness. The Levitical sacrifices were as real as though offered out yesterday, and their meaning as clear and indisputable as the shining of the August sun, and yet the center of interest is not in the Jewish offerings but in the needs of the soul, and besides them the preacher uses nothing except as God's sure remedy for sin. Every paragraph ends with a clause which says, 'He means me; he is appealing to me; he He is praying for me.'" The young preacher was Chas. H. Spurgeon. In that sermon he illustrated, as he did in all his sermons, his theory of the application. It formulates the fundamental principle in the theory of preaching. If adopted by the preacher it will be for him the cure of all mere formal discourse. The application will be a pervasive thing rather than an explicit thing. It will be suggested in the opening sentence of the sermon, and will be started on its way to the conscience of the listener. It will gather momentum as it proceeds, until its final power will appear as the sermon is concluded.

Such being the case a number of particulars may be observed with regard to it.

I. First of all the application is in the text and in the subject. The text is chosen because the preacher sees the application in it, and the subject is so conceived and announced by him as that it contains the application, in its initial form.

The preacher's power in this respect will, therefore, depend very largely upon his choice of texts and his statement of subjects, and the rules which we have already given with regard to them will be found to apply. Indeed, if his text is chosen and his subject stated as they should be, the application will very largely take care of itself, and the preacher need not be particularly concerned with regard to it. But upon the other hand there may be an undiscovered application in the text, or the application which plainly appears to the devout and earnest student of the Word may be vitiated or obscured by improper handling.

II. Again the application is in the man, that is in the preacher. It resides in his spirit and manner rather than in any language which he may employ to express it. It will be conveyed by his sincerity, his earnestness, and his fidelity to the Word of God.

This has been well expressed by Dr. Stiles of New York in an article in the Homiletic Review for March, 1908. The subject of the article is "Detached Preaching." The author begins by quoting Dr. John Watson, "While the preacher should be very sparing of 'I,' it should be possible for an expert to compose a biography of him from a year's sermons. Sometimes a single sermon should reveal his personality sufficiently to furnish material for a biography. He is not to exploit himself or to exhibit his egotism; nevertheless the preacher who does not convey himself as he conveys his message fails at the most important point." The failure to do this is "detached preaching." It consists in handing over a course of thought to a congregation with their permission to take it or discard it upon its own merits. It is as though the preacher said, "Do not be influenced by me. Merely consider whether this is true and good, and decide for yourselves what you will do with it." Some preachers, says Dr. Stiles, do this in a humble spirit because they do not desire to interpose any authority of their own, and this assumption of impersonality has an air of genuine modesty in it. Nevertheless there must be something of such assumption, or the preacher's sermon is not preaching according to Biblical models. No preacher has any right to abdicate his function and refer his hearers only to a distant and disembodied divinity. The preacher must be the embodiment of the truth which he announces, and it must have with him a vital power. The mistake that some ministers make is that of thinking that truth contains its own force; but there is no force at all in mere truth. It is only when the truth takes hold on some man, and thus becomes incarnate, that it has influence and power. It is not true that "truth is mighty and will prevail" if that truth be dissociated from a living and energetic personality. The application, therefore, is in the preacher. It has power because he is himself possessed by it. His words are in no sense autobiographical; he reveals no personalities; he is not oracular or dogmatic; and yet he is his own best argument. This is because he has chosen his text and his subject out of his deep desire to bless his fellow men in the name of Christ; because this deep desire is made manifest throughout his whole sermon, and more than all, because he plainly indicates as he proceeds with his sermon that it will not be finished with its close. He will still continue to preach that sermon, not in formal discourse, but in many ways in which he will follow it with the lessons which it contains. It is for this reason that the pulpit will never lose its power; because the power is not in the message alone; but also in the man. Printed sermons are always divested of a large part of their power. As Dr. Jefferson says, "You can not print a man, and the sermon without the man is not a sermon in the full." "Vital preaching," says Slattery, "depends more upon the will, the purpose, and the sincerity of a man's character than upon his mental attainments. Clever people can make brilliant orations, but only good people can preach sermons that will help any one. The goodness which these people must have is not an insipid innocence, but qualities of positive excellence. They display this largely in the attitude which a preacher takes to his congregation. Let us pray, therefore, that the clergy of our time may have large and strengthening sympathy for men that falter and stumble; that they may clap their hands for joy because men of other callings find their vocations sacred; that they may be self-forgetful friends and servants of all men."

Preaching is testimony more than it is anything else, and, therefore, there is more individuality in this form of address than in any other. What would be an unmannerly display of egotism outside of preaching is not only permissible in preaching but is positively peremptory.

Dr. J. Spencer Kennard's book on "Psychic Power in Preaching" deals exclusively with this element. He defines the term, "psychic power" as "the energy of the preacher's soul in contact with that of the hearer," and quotes H. W. Beecher's words "The living force of the living soul on living souls for the sake of their transformation is the fundamental idea of preaching." He also quotes Oliver Wendell Holmes, "The orator only becomes our master at the moment when he is himself captured—taken possession of by a sudden rush of fresh inspiration." He produces testimonies from many sources to the same effect.

It is, therefore, absolutely idle for the preacher who does not possess the two elements which we have reviewed to attempt an application of any other kind. Nevertheless when there is manifest application in both message and man, it yet remains that there are certain portions of the sermon in which the direct attempt must be made to press home the truths which are being uttered. Hence we consider

III. Various forms of application. There are quite a number of them. None, perhaps, are more comprehensive than those which are given by Kern, as follows: Recapitulation, illustration, inferences, exhortation, and so forth. But that form of application which deserves special attention, and which is of the greatest value, is that which is called by Broadus the application of "means

and methods," that is, the careful and specific direction
as to the way in which the provisions of the sermon are
to be carried out. It is here that the preacher sometimes
fails and incurs the just criticism of one who said with
regard to a certain sermon, "He told us to *do* it, but he did
not tell us *how* to do it."   If there is no such application the exhortation "to do it" is no more than a command to make bricks without straw. Many illustrations
may be given of this form of application, and in connection with a number of general subjects which the
preacher is apt to discuss; for example, the duty of immediately accepting the salvation offered in Christ Jesus.
The hearer should always be told just how this acceptance of Christ is to be made; in what spirit, in what
terms, and with what intentions. He can not be too
particular in discussing the details of the method whereby
one is led to exercise saving faith in the Redeemer. So
with regard to repentance and the surrender of all evil
habits and practices. So with regard to the matter of
Christian liberality. It is not sufficient to urge people
to give freely of their means: they should be instructed
with regard to the principles of Christian giving, the
objects, the times, the proportions, and above all with
regard to their indebtedness to the Lord Jesus Christ,
and their obligation to hold all that they have as a sacred
trust.   It is very particularly so also with regard to
Christian service.   Congregations are frequently urged
to do something for the Lord Jesus Christ in recognition
of all that He has done for them; but the preacher is
not often enough explicit with regard to the ways in
which Christ may be served, the avenues of usefulness,
and the time which should be set aside for distinctly
Christian work. Many a preacher who discourses upon
this subject would find it hard to give particular instruc-

tions to those who might enquire of him as to the means and methods by which his exhortations should be put in practice.

The first Christian sermon which was preached after the ascension of our Lord is a very fine illustration of all that has been said upon the subject. This was Peter's sermon upon the Day of Pentecost. Let the reader examine it from beginning to end with reference to this matter of application. He will find that the application of that sermon resided in the subject and in the man. He will also find that when Peter concluded it with the words, "Let all the house of Israel therefore know assuredly, that God hath made Him both Lord and Christ, this Jesus whom ye crucified," those that heard were pricked in their heart and exclaimed, "Brethren, what shall we do?" They were moved to action. They wished direction with regard to the way in which the exhortation of the sermon should be carried out, which directions Peter immediately proceeded to give them.

The application then should deal with particulars, particular duties, graces, fruits, and the like. This does not mean that it is to be directed at particular individuals. The only time when the preacher can adapt his application to one particular person is when there is only one person in the audience. Such was the case when Nathan preached to David, Elijah to Ahab, Jesus to Nicodemus and to the woman of Samaria. But in order that the application may be particular it is not amiss for the preacher to make the class which he is addressing very plain even as Jesus did, to limit it closely and particular as when He said, "Woe unto you, scribes and Pharisees; woe unto you, lawyers."

IV. The method of application is closely connected with what has been already said. It is a rhetorical method rather than an argumentative one. It is finally, and we believe above all, an appeal to the emotions. Men are seldom moved by a sheer argument; they are seldom moved by a mere exhortation. There must be that associated with the argument or the exhortation which deeply stirs their feelings. Ordinary preachers do not make enough of the emotions, and they may well learn a lesson in this respect from the method of the most successful evangelists. When one suffers loss in his emotional nature he suffers that which affects both his intellect and his will. Nor can the intellect and the will be as vigorous as they should be, nor as healthy as they should be, when the emotional nature is dwarfed or suppressed. This is a well recognized principle in psychology, and has been set forth at some length by Professor James. One of his finest illustrations is derived from Darwin's autobiography. This great scientist made the following confession: "Up to the age of thirty or beyond it, poetry of many kinds gave me great pleasure, and even as a school-boy I took intense delight in Shakespeare. I have also said that pictures formerly gave me considerable and music very great delight, but now for many years I can not endure to read a line of poetry. I have tried lately to read Skakespeare, and have found it so intolerably dull that it nauseated me. I have also lost my taste for pictures or music. My mind seems to have become a kind of machine for grinding general laws out of a large collection of facts, but why this should have caused the atrophy of that part of the brain alone on which the higher tastes depend I can not conceive. If I had to live my life again I would have made a rule to read some poetry and listen to some music at least once every week, for perhaps the parts of my brain now atrophied would thus have been kept alive through use.

The loss of these tastes is a loss of happiness, and may possibly be injurious to the intellect and more probably to the moral character by enfeebling the emotional part of our nature." This is a sad confession, but it is a true transcript of that which happens when the emotions are suppressed. The preacher, therefore, must not suppress them in himself , and he must keep them fully alive in his hearers by his methods in applying the truth.

And yet he must be on his guard in this matter. While we have said that sheer argument does not generally lead to action, it is equally true that a mere appeal to the emotions does not lead to action unless it be preceded by sound and cogent reasons. It must also rest upon worthy motives which take hold of the consciences of men and urge them on. It must also insist upon immediate and positive action, and the preacher must make it plain that, if such action does not follow, the hearer injures his own life. An application in which the emotions only are engaged results in what Bishop Butler calls "passive impressions," which grow positively weaker with repetition. Professor James calls our attention to the psychological reason for this. He says: "When a resolve or a fine glow of feeling is allowed to evaporate without bearing practical fruit it is worse than a chance lost. It works so as to positively hinder future resolutions and emotions from taking the normal path of discharge. There is no more contemptible type of human character than that of the nerveless sentimentalist and dreamer who spends his life in a weltering sea of sensibility but never does a concrete manly deed."

A fine illustration of all this is found in the influence of the theatre, for notwithstanding the noble sentiments that are sometimes uttered from the stage, and the heroism and integrity of character which is frequently displayed thereon, the theatre is a positive failure in moral teaching. As Dr. J. D. Moffat well remarks, "it over-feeds the emotions." Worse than that, the morality which it displays is often a mere simulation, a piece of transparent hypocrisy which may be presented by one who has no moral character, in which case the influence of the very moral sentiments which are spoken must be bad and only bad. The Rev. Charles M. Sheldon refused to have his "In His Steps" dramatized unless those who proposed to present it would guarantee that all the actors who took parts in it should be exemplary Christians. No theatrical manager could furnish the guarantee, therefore it never found its way into the regular theatre. When the emotions only are moved the soul is grievously tempted to a response which has no positive virtue. The hearer consoles himself by saying, "Yes, I have done wrong. I know I have done wrong," and he seems to regard this as in itself a form of absolution. It salves the conscience but it does not purge it. Sometimes it does not even salve the conscience. It leads not to repentance, but to despair. So, indeed, it was with Judas.

A little child said to his mother, when he had disobeyed her commands, "Mamma, I did not mean to do it." She answered him, "Yes, my boy, but you must mean *not* to do it." The resolution must be a positive one in favor of the good, and it must issue in positive action. Remember what the Savior said about the unclean spirit when he had gone out of the man. Foster, the biographer of Charles Dickens, says that the great novelist once remarked to him, "Foster, the truths which have had the greatest influence upon mankind have made people neither laugh nor cry." This certainly was a strange remark to proceed from such a source, but it has a world of truth in it. A preacher is not effective simply because his preaching produces tears. Truth is not powerful because it makes those who hear it laugh or cry. It is the truth that enters the soul like the barb of an arrow: that stays and rankles there; that can not be removed except by surgery, some moral surgery that will effect a change of conditions. Such is the truth that is effective.

The preacher, however, must remember that the emotions are not to be reached by a mere effort to reach them. We can not urge a congregation to feel the force of our application. It is useless to attempt such a thing. The application is in the man. He must feel the force of the truth himself. The feeling will not come because we bid it come. It comes chiefly through the imagination: it comes through the presentation of details: it comes from the graphic setting forth of those things with which the truth is associated, and when the preacher, dwelling upon the scene which he describes or upon the truth which he is endeavoring to expound, feels the thrill in his own soul he may be sure that the audience will feel the thrill when he presents the truth to them. When, so to speak, the "cold shivers" run over him, then, and only then, may he know that those to whom he speaks are similarly affected. Then comes that inexplicable contagion of sympathy—sympathy with the truth, and sympathy with Christ by which the application is made sure.

V. The place of the application. It is not always at the close of the sermon. It may often be distributed with profit as we have already indicated. At all events, the preacher should cultivate variety in this respect. If he is in the habit of introducing his application only at the close of his sermon, he may be sure that some people will prepare for it and be ready to evade it. The expression of the application should not be too frequent:

it should not be too complex. It should seldom be prolonged, and it should not ordinarily be accompanied with much voice or with great physical force. Best of all, it should be chiefly suggestive, so that sometimes the most effective application is an interrogative one. This was often employed by the Savior. "Which of these three, thinkest thou, proved neighbor unto him that fell among the robbers?" "The baptism of John, was it from heaven, or from men?"

And this the preacher should not neglect to do. When his sermon is in course of preparation he should frequently ask himself, Would this consideration move me? Would this argument avail in my case? Do I myself get help and comfort here? Would I do myself that which I am counseling others to do? And let him remember that the measure of his success in preaching is to be found alone in the degree in which the application of his sermon is observed and practised by his people. Not his brilliant rhetoric, not his sound arguments, not his telling illustrations, but his positive usefulness is the measure of his success.

MORAL QUALITY.

MORAL QUALITY.

The spirit and temper of the sermon.
1. Cheering and cheerful.
2. Unconventional.
3. Patient.
4. Casting no suspicion upon God.
5. Leading to Christ.

Read Jefferson's "Minister as Prophet," II ; Abbott's "Christian Ministry,"
VII ; Quayle's " Pastor Preacher," " Nevers."

XVII.

MORAL QUALITY.

By "moral quality" we do not refer to any ethical or spiritual element of the sermon, but rather to its spirit and temper. This moral quality should be exhibited in many particulars, too many indeed to specify. Let us consider some of the more important ones.

1. *First of all the sermon should be eminently cheering and cheerful.* The pulpit should be the fount of comfort and courage for all the devout and well-meaning souls who present themselves before it; and the man in the pulpit should be for them the strong, brave, and self-reliant soul, full of faith, confident in God, and absolutely self-possessed. The world is full of tired people, lonesome people, heartsick people, sinsick people, and they will throng the Church of any one who is competent to bring them help, and who is always intent upon doing so. But none of them desire him to exhibit in himself the weaknesses and pains of which they themselves are conscious. People who suffer do not want their friends to assume suffering in order to sympathize with them. People who weep are not anxious that others should weep with them because of a sort of contagion. People who are crushed with trial and temptation are never helped by those who appear to be equally crushed with themselves.

It is true that we must "weep with those that weep," but that does not mean that we weep from weakness.

There is no record of the Savior's having wept with those in sorrow, except at the grave of Lazarus. We are thankful that He did so once—it had a world of suggestion and comfort in it. But for all He wept on that occasion He was not unmanned. How strong and helpful He appears in His words to Martha, particularly when he assures her that her brother shall rise again! And so the Savior appeared on all occasions when He ministered to those in distress. Contrast Him with the mourners of that day, some of them hired mourners, whom He oftentimes rebuked, and whom on one occasion He ordered from the room in which He was about to manifest His power and His glory.

And the preacher should be as much like Jesus in these respects as it is possible for him to be. At least the same contrast should appear between his bearing and that of those to whom he ministers. There are plenty "to make ado." Let him not be one of them. Let him always be quiet, calm, and natural. It will render him all the more tender, considerate, and gracious. Let him observe those whom people in distress prefer to have about them, and those whose presence they do not desire. They invariably turn from those who whine and snivel: there is no comfort for them in such.

But this does not mean by any means that the preacher is to assume an indifference to those who are in pain, or to cultivate a sort of professional stoicism. Such preachers would remind one not of the loving Christ, but of such statues of Him as we sometimes see, representing Him in the attitude of ministering; but railed off and inaccessible. The people come just near enough to Him to fail of touching Him. A marble Christ helps no one. No more can a marble preacher.

The preacher must ever believe that "the best is yet

to be;" that no condition is as bad as it appears; and that the light will break forth in due season. No preacher can afford to be a pessimist in the pulpit, but he must always show therein what Lyman Abbott calls "a divine hopefulness." "If he is to be a leader he must set before himself an ideal, and he must have in him some expectation that that ideal can be attained. He is to have the courage to see things as they are, but he must also have faith in a God who is in the world making things better, and an incorrigible expectation that they will be better, and an invincible determination to do something to make them better. He who has no vision to see a better future, and no expectation inspiring him to its attainment, does not belong in the Christian ministry."

It is not well for the preacher to dwell too much upon the trials of others in the pulpit, not even upon those of his most devoted parishioners. If he has occasion to refer to them, the reference should be offset with a more extended reference to the relief which God has promised to those that fear and love Him. There is danger sometimes when the preacher talks too much in the pulpit about the sorrows and trials of men that he may, as Bishop Quayle suggests, "grow hysterical." It is an easy thing to do, and one may think that he is all the more considerate and sympathetic when it is done, "but hysterics," says Bishop Quayle, "are not things catalogued in the fruits of the Spirit."

Least of all should the preacher refer in the pulpit to his own trials or his own bereavements. He should never allude to them in any form of public address, either oral, written, or printed. Sometimes the preacher seems to think when he makes mention of his hard work, the difficulties of his position, or his poverty, he is winning some sort of credit for himself and making capital for his preaching, but such is not the case. On the contrary, some have even unseated themselves, and become unpopular with an otherwise kindly people by such references. "The complaining preacher," says Bishop Quayle again, "is a good specimen of a humbug. He thinks of himself more highly than he ought to think." And Jefferson adds another suggestive word, "Men who are everlastingly whimpering because of their misfortunes and trials can never lift men into the joy of the gospel, for if one is to keep his people on the sunny side of the street he must walk on the sunny side of the street himself. Jesus does not call men into the ministry with a promise of ease and comfort. No doubt He expects them to be pained and tried in order that they may be qualified to direct the multitudes of sorrowing and suffering people in this weary world." His own first sermon, which He preached in the synagogue at Nazareth, where He had been brought up, foreshadowed the character of His entire preaching work. By a happy Divine Providence the Scripture lesson for the day was taken from the 61st chapter of Isaiah, "The Spirit of the Lord Jehovah is upon Me, because Jehovah hath anointed Me to preach good tidings unto the meek: He hath sent Me to bind up the brokenhearted, to proclaim liberty to the captives, and the opening of the prison to them that are bound, to proclaim the year of Jehovah's favor." His sermon seems to have been a very brief one. Perhaps He was interrupted after its opening sentence with the surprised ejaculations of His listeners; for all that we have reported of His sermon is in these words, "To-day hath this Scripture been fulfilled in your ears." His congregation, however, were astonished. "They wondered at the words of grace which proceeded out of His mouth." And so Jesus continued upon His ministry, giving sight to the blind, setting souls at liberty, proclaiming the acceptable year of the Lord. He does not seem to have had a word of condemnation for any except hypocrites. And the preacher should strive to be more like Him. If the man in the pulpit fulfills his ministry a very beautiful prophecy of Isaiah (56:7) will be fulfilled with regard to the place of worship in which he ministers. "Even them will I bring to My holy mountain, and make them joyful in My house of prayer." A house of prayer ought to be on every occasion a very foretaste of heaven, and heaven will be infinite good cheer. It will be a holy place. Yes, it will be that first of all. "There shall in no wise enter into it anything unclean." But it will also be a happy place: no night, no heat, no thirst, no tears, no sickness, and no sorrow. There will be rivers of pleasure, a beatific vision, and eternal glory.

2. *The sermon should be unconventional.* The preacher who fulfills his mission will not be bound by any formal rules, nor handicapped by any technical requirements. We have been engaged during the chapters which have preceded this in stating these formal rules. No one can become an efficient preacher without mastering them, and it is sincerely hoped that, so far as they commend themselves to the reader, they may be adopted by him. But it is also as sincerely hoped by the author that they will all of them be ignored, if not indeed absolutely forgotten. They should be like the soapsuds in which the good woman of the old story cleansed her week's washing, but which did not appear in the beautifully clean fabrics that hung upon her clothesline. Technical formulas are only the scaffolding by means of which a structure is erected, and it is a great mistake in any department of thought to permit the scaffolding to remain

after it has served its purpose. The beginner in the art of drawing may need to make measurements, and compare distances, and experiment with lights and shades, but he will never become a draftsman until he has learned to draw with a free hand. No more can one ever become a preacher who is not what may be called a free-hand preacher. There must be no rhetorical or theological trammels upon his thought or manner in the pulpit. The course of training through which he has passed should have been sufficient to teach him what the truth is, and how it may be best proclaimed; but when once his course of training is completed he should be in every respect himself, suiting himself to the occasion, to the people to whom he ministers, and to the needs of the hour.

There is an immense amount of cant uttered from the pulpit by well-meaning preachers whose vocabulary is limited, and whose experience is scant. It is no great reflection upon them that they seem to be unable to talk in other terms, but it is a serious hindrance to their usefulness. "Cant" is the use of religious phraseology without sincerity or without pertinency. It is the adoption of certain stock phrases which when first uttered had force and meaning in them, but which lose their force and meaning by constant reiteration. It is also the adoption of a certain tone or manner, or method of doing things, which has had the same history, but which has become obsolete. Of course, there are many religious phrases which the preacher must continually employ. They are his stock-in-trade: he can no more dispense with their use than the electrician can dispense with "volts" and "amperes," or the carpenter dispense with "feet" and "inches." But these expressions are Scriptural ones. They are used by the sacred writers. Their sense has been determined by long usage, and there are no expressions which can take their place. But there are other expressions and other forms of thought which are inventions of men, and sometimes very poor inventions at that, and the preacher often continues to repeat them until they become obnoxious.

Slattery indicates that it is almost as bad to use the Scriptural phrases to which we have referred with undue frequency. It renders them meaningless and hollow. Our Savior may be properly called "Our Blessed Lord" he says, but to hear Him called "Our Blessed Lord" every time He is mentioned in a sermon with a rattling commonplaceness is shocking. "There never was a time more impatient of sham in the religious life. Men are indeed too sensitive about it, often thinking to discover it where there is only the stoutest sincerity." But for this very reason we must be the more on our guard against it.

It is not alone in the use of conventional expressions that the preacher may commit an error; but as we have already indicated by addressing his fellows in some stereotyped way that is not absolutely suited to their occupations, their aspiration, or their conditions in life. When the preacher knows how to adapt his methods as well as his language to his listeners so that they realize that he is not an alien, nor his words an intrusion, but that he is dealing with them as a fellow sinner and as a fellow saint, he becomes truly influential. He must adopt the vernacular of his congregation, so far, of course, as it is suited to the pulpit, and he must make use of such means as are suited to conditions. It is this which gives the "Bonnie Brier Bush" and the "Sky Pilot" their peculiar sweetness, and their remarkable suggestiveness. They represent men who lived among the people as the people lived, fell into their ways of thinking, and met them upon their own ground.

Jesus did not teach often where the rabbis of His

day taught; He never made use of their quibbles and refinements, and therefore the common people heard Him gladly. And after He had spoken those wonderfully fresh and unconventional words upon the mount, we are told that when He came down from the mountain great multitudes followed Him. He had taught them as one having authority, and not as their scribes.

3. *The sermon must exhibit great patience.* The preacher is very often discouraged with himself and discouraged with his people, and in consequence becomes somewhat intolerant. When he is in such a state of mind he is apt to take his people to task for their negligence, and sometimes he even goes so far as to scold them from the pulpit for what he believes to be their indifference or their shortcomings. But this is not as it should be. If his indignation is aroused he should be very careful how he expresses it. Vices and errors may stir his conscience, and seem to him to call for public reproof, but he should be very careful how this reproof is administered. If his indignation seems to be mixed with any self-sufficient spirit it will counteract any element of good which there may be in his reproof.

A book for children which was published many years ago gave four rules for parental government which these children were taught to exercise when they were engaged in plays in which they simulated the action of a father, mother, or teacher. "When you consent, consent cordially. When you refuse, refuse finally. When you punish, punish good-naturedly. Commend often, never scold." The four rules may well be employed by preachers in their pulpit work. They must ever be fully appreciative of the efforts of their people, the difficulties under which they labor, the obstacles which are in their way, the hardship of natural temperament and taste, of the callings in which they are engaged, the neighborhoods in which they live, and such like. The preacher should be diligent to find things that he may praise rather than things that he may blame. "Censure," says Bishop Quayle, "requires a small brain and a wagging tongue, but to praise requires often a systematic insight of a brother's heart. How gleeful any congregation is which finds itself possessed of a pastor who enjoys them and their church, and their children and their way of doing things, and who every once in a while remarks 'I never enjoyed a people more than this one.' It is so cheap to browbeat a congregation, and so charming and manly to enjoy one." He says again, "Do not stew. This is the best word for what so many preachers mistake for being in earnest. Stewing is no sign of earnestness. It is a sign of lack of self-control and of self-calm."

4. *The sermon should never cast any suspicion upon God.* We do not mean to indicate that the preacher has any intention of doing so. We doubt if there is any gospel minister, in our own or other lands, who would do such a thing as this deliberately. It can not be; it is an impossible hypothesis. And yet, while the preacher's intentions may be absolutely good, and his own confidence in the goodness of God be absolutely unshaken, he may inadvertently so express himself in the pulpit as that those who hear him shall be timid in their approaches to God, and doubtful of their reception by Him, or of the favorable consideration of their case and condition at the Almighty's hands. Have we altogether escaped from the heathen notion that our God might do us harm? that He is not altogether favorably disposed towards us? that He is to be appeased in some way? that His favor must be purchased at some price? Have we learned as yet the infinite difference between propitiation and repa-

ration, between atonement and compromise? Can we make it absolutely plain to our people that, while God can by no means clear the guilty, He has already removed their guilt if they are ready to believe it and accept His forgiveness? Do we realize that there is positively no sin so great that it can not be forgiven, and are we prepared so to preach to the people who listen to us that they shall feel and know in their deepest souls that there is absolutely nothing to keep them from God except that which is in themselves?

Many people are given altogether too much to an evil introspection by which their very faults are magnified, and fictitious obstacles beween themselves and their Savior are erected in their own minds. This is sometimes heightened by the condition of their health. Dyspepsia and nervous weakness often induce a condition of spiritual hopelessness, which the preacher can do very much to remove by his method of presenting the love of God. Sometimes references are made to the "unpardonable sin," giving to it a character which is absolutely unwarranted by the Scripture. Some poor souls believe it to consist in some overt act of transgression, some sort of willfulness or presumption. They imagine that they have committed it, and that they are without hope. But it is well understood now by the best thinkers upon the subject that the unpardonable sin is not an act but a condition, and when that condition is reached the soul is "past feeling," that as long as one has any fear lest he have committed it, or any wish to be forgiven in case he supposes he has committed it, the condition certainly has not been reached. Dr. R. A. Torrey has published the account of three different individuals with whom he dealt, and all of whom were brought to Christ, who had reached a condition in which hope seemed to have absolutely departed from their breasts. One of them was a "professional murderess." She attended his meetings for a time, but made every effort to throw off the conviction which she felt was fastening upon her soul. One evening she came to the evangelist and said, "You may preach now as much as you please. You can have no effect upon me. I have prayed to the devil to take away all my religious feeling, and my prayer has been regarded," and she laughed in his face; and yet in this woman's case Christ proved stronger than the devil and she was led to a living and loyal faith in the Lord Jesus Christ. "Despairing of no man," such are the beautiful words in the margin of Luke 6:35, and such should be the spirit of the preacher. It is well expressed in Faber's beautiful lines:

> "There's a wideness in God's mercy,
> Like the wideness of the sea;
> There's a kindness in his justice,
> Which is more than liberty."

What a lesson the Savior taught His disciples with regard to their confidence in God when He healed the man that was born blind. They imagined that his calamity must have been occasioned either by his own sin or by the sin of his parents. Jesus corrected their misapprehensions. He taught them once for all that providence is not always punitive, and that the purpose of providence is not always the punishment of the offender, but the vindication of the goodness of God. He said: "Neither did this man sin, nor his parents: but that the works of God should be made manifest in him." And surely they were manifested in him! The man himself was healed and saved; the power of Jesus was exhibited in a miracle which even His enemies surrendered to Him, and the way was prepared for the proclamation of a great spiritual truth, namely, that Jesus was the Light of the world; that for judgment he came into the world that they that see not might see, and that they that saw might become blind.

By the adoption of such principles as the foregoing, the preacher will make his pulpit what it should be, the source of comfort and of courage. Landseer has a very beautiful picture which is entitled "The Sanctuary." It represents a stag which has been pursued by the hunters, but which has eluded them by taking to the water. In the light of the early morning he appears just gaining the shore of an island, to which he has swum from the mainland in the distance. Poor fellow, he is the very picture of exhaustion. His head is thrown high into the air, his tongue lolls from his mouth, his legs seem scarcely able to support his weight. He is evidently staggering ashore. It has been a hard and bitter struggle, but he is safe at last. The Sanctuary! Oh, that it might be to the weary souls that resort to it what the island shore was to the wounded stag!

The finest character in all uninspired literature is Bunyan's "Great Heart." He is the ideal Christian pastor. The Pilgrim's Progress is supposed to be a juvenile book, and its use is largely limited to children, but he who has not read it since he was a child has failed to grasp its deeper meaning. By all means let the preacher read it again, especially the young preacher, before he begins upon his life work. And let him make a careful study of its principle character. He is not Mr. Big Brains, but Mr. Great Heart. He is a servant of the Interpreter—that is, of the Holy Spirit. He is attached to House Beautiful, that is the Church of God, and he does the bidding of the Interpreter for those who become his guests. Great Heart is many things, but he is one thing in particular. He is a great theologian and competent to discuss the doctrines of grace with those who are equally learned with himself. But he is more than this and other than this. He is a mighty man of valor, fearless in opposing the enemies of his master, and successful in his encounters with them. But he is more than this and other than this. First of all and chiefly, he is the considerate companion of a little company of weaker spirits than his own, and it is his business to conduct them from the House Beautiful to the river, beyond which is the Celestial City. He is their trusted friend, their loving counsellor. They look to him, lean upon him, and obey him. His tenderness and his consideration are the chief elements in his character. How lovingly he deals with Mr. Fearing and with Mr. Feeble Mind! How much is contained in the suggestion that, when he found one of these lying outside the House Beautiful, not daring to knock for admission, Great Heart went out *"one sunshiny morning"* and urged him to come in. And so on to the end. And Great Heart is but a reflection of the spirit which was manifested in the Savior Himself, and in the great apostle to the Gentiles. Paul, taking farewell of the elders of the Church at Ephesus, referred to his work in that city in terms which fully set forth what should be the moral quality of one's ministry in the pulpit. He said (Acts 20: 33-35), "I coveted no man's silver, or gold, or apparel. Ye yourselves know that these hands ministered unto my necessities, and to them that were with me. In all things I gave you an example, that so laboring ye ought to help the weak, and to remember the words of the Lord Jesus, that He Himself said, It is more blessed to give than to receive."

5. Finally, *every sermon must lead to Christ.* Christ Jesus must be unto the pulpit for all preaching purposes

"wisdom from God, righteousness, sanctification, and redemption." The sermon which does not get to Christ is not a Christian sermon. *It must get to Christ.* IT MUST GET TO CHRIST. Whatever the particular text, or theme, or place, or occasion there must ever be manifest that attraction of the Cross which shall be as persistent, as powerful, and as uniform as gravitation. Jesus Christ must be the supreme argument, the supreme illustration, the supreme application. Instruction, exhortation, consolation must all end in the Divine Redeemer. *"I preach Christ"* must be the preacher's inspiration, his guiding principle, and his greatest glory. If not, his sermon will be like the Temple when Jesus took leave of it forever, *"desolate."* So also will be those to whom it is addressed.

XVIII.

HOMILETICAL MAXIMS.

1. The essential element in preaching is the prophetic.

2. It is not so important for the preacher to find texts as to put himself in the way of texts finding him.

3. A text can not be well worked out until it has been well worked in.

4. The preacher's chief duty by his text is to find and preach its one meaning.

5. Having announced his text the preacher should attack it at once by answering the inquiry of his audience.

6. The thought of the sermon must be organized. A sermon is not a structure but a growth.

7. Beware of anticipation. It is always destructive of interest and often of profit.

8. When the preacher ceases to interest he ceases to profit.

9. The finest literary art is to simplify the profound.

10. The sermon that has no present day value has no value at all.

11. Instruction is the first requisite in sermonizing.

12. Have special care in definition; it is the beginning of proof.

13. The whole object of argumentation is "to change the minority into the majority."

14. The great value of testimony appears from this, that faith is founded on fact.

15. The illustration which adds nothing to the thought is generally worthless.

16. The best illustrations are those which have the value of proof.

17. The thought must always be as carefully prepared for the illustration as the illustration for the thought.

18. Where the application begins the sermon begins.

19. First of all the application is in the text, the subject, and the man.

20. The best feature of any text, relative to the application, is its distinctive feature.

21. Never tell an audience to do, without telling them what and how to do.

22. Usefulness is the measure of success.

23. The truths which have had the greatest influence have made men neither laugh nor cry.

24. The preacher's greatest power is derived from realizing the possible.

25. Preach Christ: do not simply preach about Him.

26. The sermon that does not lead to Christ and get to Christ is not a Christian sermon.

27. The true sermon is the result of a supernatural process; it is devoted to a supernatural work; it is made effective by a supernatural influence. Therefore,

28. "Sermonizing" becomes "preaching" in the use of that material which the Holy Spirit has engaged to employ and bless.

PART II.

THE PULPIT.

PULPIT MANNERS.

Manners in Public Speech.
  Specially important in the pulpit.
Suggestions.
  1. Punctuality.
  2. Dignity.
  3. Seriousness.
  4. Distractions.
  5. Dress.
  6. Posture.
  7. Leadership.
  8. Notices.
  9. Use of the Bible.
  10. Associate Minister.
  11. Tone of voice.

Read Preston's "Pulpit Manner;" Jefferson's "The Minister as Prophet,"
  IV; Quayle's "Pastor Preacher" ("Trivialities"); Cowper's "Pulpit
  Proprieties."

I.

PULPIT MANNERS.

New College, Oxford, was founded in the year 1378 by William of Wykeham, Bishop of Winchester. His motto, now blazoned on the arms of the college, reads "Manners Makyth Man." Just how much he intended to include in the word "manners" it is impossible to say, but he no doubt used the term in a very comprehensive sense, implying that manners are a large part of education. In the same sense it may be said that manners make the preacher.

Very much of a public speaker's power is derived from the way in which he handles himself. It is of almost equal importance with the way in which he handles his subject. His dress, his deportment, the tones of his voice, and his general bearing affect the force and influence of his message. Seneca said of Socrates that the philosophers who followed him learned more from his manners than they learned from his morals, and while so much may not be said of the Lord Jesus Christ it must at least be granted that the very manners of the Savior were most impressive in the eyes of His contemporaries, and still remain so. The Evangelists give us some account of the way in which He was dressed, particular reference being made to His seamless robe. They tell us something of the tones of His voice, of the use of His hands, and of the very way in which He looked upon those whom He addressed. The preacher, therefore, who represents Him before the public should give due attention to his pulpit manners.

It is said of Patrick Henry, pleading for a client: "His very manner in rising to his feet and his attitude before the court were themselves eloquence, which made me for the moment believe in spite of the most damning evidence, that the accused was innocent." Of John Angell James, of Birmingham, it is written: "As Mr. James slowly entered the pulpit the stranger would see in his calm and solemn countenance that his spirit was awed by a sense of God's presence." Of Dr. Kirk, of Boston, it is said: "His personal manners gave the entire tone and effect to his discourse."

It is true that some men become eloquent whose pulpit manners seem objectionable. The lady who afterwards became Mrs. C. H. Spurgeon, the first time that she saw the young preacher was affected only with a powerful sense of the ludicrous. It is recorded that "she could not understand his earnest presentation of the gospel and his powerful pleading with sinners in view of his huge black satin stock, his long, badly trimmed hair, and his blue pocket handkerchief with white spots." Spurgeon largely overcame these things, but even in his earlier years he would have been the better preacher without them.

This one thing is to be specially observed and noted with regard to the minister in the pulpit. He can not divert attention from himself. He is usually alone. The congregation are so seated that their eyes are turned to him. There are no accessories of any kind with which he may divide the responsibility. Everything that concerns him is seen, and marked, and critized. By strangers at least everything is fairly studied. His tones, positions, gestures, garments—concerning all such matters many a one in the congregation asks himself, "Why is he so?"—"Why does he do so?" The minister is, therefore, bound to give such matters attention. He must seek to be delivered from everything that is ill-mannered and out of taste, and if he does not accomplish his own emancipation from these things he is very much to be blamed.

We offer, therefore, some suggestions with regard to the minister's manners in the pulpit.

1. He should be punctual in his appearance at public worship, and equally punctual in bringing the worship which he conducts to a close. It is well for him to have an understanding with the organist, if he has one, with regard to the time when the organ shall be played and at just what point the minister may be expected to enter. If he is not punctual in opening his service he will cultivate bad habits upon the part of its attendants. If he is uniformly punctual and desires his people to be more so, all that he needs to say occasionally will be, "You are reminded that this service begins punctually at such an hour."

2. His entrance to the pulpit should be deliberate and dignified. He must be evidently self-composed. He should not appear to be disconcerted by any matter, but be himself in a state of complete repose. His own calm will be likely to communicate itself to his congregation.

3. Having entered the pulpit and taken his seat, he must not seem to be distracted by anything in the church building or in the congregation. He should not gaze around in a curious, questioning way, as though he were making some mental examination of the furniture, the windows, or the people in the pews. There should be no evidence of his looking about for particular people, as though he were enquiring within himself whether

so-and-so was at church to-day. Whether he is to assume the attitude of prayer when he enters the pulpit is a disputable question. In some Protestant Churches it is the invariable custom, ministers even kneeling at the pulpit or altar when they first enter. The minister must be his own judge with regard to this matter, and not follow any conventional custom in a perfunctory way. He certainly should have engaged in prayer before he entered the pulpit, and the spirit of prayer should possess him throughout; but whether he is to advertise that he is engaged in prayer is a question for himself to answer.

4. Having once entered the pulpit he should remain there. Only for some very exceptional reason should he come down to speak to one in the pew or at the door. Everything which needs his attention should receive it before entering the pulpit. He should have a series of signals arranged with the ushers which can be used without attracting the attention of the congregation in order to effect anything which may occur to him. A good device is a push-button in the pulpit connected with a buzzer at the vestibule door. In this way the minister can easily indicate whether he wishes the windows opened or closed, the people detained for a moment, the heat or light regulated, or if he desires that one of the ushers come to the pulpit that he may speak with him. Occasionally a preacher has a very loose way of flinging himself into the pulpit and out of it again, and tramping about the church as if he were an errand boy on service. This is much to be deplored; it detracts from the spirit that should pervade the place and makes an audience positively fidgety. Some ministers never leave the pulpit except to speak to some brother minister whom they may happen to see in attendance; but even

this is a doubtful practice. It calls public attention to the presence of the other minister, and so far forth detracts from the efficiency of the service.

5. The minister should be becomingly dressed in the pulpit. If it is the custom of his church to wear a gown the whole matter is settled for him, and this is one great argument in favor of this custom. If he does not wear a gown he should be clothed in simple black. His coat, vest, and trousers should all be black. His necktie should be either black or white, and there should be no other color whatever in it. The custom which some ministers have adopted of dressing for the pulpit as though they were expecting to attend an afternoon tea, wearing perhaps a white vest, and striped trousers, is to be deplored. The minister should be decently dressed. It is better for him to wear a frock-coat and button it during the service. By no means let him proceed to unbutton it and button it again. But the frock-coat it not imperative, He may wear a sack coat if it is more convenient, but it should be black and becoming.

Dr. Behrends has an interesting anecdote of a certain parishioner of his who was a workingman, and who was accustomed to sit with his family at home in his shirt sleeves, but when he conducted family worship he always put on his coat because, as he said, it was not respectful to appear in the Lord's presence in his shirt sleeves. Much more so it is not respectful to appear in the Lord's presence in public worship in any but the most suitable garments.

The minister should not show any article of jewelry. His gold watch-chain, if he wears one, should be concealed. The least that is permissible is a simple scarf-pin, or perhaps the wedding ring upon his finger.

6. He should care for his posture in the pulpit. He

should not sit on the middle of his back, but straight up in his chair. He should not spread his legs apart, but keep his knees together. He should seldom cross his knees in the pulpit, and never by resting one ankle upon the other knee. If he sits in a moveable chair it should not appear to be movable, and it is a gross offense for him to tilt back in it. When he rises to speak he should stand squarely upon his two feet, and he should endeavor to acquire habitual uprightness and ease in the pulpit. If in his private life, in walking, standing, or sitting, he would assume always the proper posture, he would not be likely to appear at disadvantage in the pulpit. But here at least he should have a care. His body should be absolutely self-supporting; he should never permit himself to lean upon the pulpit, though he may occasionally rest a hand upon it simply for the greater ease. By all means let him not throw himself down upon the pulpit, his arm upon the Bible. His arms should usually be allowed to hang quietly by his side. He should not fold them upon his breast, place his hands upon his hips, or bring them together and cross the fingers in a kind of defiant attitude. He should not clasp his hands over his abdomen,, nor place them under his coat-tails, nor put them in his pocket. His feet should be quite close together, one perhaps a little in advance of the other, and occasionally the position may be changed; but he should not stand with his feet too far apart, nor should there be that great rigidity which is assumed when they are placed very closely together and upon the same line. He must be particularly careful in his pulpit posture not to strike an attitude as though there were something in his posture to which he desired to call attention for the sake of effect.

7. From beginning to end his conduct of the worship

should be that of leadership. He is the ambassador of Christ. This means that he is to carefully take the middle ground between that of the priest and that of the layman. He is ordained for the very purpose of conducting public worship. He should use a certain amount of authority. It is not proper for him, for example, to announce a hymn with the words "Shall we sing?" or "Sing, if you please," nor to announce a prayer in any such terms. And at the close of the service, when he pronounces the benediction it should be as one who is qualified to do so. Let him raise both his hands, the palms towards the congregation, and solemnly pronounce the blessing in the Savior's name, but by all means let it be a Scriptural benediction, and not one which has been devised by any man. The so-called "Apostolic benediction" is the best for ordinary occasions; or it may be abridged, as it sometimes is in the New Testament, to "The grace of our Lord Jesus Christ be with you all." He may occasionally employ the Old Testament benediction, "The Lord bless thee, and keep thee: the Lord make His face shine upon thee, and be gracious unto thee: the Lord lift up His countenance upon thee, and give thee peace," or he may employ one of the remaining benedictions given in the Scriptures.

8. Let him beware of unseemly interruptions of the service. He should certainly offer none himself. It were better for him to suffer some inconvenience than to call for something to be given him, or to be done for the congregation, likely to distract their minds. One of these unseemly interruptions is the unnecessary giving out of notices, or the prolonging of the attention devoted to them. The pulpit is no place for notices other than those of religious gatherings, though it may be that sometimes the preacher may have occasion to call attention to the

business of his own congregation or something of the kind. He should not advertise from his pulpit anything that is better advertised in the daily papers. If he publishes a church bulletin, whereon the notices for the week are printed, he should not repeat those notices from the pulpit, nor call special attention to one above another. If one is more important than another let it be printed in display type. Certain notices ought always to be excluded from the pulpit, and it would be well for the preacher to make an inviolable rule with regard to such matters, and occasionally quote the rule to his congregation. It may read in some such form as this, "Notices are never given from this pulpit that relate to secular affairs. Those only are read which relate to religious gatherings or the business affairs of our own congregation."

In connection with the matter of notices a word should also be said with regard to the pastor's introduction of a visiting clergyman who is with him in the pulpit, and who is to speak to his people in the Savior's name. It is usually in bad taste for him to do more than mention the man's name, his place of residence, and the particular ministerial work in which he is engaged. He should say nothing with regard to his great reputation, his scholarly attainments, his genial character, or anything else of this kind.

9. Every church should be supplied with a large pulpit Bible, preferably of the American Standard Revision, and from this large Bible the preacher should read the Scripture lesson for the day. It gives it a certain dignity which it does not receive from a small Bible held in the preacher's hand. It is better also for him to announce his text from the large Bible, though sometimes it is more convenient for him, especially if there are several

references to other passages which he desires to make, to announce his text from a Bible held in the hand. But the text should always be read with the eye upon the page. No matter how familiar the preacher may be with the words of the text, he should so read it that the impression is given to the people that it is taken direct from the Holy Scriptures. Having opened his Bible in order to pronounce his text, the preacher should not close it until the sermon is finished. Some ministers have a way of quoting the text and immediately closing the Bible, then stepping off perhaps a few paces and commencing the sermon. The impression which is conveyed by this movement, whether it is so designed or not, is quite likely to be this, that the Word of God and its particular message is dismissed with the text. But when the Bible remains open it is as much as to say that the text itself with all its solemn meaning is still before the people: it is still the message from God with which they are engaged. Sometimes the Bible is closed when the minister is nearly through, or when he wishes the people to think he is nearly through; but it may be only a false motion, deliberately intended to mislead the congregation in the hopes of securing their further attention.

10. The minister should not talk unecessarily with another minister in the pulpit. If he is obliged to talk with him concerning some necessary matter he must at least never laugh with him, nor seem to the congregation to be saying anything of a trivial character. He should not search the Bible nor the hymn book while the other minister is engaged in prayer, and he should himself assume the same posture in prayer which the officiating minister is taking.

Finally. The minister should avoid an unnatural, artificial tone of voice—a "holy tone" as it is sometimes called. Such a tone is often an affectation; it always has the effect of one. It seems to savor of cant. It is said of Gypsy Smith that there are "tears in his voice." With him this seems to be quite natural. Let others to whom it is unnatural keep them out. We must never adopt a tone that is oily, sanctimonious, or sepulchral. It shuts the heart of the hearer against us.

EXTEMPORANEOUS PREACHING: ADVAN-
TAGES; FUNDAMENTAL PRINCIPLES.

EXTEMPORANEOUS PREACHING: ADVANTAGES; FUNDAMENTAL PRINCIPLES.

I. The method discussed.
Advantages of preaching from manuscript compared with those of this method.
1. Available.
2. Adaptation.
3. Freedom.
4. Systematic thought.
II. The nature of the art.
1. Addressing an audience as a single individual.
2. Mastering the progress of thought.

Read Bautain's "Art of Extempore Speaking;" Ford's "Extempore Speaking;" Storrs's "Preaching Without Notes;" Buckley's "Extemporaneous Oratory."

II.

EXTEMPORANEOUS PREACHING: ADVANTAGES; FUNDAMENTAL PRINCIPLES.

The best method of delivery for the preacher is that which is well stated in the words of Dr. Richard S. Storrs, "Preaching Without Notes." It is not only best in itself, but it is best for the largest number of preachers. It has been taught by the writer to the classes of the theological seminary for thirteen years, and its graduates have adopted it *con amore* with but a single exception.

I. Something may be said for all the various methods of delivery which are employed. They are discussed at length by many authorities, and it is not necessary that they should be here described, and the different arguments, pro and con, recited in full. The strongest argument in favor of preaching from a manuscript which has come to the writer's notice is that which is given by Slattery in his "Present-Day Preaching." He confesses that most laymen prefer the informality and directness of the extempore sermon, but he offsets this confession with the remark that the more discreet among the laity prefer the written sermon because they believe that the preacher gives them more thought, and thought more fittingly expressed, more "thickness of thought," as Prof. James would say. If a man finds that when he writes a sermon he can not hold the close attention of a congregation, he must feel himself an inferior preacher, however his extempore utterances may startle and thrill. Dr. Slattery confesses that it is a bore to hear a written sermon which is merely read. A written sermon, he says, ought to be preached with so much fire and freedom that the blind parishioner can not tell whether the sermonizer has a manuscript or not. "The man who thinks at all," he says, "finds after a few Sundays under the ministrations of the anecdotal preacher that he is being starved." He wishes the preacher would write his sermons. He longs for a compact written sermon, and Dr. Slattery believes that this man is a member of a rapidly growing class of laymen. The writen sermon appeals to the candid layman, who is glad to believe that his clergyman is saying what he has carefully written down in the cold moments of preparation.

Dr. Herrick Johnson gives the following reasons in favor of this method; it chastens and purifies the style; it tends to give clearness and vividness of thought; greater compactness with greater variety of material; and relief to the mind in the actual process of delivery; and that mental liberty which allows the preacher to give more undivided attention to the devotional parts of the service.

Such arguments have much force, but we believe that very much weightier ones can be presented for the other method. The use of a manuscript is scarcely tolerated in any other form of public address, and why it should be considered a help in the presentation of the important themes that have to do with man's salvation is almost inexplicable. Indeed, the habit of reading a sermon in the pulpit has very few historical precedents to which it can appeal. The great orators of antiquity, sacred and classic, made no use of a manuscript. Possibly in the case of the classic orators some orations were written before they were delivered, but as one has well remarked with regard to them, they are so exceedingly concise and compact that they must have been intended merely as a guide to the orator rather than as the actual form in which they were presented to his listeners.

The practice of the early church is clearly against the manuscript, and it was not introduced into the pulpit until the fifteenth or sixteenth century. The practice seems to have originated in the reign of Henry VIII, and subsequently increased in the Church of England, considerable prejudice being created against extemporaneous preaching because the Independents and Puritans were generally given to it. Charles II, however, attempted to correct this method, and a very curious letter was sent at his direction to the clergymen in the English church providing that the practice of reading sermons be wholly laid aside. The effort failed, however, and the use of the manuscript continued in the Church of England. At the same time, however, it was rarely employed upon the Continent. Some of those who in later times were accustomed to read in the earlier parts of their ministry regretted the practice. Jonathan Edwards in his later life declared in favor of memoriter preaching, or even actual extemporizing. Dr. Chalmers, who thought himself unable to extemporize and always used a manuscript, found that it was impossible for him to employ notes when he was addressing the operatives in the outskirts of the city of Glasgow, and Dr. Hanna testifies that Chalmers' sermons to these plain people were more effective and more truly eloquent than those which he delivered with so much applause in his own great church.

The reason why some discountenance the extemporaneous method and declare in favor of the manuscript may be that such do not fully understand the correct method of extemporizing, or that they have not been

taught to become proficient in it. Let us, therefore, define the method to begin with. By the term "extemporaneous" we do not mean extemporaneous thinking. No
matter how readily one's thoughts may come to the
preacher when he is in the pulpit upon his feet, he will
not become an effective extemporaneous preacher if his
dependence is entirely upon the occasion. The danger
in this method is much greater to the fluent man than
to the man who is slow of speech, for the man to whom
ideas (such as they are) readily present themselves while
he is engaged in the act of speaking will certainly fail
to discriminate between such as may be properly employed and such as should be carefully avoided. He will
not arrange his thoughts in logical order, and he is not
likely to succeed in producing the effect at which he himself may aim. James Russell Lowell characterizes such
men most admirably in the words of Hosee Bigelow,

> "This year I made the following observations,
>   Extrumpry like most other trials of patience."

The method which we contemplate is called by Bautain "prepared extemporaneous preaching," and by Dr.
Storrs, in the words already used, "preaching without
notes."

There are some disadvantages in this method which
are real and serious. The preacher is liable to certain
fluctuations of memory. Even he who generally has his
subject well in hand finds upon occasions that his mind
is blank; that the thought which he had hoped to present
has gone from him; and he is at a loss what to do or
say. This is a difficulty not easily overcome, though
we shall show a little later on how even this may be
managed in the pulpit.

The extemporaneous preacher is also subject to certain mental moods which he can not entirely govern. They are sometimes dependent upon the state of his health. Upon one occasion he is buoyant and cheerful, upon another occasion he is depressed and disheartened. It is not easy for one to preach a cheerful sermon when his spirit is distressed. Yet even this is not insuperable, as we shall presently see.

The preacher without notes is very much more dependent upon the sympathy of his audience than he who speaks from a manuscript, and audiences differ very widely. Their characteristics are as varied as those of individuals. Sometimes it is very apparent to the preacher that those whom he addresses are not in a receptive state of mind. He feels that it is difficult for him to obtain a favorable hearing. He is consequently handicapped and ill at ease.

Every extemporaneous preacher will confess that sometimes he labors through his discourse. It is up-hill work for him; his mind is sluggish, the right words do not come to hand; and worse than all, his own heart is not deeply stirred. But even so we believe that the advantages far outweigh the disadvantages.

1. The chief of these advantages may be well stated in the words of an old Scotchman, who, although he was but a day-laborer, was a thoughtful Christian man. He came to his pastor once with the remark, "And is n't it a good thing to give one's lassies a good edication." "Yes," his pastor remarked. "It is a good thing, sir, because it will bide with them." "Yes, indeed," his pastor answered, "it will abide with them." "And then it is so easy carried aboot." "Very true," said his pastor, "very true; there are no express charges on an education." So also these are the chief advantages of an extemporaneous method. The sermons prepared

upon this method "abide" with the preacher. They become his permanent possession. His sermons will be
in his mind whether they are in his barrel or not. And
they are available—"easily carried about," so that if he enters the pulpit—and finds the occasion absolutely unsuited
to the sermon which he expected to deliver, he is not
at a loss for a message. He has plenty of material at
hand. He may preach a different sermon. He never
need dismiss an audience as the manuscript preacher has
been obliged to do because his sermon has been left behind; nor sadly wish that he had made a different selection.

2. More than this. The extemporaneous method per-
mits of adaptation. Any given sermon may be modified
to suit the people to whom it is addressed. The extemporaneous preacher enters the pulpit prepared for the
exigencies of the hour. No matter what they may be
he brings a suitable message to the congregation. His
way of presenting the truth may be modified with reference to the number who may be present, the character
of the attendants, or the peculiar conditions of the time
and place.

3. But the method furnishes not only availability and
adaptation. It also contributes to freedom and to that
sympathetic power which is rarely exercised by the reader
of a manuscript. It is true that the manuscript may be
used in such a way as that it scarcely appears to be read
at all, and those who advocate the use invariably insist
upon great freedom therein. But no one, so far as we
have found, has had the temerity to say that one may
have the same freedom or the same power when he is
bound to a manuscript as when he is delivered from it.
It gives the preacher what has been called "the emanci-
pated eye," and this has much to do with the power of

the orator over his audience. He may take advantage
of every new form of thought and every exhibition of
interest upon the part of his auditors, and oftentimes
that which would be but a mediocre sermon, if delivered
from a manuscript, rises into positive superiority when
delivered without notes. Dr. Guthrie compared it to
the firing of a gun. The manner is the power, the matter is the shot, and it is a well known fact that a tallow
candle with a sufficient quantity of powder will pierce
a board upon which a leaden bullet would leave only a
good sized dent when fired with but a feeble charge.

4. One more advantage of the extemporaneous method
should be noted. It has its reflex effect upon the literary
character of the sermon itself. It contributes to systematic thinking. It promotes orderly arrangement and per-
spicuity. This is simply because a sermon which is not
properly arranged can not be delivered without notes unless it is committed to memory; and it is not easy even
to commit to memory a rambling discourse.

II. We pass now to consider the nature of the art of
extemporaneous preaching. If we can discover wherein
it actually resides we shall do much to promote its cultivation. While there are many things which are associated with it, and which we shall pass in review before
we conclude this subject, it may be noted that the art
consists in brief in two important comprehensive elements.

1. It consists in addressing an audience in exactly
the same way in which a single individual is addressed
in ordinary conversation. A difficulty which many
speakers find in attempting to speak without notes resides in the fact that for some strange reason they suppose an audience to be something altogether different
in kind from an individual listener. They do not regard

it as merely a large number of individuals gathered together. They regard it as a conglomerate mass, and
therefore, altogether unlike in mind and temper that which
it would be if it were separated into its component units.
The speaker who can succeed in overcoming this feeling,
and learn to speak to an audience of five hundred exactly as he would speak to an audience of one, has gone
far toward mastering the art of extemporaneous address.
If the speaker can open a subject, enlarge upon it, and
apply his thought to one person, he can do so equally
effectively to a thousand persons. The very best practice
therefore, in which one may engage in order to become
a good extemporaneous preacher is practice upon one
person, provided he can get the one person to practise
upon. The difference between addressing a number of
persons and a single person is incidental and extrinsic.
Speech is somewhat more formal, more careful, and more
deliberate, otherwise it is in no way different from ordinary speech. Mr. Balfour has well said, "Public speech is
simply conversation raised to a higher plane." This
comprehensive principle is the first to be embraced by
the extemporaneous preacher.

When the preacher first attempts the extemporaneous method his speech is very likely to become artificial
and involved. It seems to him to be necessary to be
very rhetorical and very oratorical, and he is consumed
with the desire to say what he has to say in studied
phraseology, whereas if he would pay no attention to
phraseology, except in so far as it is necessary to express his thought, he would be at ease. If the writer
may be pardoned in referring to his own experience, he
would say that he preached for ten years from a manuscript; he became convinced that it was not the proper
way in which to preach; he determined to preach

without notes. For several weeks it was a dreadful or-deal. The effort of delivering his thought after the same form which he had employed in his written discourses was exhausting in the extreme and was scarcely successful. One day he said to himself, as by a sudden inspiration, "I will not attempt to preach in this way again; I will simply tell the people what I have in mind in such language as I would employ if I were to meet them in their homes. I will tell it to them: *I will tell it to them.*" He did so, and upon the first occasion he found his freedom, and from that time on extemporaneous preaching has been for him no great effort. He has often given the advice in like terms to those who struggled with the same difficulties which he at first encountered. He has shown them the way out in the words he employed for himself, "Tell it to them; just tell it to them."

Prof. Upson of Hamilton College, one of the greatest teachers of elocution which this country has ever produced, constantly endeavored to persuade his students to deliver their orations in the conversational tone, departing from it only under the spur of feeling; and occasionally to remind the student of his desire, he would write upon the margin of their manuscripts "L and G." He explained to them that these letters stood for "Ladies and Gentlemen." It was not intended that they should make use of the words in public address, but only that they should be recalled to the natural and unaffected style. It might not be a bad idea for the preacher who finds it difficult to preach without notes to place upon the pulpit before him these letters, "L and G." The first element in the art consists in speaking to a multitude as to one person.

2. The art consists in committing to one's memory the progress of the thought rather than particular words

or phrases. In order to this the sermon must possess thought. There must be such arrangement as that one point shall suggest the next, and so on to the conclusion. One reason why some preachers are unable to master this art is because they depend upon their recollection of the form of words employed when the sermon was in course of preparation, or the phraseology of the manuscript which they have prepared but laid aside; so that when they come into the pulpit they are in danger of committing one of two errors, either of resorting to mere recitation, or of the attempt to combine that which they have written with that which may occur to them on the moment. Such dangers are positively formidable if the extemporizer does not learn at the outset to guard against them. He must pay no attention whatsoever to prearranged words or phrases. He must learn to throw his sentences into various forms. He must be able to substitute one kind of an expression for another, and this is what we call "committing the thought." Kern has well illustrated this in his chapter upon "Preparation for the pulpit." He says, "Suppose the first sentence of your sermon to be, 'This parable was not delivered directly to either the disciples or the multitude, but to one man only, a certain lawyer, or a scribe.' The memoriter preacher endeavors to fix this very thing in mind so that it should occur to him in the pulpit just as it was written. Not so the extempore preacher. He would rather avoid this, so he says to himself, 'This is only one way of expressing the thought. There are other ways, and the thought itself may be modified in this or that manner, or be omitted entirely. I may say in preaching, 'Most of our Lord's parables were spoken to a company of persons, but here we have an exception,' or I may say, 'This parable was addressed to one man, a scribe, who stood by and tempted Jesus.' Or I may leave out this sentence altogether; no matter; I am free to say what seems best at the time."

This principle applies to the entire discourse. It is fulfilled when the thought which the preacher desires to utter may be expressed by him in various ways, without his being tied to phraseology.

Such then are the two fundamental elements in the art of extemporaneous discourse—we pass to others in the next chapter.

EXTEMPORANEOUS PREACHING MATERIAL.

EXTEMPORANEOUS PREACHING MATERIAL

Material: Its acquisition, arrangement, and use.
Success depends upon:—
    (1) Large resources.
    (2) At command.

I. Acquisition of texts.
    Rumination.
    Use of an abstract.

II. Arrangement of material.
    1. Statement of subject.
    2. Arrangement of divisions.

III. Use of material.
    1. In the beginning of the discourse.
    2. Passing from the introduction.
    3. The conclusion.

IV. Additional suggestions.
    1. Sermons should be written in full.
    2. Regard to the element of time.
    3. Freedom.
    4. Avoidance of mannerisms.
    5. Impromptu additions.

III.

EXTEMPORANEOUS PREACHING. MATERIAL; ITS ACQUISITION, ARRANGEMENT, AND USE.

Effective extemporaneous preaching depends upon having an abundance of well-digested ideas, and upon facility in their suitable expression. General preparation, therefore, is vastly more important than any special preparation which the preacher may make for a given service. Dr. Archibald Alexander, who was particularly gifted in impromptu speech, was accustomed to say that if he were to stake his life upon a single effort he would familiarize himself with the general subject and then abandon himself to the impulse of the moment. If a preacher has an abundance of material he will always be ready with something, in the delivery of which he will have no occasion for embarrassment. These requisites may be stated, then, as follows:—First, the extemporaneous preacher must possess large resources, and, second, he must have them fully at command.

(1) The extemporaneous preacher must have large resources. How is he to secure them? This is very fully answered in Part I, Chapter IX, under the subject of "Materials." The preacher must be acquainted with the best literature upon all subjects. There must not merely be books upon his shelves, but books that have been read into his very soul. He must have made the acquaintance of good men and had large fellowship with them. He

must be familiar with great scenes, great buildings, great pictures, and the great events of history.

(2) He will have these at command by constant meditation upon them, by frequently rehearsing the knowledge which he has acquired. It will be well for him, whenever he has been engaged in that which is to furnish him with material, to talk about it as occasion offers. Nothing is so sure to fix information in the mind as a critical expression of opinion with regard to it in the presence of others. It will be well for him in addition to pay such particular attention to those passages in books, and to other matters of the like kind as command special attention, as that he shall virtually commit them to memory and have them upon call.

Thurlow Weed was one of the greatest politicians which this country ever produced. He had an encyclopædic mind. No piece of information with regard to political affairs escaped its grasp, and being possessed also of a good judgment his advice was sought by the men of his own party, and his criticisms honestly feared by those who opposed him. He selected and named many men for office, chief of them the great Abraham Lincoln himself. How did he come into possession of this power? The answer is a very simple one: he was accustomed at the close of each day, when he retired to his home, to talk over its events with his wife, who was equally interested with himself in the progress of political affairs. It was this daily rehearsing of events, and this daily comment upon them that gave him command of his resources.

But general preparation, although it is the most conducive to success in extemporaneous speech, is not altogether sufficient. There must be special preparation in addition. A number of particulars enter into this special preparation. Due regard must be paid to the acquisition and arrangement of material, and to its suitable use.

I. Consider its acquisition. This relates first of all to the preacher's texts. The extemporaneous preacher must always have a number of texts in hand. Observe; not "on" hand, but "in" hand. They must not be laid away in some inaccessible place, in some notebook perhaps which the preacher never consults, or in any place in which they are not likely to come again and frequently beneath his notice. They should be in his mind. He should recur to them, review them, think them over, and add any note concerning them which may occur to him in the connection. It is a good plan to have a book in which he shall record the texts which are suggested to him from time to time with plenty of blank space between them, in which he may insert any thought or argument or illustration in connection with them. It is never well for an extemporaneous preacher to use a text which has been recently suggested to him. In the vast majority of cases he will succeed much better if he defers preparation upon the text until he has proved it by keeping it in waiting for a time. The best texts will grow more and more interesting, and secure a firmer grasp upon his mind and heart as time passes by. They will keep. It may be said in general terms that the longer a text is kept the better will be the sermon that is prepared upon it, and the larger will be the preacher's facility in handling it, though we would not press this matter unduly.

This implies that the extemporaneous preacher is to "ruminate" upon these texts: an admirable word, which corresponds very closely in the intellectual process to the physical action from which it is derived. This rumination is not so important to the reader of a manuscript as it is to him who speaks without notes. Rumination is not so much formal thought as the dwelling of the mind upon the subject without any regard to its systematic development. Oftentimes a text strikes the one who finds it with a great deal of force, so much so that he determines to preach upon it at once. It is a hazardous experiment. He finds that it is soon exhausted; that there was only a certain feature of it, or a certain element in its thought which was borne in upon his mind with special emphasis. Or it may be that it is only illustrative, or furnishes no more than a certain example. If, now, this text had been laid aside for a time, its weakness would certainly have been discovered.

When the extemporaneous preacher has selected the text upon which he is to prepare his next sermon, he should begin work upon it in ample season. If he is accustomed to prepare a sermon every week, the selection should be made very early in the week and work begun at once. Let the preacher stick to his selection in spite of everything. Very much is often lost just at this point. The preacher is indeterminate and vacillating. He thinks at the beginning of the week that he will preach upon a certain text, but when a couple or so of days have passed by he discards it for another. Such a man will never make a good extemporaneous preacher; because in order to good extemporaneous preaching there must be an abundance of time given to the development of a particular subject. Select the text early in the week, concentrate the thought upon it; turn it over and over in the mind. Much of such work should be done before the preacher begins to write. It is quite important that he should work the text into his own mind and heart by such a process, that the sermon when it is finally prepared may be the outcome of his very soul.

It is said that Hook and Lamb were once walking together, as was their custom, when Hook discovered a sign over an ale-house kept by a woman. The sign read, "Wine, Ale, and Beer," but beer was spelled b-e-a-r. "That bear," said Hook, "appears to be her own bruin." This piece of humor gives the exact point to our suggestion relative to the preparation of an extemporaneous sermon. It must be the preacher's own brewing (bruin). The sermon should be brewing for some two or three days: then it should be studied with the aid of any helps which the preacher may command. Then he should arrange his material in order; prepare his plan and write his sermon out at length. He should not occupy too much time in the mechanical work. It is very important to the man who preaches without notes that the sermon be flowing. It will not be such if it is written a little piece at a time during the various days of the week. But if he has prepared for his work in the way that has been suggested, and the entire sermon is written at two or three sittings, at the most, then the sermon will more likely possess the quality which is indispensable to extemporaneous discourse. His writing should be finished at least by Friday noon. Then the manuscript is to be put entirely from him, and Saturday he should take time in which to ruminate more; go over the sermon as he has prepared it point by point, but never twice in exacily the same language or scarcely the same exact order. This, that he may not be tied to phraseology or form. Let not the preacher imagine, then, that extemporaneous discourse requires less work. This sort of preaching requires more; but he who willingly engages in it will be richly repaid. When Sunday morning comes he will be ready.

There will be no objection to preparing a brief abstract if the preacher desires to do so. Sometimes this is advisable: it relieves the mind of an undue strain upon the memory. But the abstract should be very brief. It should contain nothing but the main points of the address, and nothing in it should be in the exact phraseology of the written sermon, with the possible exception of definitions or like matter. It will be better for the preacher if he learns to indicate by some kind of catchword the thought which he wishes to express. In making out this abstract he should not consult his manuscript until it has been finished. Then, perhaps, it will not be amiss for him to verify the abstract by reference to the written sermon. We append at this point the abstract of a sermon in order to illustrate what has been said with regard to its proper character.

Matt. 28: 18-20.

I. Character.
  Not original—new: different.
    Niagara. Trolley.
  The Incarnation.
    Son—obedience.
  Temptation. Miracles.
  Reinvested.

II. Uses and Purposes.
  Purposes not apart from character.
  Missionary use of text.
    "All things whatsoever."
      Work and worship.
      His—yours.

III. Method of Dispensation.
  "Not apart," again.
  Adds force.
    Elisha's staff.

Power not all—presence.
General. Physician.
Not delegated.
No better message.

What we wish to show from this abstract is that no one who had not himself prepared the sermon could possibly discover the preacher's line of thought. It is known only to himself, and the abstract being set forth in the terms which are shown, it in no wise interferes with his absolute freedom of utterance or his choice of phraseology at the time of its delivery.

II. The arrangement of material.

1. The preacher in arranging his material for use in the pulpit should first of all be careful with regard to the statement of his subject. A suitable subject is of much more importance to the extemporizer than to the reader. It is better framed in brief terms, but no hard and fast rule can be given with regard to its form. Only it must be such a setting forth of that with which the preacher proposes to deal as that it shall give to his congregation a comprehensive grasp of the intent of the whole discourse.

The subject thus stated will suggest to the preacher the necessary order of his thought, and so promote the unity of his discourse. It will be better if the subject is particularly specific. It should be set forth not in broad and general terms, but in precise and limited ones. The limitation will help him, not hinder him.

2. The statement of the divisions of his discourse should be as carefully made as the statement of the subject. We may set it down as certain that no man can preach successfully without notes who is not absolutely methodical in the utterance of his thought. Dr. Shedd

says that the intellect must work spontaneously in a logical manner in order to successful extemporaneous preaching. Consecutive reasoning must be natural to the mind. "Truth must be logically connected and related, so that its separate parts are unfolded with a facile and effortless precision." The separate points of the discussion should follow each other by a kind of necessity, so that the one shall follow the other as a matter of course. The whole sermon becomes like a row of bricks set up in order. The falling of the first necessitates the falling of the rest.

Each separate point must be very clear and precise like the subject itself. Their mutual relations must be close and intimate, not loose or superficial; and they must be positively progressive. Bautain says: "Formerly the fault was in a dialectical turn and frequently the style became spoiled by dryness, heaviness, and an appearance of pedantry. Still men knew how to state a question and how to treat it. They knew at which end to begin in order to develop it and solve it, and the line of argument, distinctly marked out, led straight to the object and to a conclusion. The fault nowadays is in an absence or deficiency of method. People remain a long time before their subject even though they rightly understand its very terms. This induces interminable preparations, desultory introductions, a disorderly development, and finally no conclusion or at least nothing decisive."

The preacher, therefore, before he makes his abstract should review his sermon work and make sure that its separate parts advance in a methodical manner. In order to this it is usually better that the sermon should be constructed upon the textual plan. This is because the separate parts of the text will furnish the preacher with his separate divisions, and he is not likely to forget their

order, or violate the unity of his plan. Recur to the
abstract which has been given. The text is the Great
Commission, "All authority hath been given unto me in
heaven and on earth. Go ye therefore, and make disciples of all the nations, baptizing them into the name of the
Father and of the Son and of the Holy Spirit: teaching
them to observe all things whatsoever I commanded you:
and lo, I am with you always, even unto the end of the
world." The subject of the sermon is "The Authority
of the Risen Christ." The first division is "The Character of this Authority or Power." It is connected with
the words, "All authority hath been given unto me in
heaven and on earth." It is His mediatorial authority
and power. The second division is "The Uses and Purposes of this Power,"—the evangelizing of the nations.
The third division is "The Method of Dispensation." It
is immediate. "Lo, I am with you always, even unto the
end of the world." It will be seen that the textual treatment in this instance is of such a character that the
preacher can never forget it, and if he has made sufficient
study of the text his material will always be in hand.
Dr. Alexander McLaren has a sermon upon John 16:33,
"Be of good cheer; I have overcome the world," in which
the same principles are illustrated. His subject is "The
Victorious Life." It is treated topically, but in a way
absolutely adapted to the uses of the extemporaneous
preacher. He proposes three questions: First, "What is
a Victorious Life?" Second, "Was there ever such a
Life?" and third, "If there was, what does it matter to
me?" This is very simple, but very comprehensive.

One caution should be observed in this connection.
It is a great mistake for the extemporaneous preacher to
multiply his divisions, and he should be particularly ap-
prehensive of subdivisions. Let him remember what has

been already said, that it is better to amplify than to multiply.

III. With regard to the use of material.

1. The extemporaneous preacher should be particularly cautious in the beginning of his discourse. He must be content, when he first begins to speak, to be very modest and deliberate. As Dr. Lyman very suggestively remarks, "Even on the ladder that reaches to heaven it is not well to stand half way up the ladder, above your people's heads. In any case you must start with them." Let him begin with the very lowest round in the ladder. This may not be so essential to the reader. The extemporizer must be willing to seem weak in comparison, in the beginning of his discourse, but he must be conscious of having a reserve or he will not be able to succeed.

2. The process of passing from his introduction to the discussion of his theme is usually the most difficult thing for the extemporizer to manage. It is here that he is usually wrecked if he is wrecked at all. He is stranded upon the harbor bar as he leaves for the deep sea.

What is his safeguard? Simply this, that the passage from the introduction to the discussion should be more carefully thought out than any other portion of the discourse. He must make sure of it. He must have rehearsed it in various terms in private before he appears in the pulpit. It will not do for him to say as a certain preacher was once heard to say, "I require twenty minutes to get into a subject, and then it takes twenty minutes to get out." A preacher should be able to get into his subject within five minutes at the utmost, usually within two or three, but once into his subject let him have full courage. Let him not think of sparing his material. If he has prepared for the pulpit as he should have done, he need have no embarrassment or hesitation. Let him give the audience the best that he has. If he has really struck a lode he need not fear that it will run out.

But suppose that at some point in his discourse his mind suddenly becomes a blank! We have already said that this is one of the disadvantages of this form of speaking. What is he to do? He can not recall the thought which was next in order, and it may be a very important one. All his ideas seem suddenly to have abandoned him. This he may do: assure himself that he will be at a loss for a moment only, if he maintains his self-control. He may certainly trust his mental processes. If his mind has not positively given way it will assert itself. He may be sure of its doing so. Let him not appear disconcerted: let him not hesitate or stammer, but let him in an easy and apparently natural way use the time for a brief moment with some sort of harmless repetition of what has already been said, some needless amplification of a point, or something of that sort, and the thought which he supposed to have been lost will thrust itself upon him. Let him seize it at once and proceed.

3. With regard to the close of the discourse, let him be sure to stop when he is through with his subject. Some time ago an article appeared in one of our magazines with this title, "The Fine Art of Leave-Taking." It had respect simply to the social custom, and spoke in a very thoughtful and judicious way of the embarrassment frequently caused by visitors who wear out their welcome by prolonging their farewells; who when they attempt to leave find it hard to do so, halt and hesitate, introduce perhaps a new subject of conversation, even rise to leave and take their seat again, or stand a while at the door

and thus defer the good-bye. The author of the article suggested that visits be never prolonged beyond a suitable time, and that when the visitor desired to leave he should rise and with a brief remark, as, for example, "It is time I should be going; good evening," take his departure without more ado. The same fine art of leave-taking should be cultivated by the extemporaneous preacher, and it is a fine art indeed.

It often happens that the preacher who has prepared his sermon with great care, and who in his manuscript has brought it to a suitable conclusion, is assailed when when he is upon his feet with some thought which he thinks he may profitably introduce near the close. It is almost always a misfit. It interrupts the progress of his thought, it impairs its unity, and it is generally unprofitable. Bautain has a very fine passage with respect to this matter which he calls "After-growth," (see pages 280-281). The substance of his remarks is this, the preacher feels that he should end, but he has a confused feeling of something which has been omitted. He is anxious to recover his lost ground, and he begins some new development when he ought to be concluding. The effect upon the audience, already fatigued, is very bad. It becomes impatient; it ceases to listen, or possibly, with a certain interest in the preacher, the audience follows him with uneasiness as men from the shore watch a boat which seeks to make port and can not. "It is a less evil," says Bautain, "to turn short round and finish abruptly than thus to tack incessantly without advancing. The greatest of a speaker's misfortunes is that he should become a bore."

IV. A few additional Suggestions.

1. It will be well for the preacher to habitually write out his sermons in full before delivering them. This

suggestion should be heeded especially by the younger preachers. Although Spurgeon himself in his later ministry never wrote his sermons in full before entering the pulpit, yet in his advice to students he says, "I recommend as a most healthful exercise, and as a great aid toward obtaining extempore power, the frequent writing of your sermons. Those of us who write a great deal in other forms, as for the press, may not so much require that exercise, but if you do not use the pen in other ways you will be wise at least to write some of your sermons and revise them with great care. Leave them at home afterward, but still write them out that you may be preserved from a slipshod style." When Spurgeon was asked by Dr. Cuyler whether he wrote his sermons, he answered, "I had rather be hung." But Spurgeon obtained the same discipline by his frequent use of the pen in the expression of thought. In addition to this he always revised his sermons as taken by his stenographer for publication. In his earlier ministry Spurgeon himself did as he advised his students to do.

The old proverb has it "Reading maketh a full man, writing an exact man, speaking a ready man." Bautain says: "The pen is the scalpel which dissects the thoughts, and never, when you write down what you behold internally, can you yourself succeed in clearly discerning all that is contained in a conception, or in obtaining its well marked scope. You then understand yourself." In a certain sense the thought becomes objective, or, as some would put it, "concrete." At least it presents itself to us in a very different way, so much so that one will often refuse to say what he expected to say after he has seen it in black and white. Do we not sometimes write a letter according to the very notion which we have in mind, but afterwards destroy it because we discover upon writing that even if we have said exactly what we expected to say we have not said the right or proper thing?

Writing reveals our deficiences. We suppose that we have the thought clearly in mind, but when we attempt to write it we do not have the words at command for its expression. We may then pause and search for the proper expression. Whereas if we were to enter the pulpit without this discipline, the hesitation would occur when we were upon our feet, to our own embarrassment and to the annoyance of those to whom we speak, or if to avoid hesitation we hasten to use the improper word the very point which we are anxious to make is obscured or evaded.

2. Have regard to the element of time. Those who do not carefully prepare their addresses in advance are always likely to err in this respect no matter how long their experience may have been. Before entering the pulpit the preacher should always ask himself, how long will it require for the utterance of this particular message? On some occasions it will require more time than others, but how long will it be on any occasion? How many minutes shall I speak, and how shall I divide my sermon so that it may be properly balanced as respects time? How long shall I dwell upon the first division? upon the second? and so on. And the preacher must remember that he is likely to elaborate more when he is upon his feet, and that it will require more time to deliver the sermon without notes than it would have required to delivered it from a manuscript.

Amplification must be most carefully studied in extemporaneous preaching. The preacher should cultivate his ability to dwell upon an important point or principle until he can perceive from his observation of the con-

gregation that they feel the whole force of it. But sometimes, because the preacher himself is not satisfied that
he has really carried his point, he is tempted into an
amplification which is really not amplification at all but
iteration and repetition, and so the time slips away from
him. It is not unusual to hear one say something like
this, "Now I have dwelt so long upon this point that
I shall be obliged to curtail my remarks upon the next."
This is a confession of extempore weakness. The
preacher who makes it is an undisciplined preacher. He
has not learned to be governed by what he himself has
prepared, but has introduced extraneous and often unimportant matter. Uncontrolled fluency is a positive
blemish in extemporaneous discourse. Josh Billings, has
summed up the whole matter in one of his suggestive
mots: "If a man bores half an hour in one place and
does not strike anything, one of two things is the matter;
either he is not boring in the right place, or he has not
got a good auger."

3. It is very important for the extemporaneous
preacher to enter the pulpit with the largest possible freedom. If he is to succeed in any measure he must be
in a certain sense careless of results. If he is fearful
or hesitant with regard to his theme, or the way in which
he is to express himself, or the possible effect upon his
congregation, he will be the more likely to fail. Let him
be content for the time being to summon to his aid the
best that he has in hand, and deliver himself of it without apprehension. Once upon his feet let him cast away
concern for everything except God's help and blessing.
Especially let him be very careless with regard to any
criticism which he imagines may be passed upon his
thought or his delivery. If it be not so, he can not
succeed. A most interesting story is told in this con-

nection of the celebrated Baptist minister, the Rev. Dr.
P. S. Henson, not only a great preacher but a great wit.
The story well illustrates the point which we are trying
to make. On one occasion he was himself conscious of
the fact that his thoughts did not flow as freely as usual,
but he would not permit himself to be embarrassed on that
account. When he descended from the pulpit, one of his
parishioners came to him and with assumed humility
remarked, "Well, Doctor, I was quite sorry for you this
morning. What was the matter with you?" "Nothing
whatever," replied the Doctor. "Oh," said the parishioner, "I am glad to hear that, but something seemed to
me to be going wrong with you." "No," replied the
Doctor, "nothing went wrong." "Well, I thought perhaps you were not feeling well or something of the sort,
for you seemed to have lost your liberty." "Well, my
good friend," said the Doctor, "you have evidently not
lost yours;" and the parishioner retired discomfited.

Hosee Bigelow remarks, "Folks that's afeared to fail
are sure of failin'." More than this, the audience oftentimes will not discover that the preacher is ill at ease,
and many times his apprehensions are altogether needless. Let him not attempt to cover up his embarrassment by prolonging his sermon. Let him not be anxious
to fill the usual time consumed by it. If he has forgotten
one half of what he has prepared, and can not command
it when he is upon his feet, let him not worry with regard to it. Let him preach what he can preach easily
and without embarrassment, and stop.

4. The preacher should be on his guard against certain bad mannerisms into which the extemporaneous
preacher is very apt to fall. With very few exceptions,
men who preach without notes adopt certain favorite
words or expressions which they use again and again

and again; or they contract a habit of qualifying their statements because, when they are first uttered, they do not sound to them exactly correct or forcible, and they are obliged to interpolate "That is to say" or "In other words" or something of the kind. Sometimes they make use of needless connectives, especially in the introduction of sentences which have not been carefully thought out. How very often would they find such words as these in a shorthand report of their addresses: "Now," "Now then," "Well then," "Again," "To proceed" and so forth.

Some extemporaneous preachers have a strange hesitancy in the utterance of their sentences, often shown even in the middle of a sentence with a peculiar drawl or the prolongation of the final syllable in a word; pauses which are not rhetorical, and a break in the delivery which indicates that the word desired is not at command. This arises from the fact that the preacher has not learned to think by phrases and sentences, but is delivering himself only of words or brief clauses, and attempting to form a sentence by adding the one to the other. This results in a sort of *staccato,* which is annoying both to preacher and people. It can be easily avoided if the preacher will not start upon a sentence until he has thought it through and knows exactly how it is to be framed and finished. When first suggested it might seem that this would require considerable time, and render the preacher's phrases altogether too deliberate but such is not the case. It requires the briefest instant: the time consumed by foreseeing the thought is negligible, but the practice once adopted will entirely correct the hesitancy to which we have just referred.

5. The last suggestion to be made, in order to effective extemporaneous preaching, is that the preacher avoid the introduction into his sermon at any point of extended

paragraphs embodying the thought which occurs to him suddenly while he is upon his feet. They may appear to him most attractive, but they are usually only a blemish upon his discourse. They lead to digression. They carry the people away from the subject in hand. This remark applies particularly to cheap anecdotes, or flashes of enticing but useless wit.

In an article on "Public Speaking," in the *Saturday Evening Post,* United States Senator Albert J. Beveridge says: "It is a remarkable thing that there is neither wit nor humor in any of the immortal speeches that have fallen from the lips of man. To find a joke in Webster would be an offense. The only things which Ingersoll wrote that will live are his oration at his brother's grave and his famous 'The Past Rises Before Me Like a Dream.' But in neither of these productions of this genius of jesters is there a single trace of wit. There is not a funny sally in all Burke's speeches. Lincoln's Gettysburg address, his first and second Inaugurals, his speech beginning the Douglas campaign and his Cooper Union address in New York are, perhaps, the only utterances of his that will endure. Yet this greatest of story-tellers since Æsop did not adorn or deface one of these great deliverances with story or any form of humor. The reason for this is found in the whole tendency of human thought and feeling—in the whole melancholy history of the race—where tears and grief, the hard seriousness of life and the terrible and speedy certainly of our common fate of suffering and of death make somber the master-chord of existence. The immortal things are all serious—even sad!"

ATTENTION: PRELIMINARIES.

ATTENTION: PRELIMINARIES.

Attention the indispensable condition of effective speech.
   Attention defined.
      It is not mere silence.
      Nor interest in the general subject.
      But mental application with a view to instruction.
I. The Source of Attention.
   1. It is in the preacher alone.
   2. It is not a condition but a result.
   3. It resides not in "magnetism" but in method.
II. Preliminary Considerations.
   1. Pulpit and Furniture.
   2. The Room.
   3. The Preacher himself.
When all things are ready, he may begin.

Read Fitch's "Art of Securing Attention;" Arnold's "Attention and Interest;" James' "Talks to Teachers," X and XI; Quayle's "Pastor-Preacher" (Wonder); Buckley's "Extemporaneous Oratory" (Attention).

IV.

ATTENTION: PRELIMINARIES.

Attention is the indispensable condition of all effective speaking. Its logical place in the matter of pulpit delivery is first. This agrees with many statements of the Scripture upon the subject. "He that hath ears to hear, let him hear," "Come, ye children, hearken unto me: I will teach you the fear of Jehovah." The Savior Himself used words in connection with certain of his parables (see Matt. 15: 10) which the preacher might well adopt as his guiding motto—"Hear and understand." It would be well if they were printed in large type and set before his eyes upon all occasions. Will he so speak that the people shall *hear* easily and readily? and will he so speak that they shall *understand* and desire more?

It is a noticeable fact that preachers do not always hold their audiences, and even when they do, their sermons, and sometimes the very texts, are forgotten by the people. A preacher sometimes congratulates himself upon the fact that his sermons can be repeated after a comparatively short interval without being recognized. He should rather commiserate himself. It is evident that he has not had the attention which he should have sought and received.

What then is attention? This preliminary question should be carefully answered because some things are taken for attention which do not deserve the name. Mere silence is not attention. It is said sometimes of an au-

dience that one "can hear a pin drop." This is no sign
that the audience is really attending to the words of
the preacher. Possibly they are asleep; possibly they are
deeply engrossed with other subjects. At all events,
silence is not attention. There is silence in a grave-
yard. Neither is an interest in the general subject attention. One may display considerable interest in the
theme which the preacher announces and follow him
very carefully, while real attention is not secured. Sometimes their eyes may be upon him, and they may be apparently listening with eagerness to the words which he
speaks, when their minds are not following his thought.
Professor James, in illustrating this matter, tells a very
amusing story of a teacher, who told him that upon one
occasion when she was giving a lesson she was delighted
at having captured so completely the attention of one
of her young pupils. He did not remove his eyes from
her face. But after the lesson was over he disabused
all her impressions by saying to her, "I looked at you all
the time you were talking, and your upper jaw did not
move once." That was the only fact which he had
taken in.

Attention is positive mental application. The mind
which is engaged with it is diligent and active. More
than that, it is intelligently employed with a view to
instruction. Nothing less than this is worthy of the name
of attention.

The particular art in securing this attention is to
so awaken this mental effort that it shall be as natural,
as easy, and as delightful as possible. Herbert Spencer
founds the whole theory of effective public speech upon
what he calls the "economy of the mental force of the
hearers." This means that their mental force should
not be subject to an undue strain. It must not be taxed

beyond that which it will bear. The best attention, strained beyond its limit, is lost. One made a very significant remark with regard to a certain book in which he had become interested, that it "read down-hill." So it must be with public speech. It must move down-hill, at least at times, and even though the preacher may induce his congregation to climb some very steep ascents, there must be occasionally such frequent easy descent that what might be called the mental muscles shall be rested by their relief from prolonged strain.

I. We consider first the source of attention.

1. The source of attention is in the preacher alone; that is to say, it is in the preacher alone at the outset of the discourse. The conditions may be somewhat altered as the discourse proceeds, but in the beginning the preacher is wholly responsible.

It will not do, therefore, for him to say, "The subject is of great importance," or "The people ought to listen to the discussion of this theme." This may be very true, but it does not minister to attention. The remark of Beecher's is in place in this connection. When he was asked how he felt when he saw some one asleep in his congregation—did he not feel like sending some one to wake him up? Beecher replied, "No, I think some one should be sent to wake *me* up."

"Can you sell goods," said the merchant to an applicant for the position of clerk. "Yes, sir," was the reply, "I can sell goods to any one who wishes to buy." "You are not the man I want," replied the merchant, "Any one can sell goods to a man who wishes to buy. The true salesman is one who can sell goods to one who does not wish to buy."

Let the preacher understand then that he can not demand attention, he can not entreat attention, and he ought not even to invite it except under very unusual circumstances. Professor James says, "Do not beg attention as a favor, nor claim it as a right, nor endeavor to incite it by preaching the importance of the subject. Sometimes, indeed, you must do these things, but the more you are obliged to do them the less skillful you show yourself to be." "Lend me your ears" may sometimes be in place when there is prejudice to be overcome, or distracting conditions to be met, or something of the like, but ordinarily nothing of the kind is properly in place.

2. Attention is not the condition of good preaching, but the result. There are audiences which have the reputation of being good listeners. They have been well disciplined by the preachers who have ministered to them, or they have been so accustomed to those who secured their attention in the proper way that they have learned to give it, even when it is improperly sought. But the fact that they are good listeners is no credit to the preacher who, for this reason, secures their attention, and if he does not proceed upon proper principles he will undo the good which his predecessors have done.

Let no one say, then, as he enters the pulpit, "If the people will listen I shall preach well." Let him rather say, "If I preach well, the people will be sure to listen." This should be his gauge of the quality of his own effort. If he is quite sure, from the interest and intelligence expressed in the countenances of those before him, that they are applying themselves to the truth which he is presenting he may be content, otherwise not.

But as we have already suggested, attention is the first result of good preaching, and when it is thus gained it becomes also the condition. But it must be first gained. Then it unqestionably helps the preacher, as every preacher will testify. And yet it is only the condition to a certain extent, and at no point in the discourse is it so much the condition as the result, because the condition will not long continue if the result does not continuously appear.

3. Attention resides not so much in "magnetism" as in method. Herein we lay bare a very common error, and yet one for which there is some show of reason. Unquestionably some speakers have a greater power because of some mysterious faculty of public speech which we can not fully define. The very tones of their voice are appealing, the play of the countenance is attractive, and the flow of language is naturally so engaging that the people listen often in spite of themselves. We say this is magnetism. There is, indeed, considerable power in it. But what we wish to emphasize is this, that there is not nearly so much power as has been credited to it. Poets may be "born, not made," but it is not so as a rule with public speakers. Good public speakers are largely the product of training. We say "public speakers;" because we wish to distinguish between those men who seem to be particularly gifted, and those upon whom no special genius has been bestowed. Orators are in a sense "born," but some orators are poor public speakers. Not every man can be an orator in the full sense in which that word is commonly understood, but any man and every man who has the ordinary degree of talent can become a good public speaker—interesting, instructing, and molding the thought of those who hear him, if he will submit to suitable training. There is no reason, therefore, why any one who proposes to become a preacher should be discouraged.

Still further, it is impossible for any one to say at any stage of his progress whether he is an orator or not. The gifts of oratory do not always appear at the first. There are too many instances on record of those who positively failed in their attempts to sway an audience in the early portion of their career who yet became proficient in oratorical arts and influences. To prohibit any dogmatism on this subject, the old story of Demosthenes may be recalled. We may also remember that when Disraeli made his first address in the House of Commons he was received only with derision, and they would not hear him. But we are told that he shook his fist in the faces of his hearers and exclaimed, "The time will come when you will be glad to hear me!"

Even so may it be with some in whom the gifts of oratory have not as yet appeared, and no one need despair of attaining them.

II. Some preliminary considerations. If the preacher is to secure the attention of his congregation there are certain matters to which he must pay regard before he utters his first word. The comprehensive question in this connection is this, "Am I ready to begin?" And this involves yet another question, "Are all things ready for me to begin?" Let us consider them then in inverse order, naming first certain matters outside the preacher's own self.

1. The pulpit, its furniture, and its surroundings. Is everything in place, and are there no distractions to divert the attention of the people? Is the Bible open to the page from which the text is to be taken? Is there anything to be adjusted? and so on.

One of the most usual and unnecessary means of diverting attention, strange to say, is the arrangement of flowers about the pulpit. The writer is a great lover of flowers, and it is his delight to see them brought into the house of God for its adornment; but very frequently they are so placed that the people can not fail to notice them, to admire them, and perhaps to study them, even while the sermon is beginning, and certainly during its progress. Sometimes they interrupt the range of vision, so that certain parishioners can not see the preacher's face for the intervening flowers.

2. The room. Is the light, the heat, and the ventilation so arranged as that there shall be no disturbance while the sermon is in progress? If it is an evening service and the congregation have found it necessary, in order to economy, to turn out certain of the lights when the people do not need them for their own use, by all means let the preacher wait for this to be done before he arises to his feet. If there are windows to be opened or closed, or registers to be adjusted, let this be attended to before the sermon begins.

It is to be hoped that the congregation shall all have arrived before the sermon is begun. If late-comers appear they should never be shown to advanced seats. There should be no walking up the aisles by any one when the preacher rises to address the people.

The audience also should be properly distributed. This is in most churches the work of the ushers, particularly where the church is frequented by a number of strangers. They should not be largely seated in one section of the church to the neglect of another.

The preacher should not rise to his feet to announce his text until the people themselves are ready for him to begin. There is an exact moment for which he should wait, and beyond which his rising should not be prolonged. Perhaps they have just sung a hymn, and have been standing upon their feet. Let him give them time to take their seats and to adjust themselves to their positions. Let him wait until the general coughing that often follows congregational singing is finished. Let him delay until that precise point when they turn their eyes to the pulpit almost with one consent, as much as to say "We are ready." Then let him rise and begin.

3. Now as to the preacher himself. Is he ready? Is his dress such as not to distract attention? We have referred to this under Pulpit Manners. Let the suggestions made in that chapter be observed in connection with this matter. Let him by no means call attention to anything whatsoever in his dress or person. Let him not pull down his cuffs, pull out his watch, finger his necktie, adjust his moustache. Let him not even turn the leaves of his Bible in a preliminary way. The place from which he is to preach should have been already found. Let him not rise with his notes in his hand to adjust them to their place upon the pulpit; they should be already there. Let him have clearly in mind the very words with which he is to introduce his text, and as he glances over his congregation the moment before the text is to be announced, let them read in his countenance his positive preparation for the work which he has in hand.

Said Commodore Dewey to the captain of the Olympia just before the battle of Manila Bay, "Captain, whenever you are ready you may begin firing." Even so the preacher.

SECURING AND HOLDING ATTENTION

SECURING AND HOLDING ATTENTION

I. Say something at once.
  (1) That is worth hearing.
  (2) That the audience shall think worth hearing.
      Announcing the text.
      The next utterance.

II. The concrete before the abstract.

III. Promote curiosity.
      The "Sense of Wonder."

IV. Holding the attention gained.
      Expectation. Desire.

V. The three qualities of discourse.

V

SECURING AND HOLDING ATTENTION

We now suppose that the preacher is ready and may "begin firing."

He must be sure before he opens his mouth that he will be certainly heard, heard easily, and heard pleasantly. His opening sentences must not be incomprehensibile on any account, either of matter or manner. His opening words must be well chosen, and so uttered that no effort shall be required to identify them. Sometimes, as Dr. Buckley remarks, the preacher begins under an accumulation of energy resulting from temporary excitement. His nervous equilibrium is disturbed. Consequently he employs one of two objectionable tones, either his voice is pitched too high or too low. He begins with a shriek or murmur. But to attain high success the speaker must be heard agreeably. There should be, if possible, music in his voice. There must not be any positively objectionable features. The vital thing for him to consider is that all hearing is voluntary, and that nowhere outside of a state's prison is the presence of the auditor obligatory and listening compulsory. Attention may be destroyed in the opening sentence by a disagreeable manner or a disagreeable voice.

This matter having been suitably attended to, certain rules may be given for the securing of attention at the outset.

I. Say something at once. "Real attention," says

361

Fitch, "must always be founded on the fact that you have something to say which is worth hearing, and that you say it in such a way that the hearer shall feel it to be worth hearing."

Observe the two elements in this statement. They are related to both matter and manner. As to matter, the subject must claim attention for itself, not the preacher for the subject. "Real attention must always be founded on the fact that you have something to say *which is worth hearing.*" And yet while the preacher does not claim attention for the subject by any formal method, he does do so by the way in which he says that which is worth hearing. He makes no positive plea. His plea is *in his manner.* The attention of his congregation will largely depend upon his very first utterance. One of the most impressive openings of an address to which the writer ever listened was made by the Rev. Dr. H. C. McClelland of Pittsburg at the memorial service for President McKinley, in the Shadyside Presbyterian Church. When he rose to speak he advanced deliberately to the front of the platform at the side of the pulpit, and in a voice that could be distinctly heard by every one present he said, "We were so busy with our occupations and our prosperity, and he was so busy with his official cares and duties, that we did not know how much we loved him until that fateful afternoon when he thrust his hand into his bosom and drew it forth reddened with his own blood." As these words were uttered the preacher illustrated them with his gesture. He slowly thrust his own hand into his bosom and drew it forth again. The gesture was not descriptive, but rather emphatic, and the effect upon the audience was indescribable.

But one will say that the first utterance is usually the quotation of the text. This is true. In what sense,

then, will the maxim of Professor Fitch apply? How
can it be said with regard to the text that it must be
worth hearing, and that it must be said in such a way
that the hearer shall feel it to be worth hearing? Is not
the text always worth hearing? No, not necessarily.
Of course there is a sense in which every text, which
is the very Word of God, is emphatically worth hearing,
but the occasion, the place, the preacher, the people,
have very much to do with the quality of the text, apart
from its position and meaning in its connection in the
Word of God. If it is not skillfully chosen, so that it
is suited to its purpose under present circumstances, it
is not, in the sense in which we use the words, worth
hearing.

But suppose it to be eminently adapted to the
preacher's use, and to the people whom he addresses.
The important question still remains, Will they feel it
to be worth hearing? Much depends upon the answer
to this question. In order to insure attention it must
be properly announced and well uttered. If a preacher
begins by indicating the portion of Scripture from which
it is taken, this should be done in a suitable way. There
are many in every congregation who desire to remember
where the text is found, yet many preachers announce
their texts in such a way as to positively preclude their
recollection of the place. Oftentimes the verse is given
first, the chapter second, and the book last, as when the
preacher rapidly says, "My text will be found in the
twenty-first verse of the twenty-fifth chapter of the book
of Proverbs." The inverse order should always be followed. The name of the book should be given first, the
number of the chapter second, and the number of the
verse last, and there should be a slight pause between
each announcement, after this fashion, "My text is found

in the Book of Proverbs, * * * the 25th chapter, * * *
the 21st verse." It will not be necessary to repeat this
if it is properly uttered. Then follows the quotation of
the text. Let it be done deliberately, simply, but impressively.

Shall the text itself be repeated in order to atention?
Ordinarily not, because if the preacher leads the people
to believe that the text is usually to be repeated they
will fail to give it proper attention upon its first quotation.

It is the custom of many English preachers to repeat
their text for a special reason, especially if it be one
embracing several sentences. When it is quoted the
first time it is for purposes of simple information, that
the people may have the mere words of the quotation.
Then it is repeated the second time with certain proper
inflections and emphasis in order to bring out its special
meaning and application. Some preachers have been
known to repeat their texts more than twice with increasing emphasis, and in the hands of some men this
adds power to the announcement. It is usually, however,
a dangerous expedient, and it is far better for the ordinary
preacher to quote his text but once, but to quote it in
such a way that the principle already announced shall be
fulfilled.

Following the text comes the first utterance of the
preacher. That he may secure the attention of the congregation it is highly important that he attack his text
at once in the manner which has been already shown in
Part I, Chapter V. In this respect the first sentence
which the preacher utters is certainly the most important
in the entire sermon. Let him indicate at once what he
proposes to talk about, and let his subject be stated in
such terms that it shall foreshadow his entire discussion.
The first sentence must be germane, positive, weighty,

and worthy. The people will then feel that he has something to say upon this text which it is worth their while to hear.

II. In order to gain attention the preacher must introduce the concrete before he proceeds to the abstract. In the opening paragraphs of his sermon, and for some little time, say three to five minutes, there should be no abstruse statement, no philosophic proposition, no theological formulæ—nothing of this sort, but something that shall relate to persons, scenes, or things, and not to what is ordinarily called "thought."

One of the finest illustrations of this rule which has fallen under the writer's observation was a sermon delivered by President J. D. Moffat in his hearing. His text was Col. 2:8, "Take heed lest there shall be any one that maketh spoil of you through his philosophy and vain deceit, after the tradition of men, after the rudiments of the world, and not after Christ." If ever there was a temptation for a preacher to begin a sermon with a philosophic statement here was one. But the preacher upon this occasion was a master of the art of pulpit rhetoric, and his opening sentence was in these words, "That against which the apostle warns us in this text is not philosophy, but *a man with a philosophy.*" The audience, who might have anticipated, when the text was announced, some metaphysical discussion, were at once set at ease; their positive prejudices were immediately allayed. The concrete was presented to their notice, "a man with a philosophy."

III. It is important that the preacher in his opening paragraphs should promote the curiosity of the audience. We use this word "curiosity" with hesitation, but there is no other term which will take its place. Let it be understood then that it is not used in the sense of idle curiosity, but in that of diligent enquiry. "What does it mean? What will he say about it?" "Curiosity," says Archbishop Whateley, "is the parent of attention." Many illustrations could be given of the service which it performs. H. Clay Trumbull testifies that the first preacher who secured his immediate attention in his younger days was a converted Jew. In broken English he announced the words of his text before saying where it was found. "And ven dey hurd dat he shpake in de Hebrew tong to dem, dey kep de more silance." These words in their peculiar fitness to the man and the hour commanded the attention of others in the audience besides Trumbull himself. Dr. M. B. Riddle began an address upon the public opening of the theological seminary, with the quotation of a text so singularly appropriate to the time, and so thoroughly in keeping with his own record and work, that it commanded at once the attention of the congregation which he addressed. This text was in the words of the the chief captain who was bringing Paul from the Temple court into the castle, Acts 21 : 37, "Dost thou know Greek?"

The great value of this principle is derived from the fact that the mind of the worshiper is always disposed to listen to that which satisfies its need. It is truly hungry, anxious, and inquiring. The preacher who takes advantage of this condition will certainly secure attention.

One of the writer's students, some years ago, was called to recite upon this point. The teacher asked, "What next is required in order to command attention." The student, who was a Scotch-Irishman, roared out his answer in marked accent, "make them wander!" (wonder). The class was convulsed with laughter. Even the professor could not restrain himself. Nevertheless the student had aptly and emphatically expressed a great principle. Bishop Quayle enlarges upon it, in a chapter whose heading is "Keeping alive the sense of wonder." Referring to Ezekiel's vision he says, "When wonder is dead the soul is become a dry bone." And again, "The preacher's credential is that he is alive to wonder." In such aphorisms is wrapped up a store of instruction in the art of securing attention. From first to last the interesting preacher keeps alive the sense of wonder. It is not simply that his theme brings him into touch with what are ordinarily called "mysteries" and "miracles," but that in all spiritual matters he leads his hearers to the very edge of wonders more wonderful than these; just as Jesus with Nicodemus, when he aroused his wonder over such a commonplace thing as the sighing of wind.

The principles which have been given find complete illustration in many of the addresses recorded in the Scripture, none better from any mere man than Paul's sermon on Mars' Hill. He had something to say that was worth hearing. He presented the concrete before the abstract, and he aroused the curiosity of his hearers. "Ye men of Athens, in all things I perceive that ye are very religious. For as I passed along, and observed the objects of your worship, I found also an altar with this inscription, To an unknown God. What, therefore, ye worship in ignorance, this I set forth unto you." Let the reader examine these opening sentences in the light of the principles which have been announced.

The Savior Himself, however, is the supreme illustration of these principles. He certainly recognized the fact that the source of attention was in Himself rather than in His hearers, and He never talked, even as His great apostle once did, to a sleepy listener. Never before, nor since, has any one said so much that was worth hearing in a way which led the hearer to believe that it was worth hearing. Never before, nor since, has the concrete been so wisely and impressively used to convey the lessons of the abstract; and never before, nor since, has curiosity been so whetted by a teacher's words. When Jesus began to speak to the people He called attention, first of all, to the birds of the air, or the lilies of the field. When He would instruct Simon His host, He addressed to him the question, "Seest thou this woman?" "Behold, a sower went forth to sow" were His first words by the seaside. We do not need to multiply the illustrations. Jesus did not ask attention for His cause or the subject. They secured it for themselves. When Jesus began He began, that was all. Without delay, without circumlocution, and without apology. The preacher should follow His example.

IV. The attention having been once secured by the means which we have indicated, how is it to be held? How shall a congregation be induced to give continuous attention until the sermon is finished? The best writers upon this subject indicate two things which must follow the initial curiosity, and continue to the end of the discourse. These are expectation and desire. The skillful speaker begins with that which is entirely known, but proceeds to that which is partly known and partly unknown. The known elements in the preacher's discourse are combined with great skill with those elements that are but partly known. So it was with the apostle Paul's address upon Mars' Hill. He began with the altars in common use, and immediately connected them with the altar to the unknown God. This at once produced expectation and stimulated desire. The audience looks forward under such circumstances to a situation which is not immediately present, but which it awaits with feelings of anticipation, and sometimes of anxiety. The desire to have the expectation gratified is aroused. Arnold likens it to the pot of gold at the foot of the rainbow, only that it has a reality when once reached. But its presentation lures the audience on. The perspective situation arouses their minds to positive activity. Their interest in the subject passes beyond their own control. They are in the hands of the speaker: he moves them at his own will.

Herein, then, will be found the connection with the principle announced in the opening of the preceding chapter, in our definition of attention. The mental application of the hearer is stimulated with a view to the instruction which he expects to receive. His interest impels his mental effort, and if this interest be properly controlled he is led into an intellectual state of pleasure and of ease. His intellectual effort becomes a positive delight. Herein lies the secret of holding attention.

But the preacher must remember meanwhile that the strain upon the mental effort of his listeners can not be unduly prolonged. Professor James says: "A little introspective observation will show anyone that voluntary attention can not be continuously sustained. It comes in beats. The mind tends to wander. Its attention must every now and then be again secured by distinct pulses of effort which revivify the topic for a moment, until some intercurrent idea captures it and takes it off. Then the processes of recall must be repeated once more. Voluntary attention, in short, is only a momentary affair. The process, whatever it is, exhausts it self in the single act, and unless the matter is then taken in hand by some trace of interest inherent in the subject, the mind fails to follow." The remedy for this mental wandering is found in variety. The subject must be made to show

new aspects of itself. The curiosity must be transferred
to some other point or some other aspect of the theme.
New questions must be promoted and new ideas suggested. The attention wanders when the subject is un-
changed, and this may be attested in the simplest possible way. One may test it for himself. Let him endeavor
to attend steadfastly to some dot in the paper on the
wall. He can do it for a very few moments. Either
his field of vision becomes blurred so that he sees nothing distinctly, or else, no matter how hard he tries, he
has involuntarily ceased to look at the dot in question
and is looking at something else. Yet his attention may
be continued by suggesting new and different questions
with regard to the dot. How large is it? How far
is it from the eye? What is its shape, its color? How
is it related to other figures in the wall-paper? Is it
part of a pattern? Is it often repeated? and so forth.
If the observer turns it over in various ways, and with
various associations, he can keep his mind upon it for
a comparatively long time, and this is exactly what the
skillful speaker does with the theme which he presents
to his hearers. He varies the method of presenting it.
He bids his audience look at it from one side and from
another. He interrupts their continued thought with
some interesting illustration. He associates it with some
other interesting subject, and so on. In this way the
hearer's own mental activity is promoted. Relief from
continuous strain is afforded, and if to this be added oc-
casional recapitulation of the truth presented, but stated
in some other form, the attention will not be likely to
flag. These principles relating to the holding of an attention once secured are fully illustrated in the preaching of Jesus. The activity of His hearers was always
promoted, sometimes in ways which the preacher in the

pulpit can not adopt, as when the disciples were instructed to distribute the bread to the hungry multitude, or the scribes were sent to bring the tribute money. And as to variety, when was it ever so beautifully displayed as in the teaching of Jesus? Parable and miracle, the formal and the colloquial, the city and the desert, the land and the sea. We could form many such antitheses. Every address had variety in itself, and each was a change from every other. How the example of Jesus should shame the dull monotony which too often characterizes the preaching of His ministers!

V. In conclusion, then, in order to hold attention the sermon must display those three necessary qualities of a discourse to which we have already referred—unity, organization, and progress; but progress more particularly. The preacher must begin, he must then continue, and he must finish. These three things should be apparent to those to whom he speaks as plainly as though he were to say to them, "I now begin my discourse; I now proceed to continue the elaboration of my thought; I now propose to finish what I have to say."

PART III.

VARIOUS KINDS OF SERMONS.

THE NARRATIVE SERMON.

Instruction by means of example.

I. Material must be arranged in sermonic form.

II. The subject must be stated in religious terms.

III. The divisions likewise.

IV. The historical material should be employed only so
far as it relates to the subject.

Historical imagination.

Read Broadus, Part I, Chap. VI; Watkinson's Sermons; McNeil's Sermons.

I.

THE NARRATIVE SERMON.

In the Narrative Sermon instruction is conveyed by means of example. It deals with some Biblical character or some Biblical scene. In structure and method it is the simplest form of sermonizing, but even so it is often the most interesting and the most profitable. This is because there are very many among the preacher's auditors to whom spiritual truth is very much more palatable when it is associated with living material. We are always interested in biography, even in common conversation. The incidents which are associated with one's experience are frequently told and gladly heard. The little child is never more amused than when he climbs into his father's lap and requests some story of his childhood. Just so in sermonizing. Many a truth to which little attention would be given, if conveyed in abstract form, becomes not only acceptable but positively enjoyable when it is associated with actual life.

It is important in order to the suitable preparation of the narrative sermon that the preacher should be in possession of all the Scriptural facts. Full information must be had to begin with. The relation of these facts to each other should be distinctly understood, and the main fact about which the others revolve should be very particularly identified. Having possessed himself of these facts the preacher may subject the preparation of his discourse to certain rules such as the following:

I. He should arrange his material in sermonic form. The discourse is not to be a "lecture," but a "sermon." If he is engaged in the construction of a lecture he may content himself with an orderly review of consecutive events. This will make a narrative, but not a narrative sermon. Narrative is all well enough in its proper place, and there may be occasions when the preacher will desire only this; but a sermon must be something else and something more. It is intended to arouse the conscience, act upon the will, and persuade to belief and action. It requires much more skill to construct a narrative sermon than a mere narrative, but the effect will be much the more emphatic and permanent.

It is one of the notable peculiarities of the Holy Scripture that its characters are essentially human. Although its men and women, many of them, lived in ages long gone by, yet their actions may be so presented as that they shall seem to be our contemporaries. Even Cain, the first-born of the race, is not an antediluvian when viewed through eyes that are capable of seeing that which he holds in common with all mankind. He is a postdiluvian. His indifference to sin, his self-righteousness, his jealousy, his anger, his self-justification, and much else, are found in the men whom we know to-day. Therefore a narrative sermon, though it deals with Cain, may be as fully up-to-date as though Cain had but just departed this life.

II. The subject of the sermon should be stated in religious terms. This, because it is a sermon and not a mere narrative. It is the statement of this subject in terms that are applicable to human life as we see it, that gives the sermon its immediate value in its very opening sentences. To announce a title which is merely historical, or associated only with the scene or the man which furnishes the example, is to defeat the preacher's object at the outset.

And yet the subject must have direct reference to the scene which is to be described or to the man whose character is to be employed for the purposes of the sermon. Take, for example, such a text as this, Ex. 5 : 22,23, "And Moses returned unto Jehovah, and said, Lord, wherefore hast thou dealt ill with this people? Why is it that thou hast sent me? For since I came to Pharaoh to speak in thy name, he hath dealt ill with this people; neither hast thou delivered thy people at all." This text is purely historical. There is no exhortation in it. No duty is commanded; no grace commended; no doctrine presented. How then shall the subject be stated in sermonic form? If the preacher announces his subject in some such terms as this, "The Complaint of Moses," the subject is a historical one and open to objection; since it relates wholly to the past. But let the subject be announced as "The Delay of Divine Deliverance," and every hearer will feel its immediate present application and force. Or take 2 Tim. 1 : 5, "Having been reminded of the unfeigned faith that is in thee; which dwelt first in thy grandmother Lois, and thy mother Eunice; and, I am persuaded, in thee also." The subject may not be "The Parentage of Timothy," but "The Entail of Faith."

And yet sometimes the subject may be stated in terms that appear to be merely historical when they are not. For example, Heb. 11 : 22, "By faith Joseph, when his end was nigh, made mention of the departure of the children of Israel; and gave commandment concerning his bones." The subject in this case may be "The Faith of Joseph," and it will be apparent that the preacher proposes to discourse not upon Joseph's faith as a strictly individual characteristic, but upon such faith as that which Joseph showed, and which we ourselves may well show in imitating his example.

III. The sermonic principle must be applied to the statement of the separate divisions of the sermon also. They should not be divisions of the scene, or of the life of the man under consideration, but divisions of the sermonic subject which has been announced. And yet as the subject of the sermon must be directly related to the character employed, so also the divisions of the subject must have direct reference to the successive events in the man's life, or the successive elements of the scene. Recur to the text from Exodus. One may not take for his subject "The Delay of Deliverance," and then, returning to the historical, announce as his first division, "The Complaint of Moses;" for his second, perhaps, "The Severe Treatment of Pharaoh;" and for his third, "The Answer of Jehovah;" but better to divide the subject as follows: 1. How this delay may be interpreted by the wicked and unbelieving, (as Pharaoh). 2. How it may be interpreted by God's own people, (as Moses). 3. How it will be interpreted by God Himself, (as shown in His great and complete deliverance).

IV. The historical material should be employed only so far as it has to do with the subject; and

V. It should be employed in strict connection with the progress of the thought. Certain particulars with regard to these two points.

1. The introduction should make use of no more of the historical material than is necessary to make the situation intelligible. Certain general statements may be employed with very little of the detail.

2. In the separate divisions as they progress only that historical material should be employed which is immediately connected with each division.

3. The preacher should reserve for the application or conclusion of the sermon that which was the culmination of the career, or the crown of the character employed.

It is very important to avoid anticipation in this matter. It is not necessary for the preacher to follow the events of the Scripture passage in historical order. It is not well for him to tell the whole story at the outset. All the material is to be disposed according to the demands of the subject as it is developed. If he finds this difficult, it is generally because his subject is not well chosen, or his divisions are improperly arranged. In one word, the subject should be made the governing factor from the beginning to the end.

The method may be set forth by means of a somewhat extended illustration better than by any formal rules. Let us suppose that the text is taken from Paul's address before King Agrippa, Acts 26:27, "King Agrippa, believest thou the prophets? I know that thou believest." The subject at once announced is not "Paul Before Agrippa," or "The Apostle's Defense," or any such thing, but "Our Deeper Convictions." The subject is first given and explained. The introduction is occupied with a very brief statement of Paul's arrest, and his experiences during his two years' imprisonment, closing with some account of Festus' confessed inability to deal with his case, the arrival of Agrippa, and the proposition that Agrippa should have an opportunity to hear him, the trial in brief and the questions of the text. It is then asked, "Why do not men yield to their deeper convictions?" If we may discover why Agrippa did not yield to his convictions we may be able to answer the question for ourselves. There were two principle reasons why the king was false to his convictions. These are the great reasons why men prove faithless to them to-day. The first division is now stated. "We do not yield to our deeper convictions because of our pride of opinion." This is at once associated with King Agrippa. It is shown how he was the leading Jewish lawyer in the world; that he had already rendered certain decisions which had established him as an authority in matters of Jewish jurisprudence. His pride was manifested in the fact that it was he who offered to hear the Apostle, even before Festus had proposed it, saying, "I also could wish (margin, "was wishing") to hear the man myself." It is evident that Agrippa in his vanity expected to solve the problem which Felix and Festus had been unable to settle. More may be given in the same line. It is then shown how the tables would have been turned had King Agrippa yielded to his convictions. He would have been discomfited by the very man whom he sought to try. So to-day it is pride of opinion which keeps many a man from Christ. The second division will be, "Because of our manner of life." Observe that nothing has been so far said with regard to Agrippa's personal character. It is now to be introduced. His character was as base as his talents were conspicuous. He had early become a profligate; his consort Bernice is his own sister; and at the very time when he sits to try the Apostle Paul he is engaged in a secret conspiracy with Rome, plotting the dismemberment of his own nation. He is a traitor, an adulterer, and a debauchee. He can not yield to his convictions without confessing his sins and abandoning them. Even so to-day. And the comparison can be carried out to some extent. The conclusion is found in the sequel to the story, and more particularly in the closing events of Agrippa's life as they are gathered from secular history. Only once did the orbit of his life approach so near to the Sun of Righteousness. This was his moral perihelion. Thence he drifts away into hopeless infidelity and vice, a "wandering star," as Jude puts it, "for whom the blackness of darkness hath been reserved for ever." But he will need no more for his condemnation at the last than to be again confronted with the Apostle Paul, and again to hear the same question, with the same answer, "King Agrippa, believest thou the prophets? I know that thou believest." The close connection between the sad climax in the career of Agrippa and that of every sinner's life is manifest and emphatic. So it is with those who will not yield to their deeper convictions.

W. L. Watkinson has no superior in the art of narrative sermonizing. Many of his discourses are of this character. In the one volume entitled "The Bane and the Antidote," out of sixteen sermons, five, (almost one-third), are narrative, and they are all treated according to the principles which we have recommended. Let us consult some of them. Mark 12: 34, "And when Jesus saw that he answered discreetly, He said unto him, Thou art not far from the Kingdom of God." Subject, "Nearness to the Kingdom of God."

I. The Kingdom of God. Let us briefly inquire into the meaning of this phrase.

II. Near the Kingdom.
  1. There is a nearness to personal godliness that is brought about by intellectual sincerity.
  2. There is a nearness to personal godliness that is brought about by moral integrity.
  3. There is a nearness to personal godliness that is brought about by ceremonial faithfulness.

III. Entrance into the Kingdom.
  1. A word of admonition.
  2. A word of direction.
  3. Finally, a word of encouragement.

Gen. 42 : 11, "We are true men." This is a sermon concerning the brothers of Joseph, who made this statement when they imagined that they were under suspicion. The subject is, "Revised Estimates." We have already referred to it.

I. The Mistaken Estimate.
    1. They rested in their superficial goodness and forgot their deeper wickedness.
    2. They rested in their exceptional goodness and forgot their prevailing wickedness.
    3. They rested in their present goodness and forgot their past wickedness.

II. The Corrected Estimate.

A careful examination of these sermons by the reader will illustrate the method to the full.

In order to achieve great success in the composition of this class of sermons, the preacher must diligently cultivate his imagination. As to this matter see Part I, Chapter XV. What we have called the historical imagination is almost indispensable to effective preaching along this line. It is necessary to realize the scenes which are depicted, to enter into active intellectual sympathy with the character presented. Ruskin has well said that hundreds of people can talk for one who can think, but thousands can think for one who can see. So when we say that the narrative sermon is the simplest form of pulpit address, we do not mean that it is not capable of becoming one of the highest forms. If the preacher is one of those thousands who can see as well as think, whose vision penetrates the example considered, he may elevate his style of address to a very high point. In such a case his presentation of character is not a mere sketch, the barren recital of successive events, or certain moralizings concerning them; but it is profound analysis which enters into the very spring of human life, dissects the motive, and lays bare the heart. The preacher must gather about the character much that the sacred narrative does not directly record, but which it distinctly implies, to heighten description, and render the lesson the more comprehensive and impressive. The sermons of John McNeil are among the finest examples of this historical imagination. Take, for example, a few lines from the one entitled, "What aileth thee, Hagar?" "Notice the scene. A dusky woman, an Egyptian, dark of skin and darker of heart at this moment, sitting in loneliness and bitterness: a bow-shot off, a young lad. At first he was all the hope, but now he is all the trouble. Utterly spent with the heaviness of the way, he has been cast under a shrub that his mother may not see him die. Nothing all around but sand and barren scrub and baking rocks, reflecting and beating down more keenly the fierce heat of the sun. A great over-reaching empty heaven. If anything to be seen, away yonder in the distance a black speck or two which by and by will turn out to be the swift wings, gleaming eyes, and sharpened beaks of the vultures hastening to their prey. Many a time they have got a meal here. From afar they scent the feast, and are just beginning to darken the sky, and there—oh, wonder of wonders, it is right there! heaven is near! there God is, there salvation is, there the voice of promise and hope and revival!" The writer can never forget the impression which was made upon his mind when he heard John McNeil preaching upon the stilling of the waves. He described the Savior awakened by His disciples, and among other things he put these words into the mouth of Jesus, "Am not I wet too?" and as he said this he seized his coat-tails with his hands and wrung them out as though he was wringing the sea-water from them. All preachers can not exhibit the power of imagination to the extent of John McNeil, but all should endeavor to attain somewhat of it in order to success in narrative preaching.

THE EXPOSITORY SERMON.

THE EXPOSITORY SERMON.

The Expository Sermon defined.

I. Advantages.
  1. Fulfills the very idea of preaching.
  2. Gives complete and exact knowledge of the teaching of Scripture.
  3. Affords opportunity to treat neglected passages.
  4. Contributes to interest in other sermons.

II. Requisites.
  1. Unity.
  2. Structure.
  3. Mastery of details.
    (1) Not too many.
    (2) Pertinent.
    (3) Comprehensive.

III. Further effectiveness.
  1. The preacher must not lose sight of his theme.
  2. Parallel passages.
  3. Obscurities.

IV. Various length of passages.
  Three kinds of sermons.
    1. Treating all the details.
    2. Selecting certain details.
    3. Massing the details.

Read Prof. Sewall's Chapters in "Preachers and Preaching," Shedd VI. Broadus, Part II, Chap. III.

II.

THE EXPOSITORY SERMON.

The expository sermon is the product of exegesis, but it is in no sense its exhibition. It is not a running commentary upon some passage of Scripture in which its separate parts are taken up seriatim and explained, but, as its name implies, it is a piece of rhetoric: a sermon. It differs from the topical sermon in that it is all derived directly from the Scripture; and it differs from the textual sermon in that more of the details of the Scripture passage are employed. But the textual sermon runs into the expository sermon, and it is not very easy to draw the dividing line. Professor Sewall well remarks: "Make the exegetical part of the sermon brief. Do not let the interpretation spin itself out into garrulity. Put it as compactly as clearness will permit. Exegesis is not the ultimate aim of the discourse: it is simply the instrument which we use to dig out the truth on which we intend to preach. When the truth is dug out, then preach. It is folly to keep on digging. Many a good sermon has been spoiled by too much exegesis."

The narrative sermon prepares the way for the expository, and it will be well to have some experience in the composition of narrative sermons before expository sermon work is begun.

It is true that this class of sermons is one of the hardest properly to prepare. It requires more careful, extended, and skillful study than the young preacher may be ready to give to it. Yet the attempt should be made, simply because all good preaching is the result of exposition. No sermon of any class can be properly prepared upon faulty exegesis.

I. The advantages of expository preaching.

There are certain reasons why expository preaching is not more general. It is apt to be severely criticized, and some parishioners do not hesitate to express their dislike for it. This fear of criticism is the first reason why more expository sermons are not preached. But another reason, and perhaps a greater one, is the preacher's own sense of his lack of skill in the matter. Naturally he prefers to do that which he can do easily and well, and he shrinks from attempting a work in which he fears he may be unsuccessful. But the advantages of this kind of preaching, and the very great interest which it does elicit when it is properly performed, are sufficient reasons for undertaking it.

1. In the first place it fulfills the very idea of preaching, because preaching is first of all instruction in the word of God, and the application of its truth to the heart and life. The author quoted above says with regard to this matter: "The expository sermon gives the truth an opportunity to speak for itself. Here is a great body of divine revelation that wants to get itself uttered and understood. How can that best be done? Look at other enterprises. How can we learn most of geology? By quarrying among the rocks themselves. How can we best study astronomy? By going directly to the stars. Why not apply that method here? We can take the principal things of the Bible and discourse upon them eloquently in our topical sermons, and that is a very useful thing to do, but how much of the real Bible do our people get in the process?"

2. It gives more complete and exact knowledge of what the Scripture actually teaches. In this work the preacher does not merely give the substance of truth, or declare that this or that doctrine is set forth in the Bible, but he gives the Bible a chance to speak for itself. This is a decided advantage every way. The Bible has often been held responsible for errors and absurdities of which its representatives were the sole authors. But when the people derive their knowledge of its contents at first hands, their knowledge becomes the more exact; and when they derive their knowledge from a large exhibition of its teachings, their knowledge becomes the more complete.

3. It gives the preacher the opportunity, and more than that—the disposition to use those portions of Scripture which are very generally left unused. He is graciously tempted into some books from which texts are not often derived; or even when the passage is selected from a book which is frequently employed, he is encouraged to dwell upon certain texts upon which he would not otherwise preach at all, because they are contained therein.

4. The last advantage to be mentioned, and one which is by no means the least, is that it contributes very greatly to the interest of the people in other sermons not expository. This is because the people have been trained in the Scripture, have learned to put more of it together, have been led to understand its relations, and the sermon in which the larger connection can not well be employed by the preacher is fitted into its proper place by those who hear it, and their profit and pleasure indefinitely extended.

It is not possible to say just how much Scripture should be used in each expository sermon. No rule can be given with regard to the length. Sometimes a single verse will contain may terms that need interpretation, and set forth a variety of truths that need to be co-ordinated, and will thereby furnish sufficient material for an ordinary sermon. It is only that a longer passage is not to be treated in exactly the same way as a shorter one, but this will be discussed further on.

II. The requisites of an expository sermon.

1. The chief requisite is unity. This is not exactly that ordinary unity of which we have already spoken as one of the fundamental qualities of discourse. Ordinarily unity pertains to one's own material, the various thoughts which are the product of his own brain, and which he must be careful to correlate so that they shall bear the same or a similar relation to each other and to the subject in hand; but in the case of the expository sermon the preacher is dealing with details which are furnished to him. The problem is not that of unifying his own material, but another's. All that is included in the paragraph which he is expounding resembles a pile of stones dumped down before the mason who is engaged in erecting a wall. He must choose his material stone by stone, select it with reference to the place in which he is to put it, trim it, fit it, and settle it in position.

Without this unity the sermon is likely to be only a collection of disjointed remarks, some upon one expression, some upon another, and instead of the preacher producing one sermon he will find that he has produced a number of little sermons, brought together in a mechanical or artificial way.

What must he do to secure this unity? Just what the mason does. He must select the material which is suited to his subject and reject the rest. Let him not suppose that in so doing he offers any violence to the word of God. If he were producing a commentary he would be bound to neglect nothing contained in the passage. But he is not doing this. He is preparing a sermon upon a given subject which he finds in the passage considered, and in order to the clear and emphatic presentation of this subject he chooses that which is related to it.

2. The second requisite is what has been called "structure." This corresponds to what we have called "organization" in giving the three fundamental qualities of discourse; but it differs from ordinary organization just as the unity of expository work differs from the unity of topical work, and for the same reason. By "structure" we mean that the materials which the sermonizer has selected from the passage are to be put together upon a system—that system suggested by his subject. They are to be so put together as that the one shall agree with the other, and all proceed together toward the conclusion.

These are the two more important requisites in expository preaching, but the question arises, Just what is to be done in order that the sermon may possess these qualities? How shall the preacher proceed to expound the passage in a sermonic way? This is answered in the next point.

3. The mastery of details. All the details in the passage must be studied, whether they are to be employed or not. None of them may be slighted. If the sermonizer does not carefully inquire concerning all of them he will be unable to make a proper selection and a proper grouping of any of them.

He must study these details with the author's point of view in mind. What was the subject discussed by the author? What was his purpose in discussing it? These may neither of them be the preacher's; but the preacher must be acquainted with them in order to form his own. The author was writing at a different time, to a different people, and with a different object in view; but if the preacher does not understand the adaptation of the author's words to his own time, people, and purpose, he will not be able to make his own adaptation to his own time, his own people, and his own purpose.

When the details have been all studied, and studied with the author's point of view in mind, the preacher will select the subject which seems to him to be the most appropriate upon which to discourse. It must be true to the passage. It must be a veritable subject as heretofore explained, but the selecting and grouping of material can not, of course, be done until this subject has been found and stated. Then the work will proceed. The details will be chosen in accordance with such rules as the following:—

(1) Not too many details. There is great danger of overcrowding in expository sermon work, and of presenting so many thoughts and points that the hearer shall follow with difficulty. The preacher may be absolutely true to his passage, and his exposition may be positively Scriptural, when many of the details are left untouched. Professor Shedd well remarks that in expository sermon work there is often too much dilution and too little exposition. "That is to say, the very multiplication of details impairs the force and weight of the principle contained in the subject."

(2) The details must be pertinent. Here is where the particular skill in expository work is required. Really the great question which confronts the sermonizer is, Which details shall I select? And he may go far astray in his answer, because the details which are the most important may at first sight seem inferior. It is not the

big word, nor the peculiar term, that is always of chief importance. The very gist of the truth which the preacher should express may be found in a tense, or a preposition, or some other insignificant part of speech. It may be this very thing, inferior at first sight, which ministers special vividness and power to the presentation of the subject. A student in the seminary prepared a sermon upon 1 Peter 2: 25, "For ye were going astray like sheep; but are now returned unto the Shepherd and Bishop of your souls." The student secured the commendation of his professor because, in expounding the passage, he had noted the fact that the verb in this verse was in the passive voice, indicating that they had not returned of themselves, but had been graciously brought back. "Your going astray was of yourselves; your being returned was of the Lord."

In the search for pertinent details the preacher is subject to certain dangers, against which he must be on his guard. He may not choose enough to ensure fidelity to the passage, or he may choose too many for the preservation of the unity of his discourse; or, in his ignorance or indolence, he may neglect the most important. To this work then the most careful study is to be given.

(3) The details should not only be pertinent but comprehensive. He must look carefully for the broad and suggestive teaching, and not for that which is incidental or comparatively insignificant.

If these rules be carefully followed the sermonizer will discover that he has material which may be easily grouped and built into a harmonious whole.

III. In addition to these primary requisites in expository preaching some other matters should be observed to its further effectiveness.

1. The preacher must not lose sight of his theme.

Indeed, if he does lose sight of it, it is probably because the theme itself is not well chosen. And yet there is sometimes a temptation to depart from it because of the numerous suggestions of other subjects contained in the passage. But the theme should be constantly kept in view. It will be well to specifically recur to it occasionally, more frequently indeed than in any other form of preaching, so that the congregation may be reminded of it while the sermon is in progress. This reference to the theme is like the "tie-course" in a wall, binding its separate parts together.

2. A generous use should be made of parallel passages. They should be more frequently employed in expository preaching than in other kinds, just because it is expository. Being such, the best exposition is the Bible itself. They also minister variety to the discussion of the subject by permitting the mind occasionally to break the bonds which the expository method may seem to impose upon it. But these parallel passages should be carefully selected. They should contain some analogous truth. They should be well digested, assimilated, and carefully incorporated in the sermon. More particularly, let not the preacher at any time depart from the passage with which he is engaged and proceed to preach, as it were, a little sermon upon the parallel passage.

3. Be careful not to make the difficulties of the passage, if there are any, the more obscure. Do not attempt any exposition because of a personal interest in the matter. The interest of the people is the first consideration. But if there be difficulties whose discussion can not well be avoided, let the preacher be honest in his exposition, honest first of all with himself, and then with those whom it is his privilege to address.

4. Remember that the end and object of expository

preaching is that of any other preaching, practical help-fulness. It is done to save and edify those to whom it comes.

IV. We have already indicated that there· is no rule with regard to the length of the passage to be expounded. Generally speaking, however, expository sermons may be of three kinds, relating to the varying length of the passage considered.

1. The first kind is that wherein the details of the passage are very fully treated. This is the hardest of all to prepare because the unity is sometimes quite obscure, and yet thought and care will prevail even in this case. Dr. Maclaren, of Manchester, has a sermon upon a passage which seems to contain certain exhortations which have no direct connection with each other; Col. 4:2-6, "Continue steadfastly in prayer, watching therein with thanksgiving; withal praying for us also, that God may open unto us a door for the Word, to speak the mystery of Christ, for which I am also in bonds; that I may make it manifest, as I ought to speak. Walk in wisdom toward them that are without, redeeming the time. Let your speech be always with grace, seasoned with salt, that ye may know how ye ought to answer each one." Dr. Maclaren's subject is, "Precepts for the Innermost and the Outermost Life." The text has to do with matters of experience and matters of duty. His main divisions are two, which, with their sub-heads, are as follows:

I. The Innermost Life.

   Prayer.

      1. For ourselves.
      2. With watchfulness.
      3. And for others.

II. The Outermost Life.

    1. A wise walk.

    2. A gracious speech.

Dr. Maclaren treats in this sermon all the details, yet all are methodically arranged.

2. The second class is where the details are all set forth, and then certain are selected as illustrative of the others. An example is found in a sermon upon Rom. 9: 1-5, "I say the truth in Christ, I lie not, my conscience bearing witness with me in the Holy Spirit, that I have great sorrow and unceasing pain in my heart. For I could wish that I myself were anathema from Christ for my brethren's sake, my kinsmen according to the flesh: who are Israelites; whose is the adoption, and the glory, and the covenants, and the giving of the law, and the service of God, and the promises; whose are the fathers, and of whom is Christ as concerning the flesh, who is over all, God blessed for ever. Amen." Eight particulars are here mentioned which distinguish the Israelites in their religious heritage—the adoption, the glory, the covenants, the giving of the law, the service of God, the promises, the fathers, and the coming of Christ. These are the distinguishing privileges of believers—members of the Church. Each of the eight is carefully explained in a few words, then four of them are selected for special treatment and larger amplification. These four are the adoption, the promises, the fathers, and the coming of Christ. The connection between the Old Testament and the New is pointed out, and the first coming of Christ connected with His second coming as the great hope of the Church.

3. In the third kind of expository sermon work the details are none of them treated separately, but they are massed and their general teaching and import is set forth

without reference to particulars. This is generally done when the passage is quite extended, say twenty or thirty verses or more. The method may also be employed when one desires to expound a certain book of the Bible, or a number of books closely related to each other.

Some preachers seem to imagine that in a course of expository sermons it is necessary for them to treat every chapter successively, and sometimes to prepare several sermons upon the same chapter. In this way the course may be indefinitely extended. A preacher may occupy half the winter, or even more, in discoursing, let us say, upon the Gospel of Matthew, or the Epistle to the Romans. Unless he is very highly gifted, and a man of unusual spiritual power, this will become intolerably wearisome. But the preacher may learn to do this kind of work comprehensively by massing the details, so that an extended portion of Scripture, running perhaps into an entire book, may be covered in three or four sermons. If then the preacher desires, some time later, to take up special passages from the book and enlarge upon them, it may well be done to the pleasure of those who listen. This method may be illustrated in a sermon upon the 73rd Psalm, beginning, "Surely God is good to Israel, even to such as are pure in heart. But as for me, my feet were almost gone; my steps had well nigh slipped." The subject of the sermon is "Asaph's Error," as illustrating the error into which any Christian may fall. The preacher observes that the psalm is equally divided into two parts. It contains twenty-eight verses: the first fourteen give the reason for Asaph's error, and the method of its expression. The last fourteen show the way in which it was corrected, and the spiritual effects. The preacher observes that in the first half of the psalm Asaph's mind is entirely occupied with the physical and temporal condition of the wicked, as contrasted with that of the righteous; but in the second part nothing whatever is said with regard to either the physical or temporal. Asaph's error has been corrected by going into the sanctuary of God. The spiritual benefits, and the eternal prospects of the righteous, occupy his mind and fill his soul.

These thoughts amplified and illustrated, with some references to the details of the psalm and some quotations of its expressive verses, furnish a sufficient exposition, though its particular words are not explained and its details are not treated at length.

The only way in which one may become a skillful and useful expository preacher is by candidly recognizing the difficulties which are connected with this work, resolutely facing them with the determination to master them, and much practice. He may then expect to be what others have been before him, for some of the most useful preachers in the history of the Church have been those whose sermons were largely expository. Among these may be mentioned Monod, Hanna, W. M. Taylor, F. W. Robertson, Ryle, Joseph Parker, Maclaren, and F. B. Meyer.

THE EVANGELISTIC SERMON.

THE EVANGELISTIC SERMON.

The evangelistic sermon defined.

Its form as preached by the settled pastor.

Its subjects.

    The eighteenth and nineteenth centuries compared.

      Edwards. Spurgeon.

Special features.

    I. Addressed to the conscience.

    II. Positively instructive.

    III. Exceeding simple.

    IV. Experimental.

    V. Variety in form.

    VI. Not confined to the evening service.

    VII. The pastor his own evangelist.

Read Torrey's "How to Promote and Conduct a Successful Revival;" Spurgeon's "Twelve Soul-Winning Sermons;" Pattison's 'History of Christian Preaching," Chap. XIV (Jonathan Edwards); Headley's "Evangelists in the Church;" Chapman's "Present Day Evangelism."

III.

THE EVANGELISTIC SERMON.

We use this term "evangelistic" in a special sense. It is true that every sermon in which the gospel is proclaimed is an evangelistic sermon, but the term has been narrowed to that particular form of sermonizing in which the unconverted are directly addressed. It is in this sense, therefore, that the term is now employed. The evangelistic sermon is one which seeks to promote the conviction of sin and to lead men to an immediate decision for Jesus Christ.

But even so, the evangelistic sermon as preached by the settled pastor is not exactly the same thing as that preached by the professional revivalist, and we must recognize the difference between the two at the outset. A professional revivalist usually takes it for granted that the people whom he addresses have been sufficiently indoctrinated. It does not ordinarily appear to him to be necessary even to define his terms. He proceeds at once with an extended appeal, usually abounding in anecdote and illustration, and by such means he seeks to bring the unconverted to a positive choice. But it has been demonstrated again and again that the settled pastor can not pursue this plan in his evangelistic preaching, and even those revivalists who have become for a time settled pastors have abandoned this method for that which is better suited to the pastoral office. This is all well set forth by the Rev. Wm. Patterson, pastor of Bethany Presbyterian Church, Philadelphia, in a chapter on "The Minister as

an Evangelist," in Dr. R. A. Torrey's book "How to Promote and Conduct a Successful Revival." He says:
"The work of the minister according to the teaching of
the New Testament is three-fold. First, he is to feed the
Church of God—the babes with the sincere milk of the
Word, and those who are more advanced with the strong
meat of its doctrines. Second, he is to care for those
over whom he has been placed as an overseer or under-
shepherd. We are all agreed as to the importance of
these two departments in connection with the minister's
work: in fact, we can hardly over-estimate the importance
of building up Christian people in faith and in knowledge. Third, he is commanded to do the work of an
evangelist, in other words to reach out after the unsaved,
and to bring into the fold those who are outside." There
can be no doubt that this is the proper order of precedence. While we can scarcely discriminate between the
pastor's pastoral work and the pastor's evangelizing work,
there is no question that the feeding and upbuilding of
the Church of God is the pastor's first duty. It is laid
upon him as of primary importance by the Savior Himself, and by the apostles who followed Him. Its chief
importance also appears in this, that it is absolutely essential in order to the success of pastoral work that the
pastor should organize a corps of intelligent and zealous
workers, competent to instruct others in the way of salvation, and that through them he should seek to do a large
part of his evangelizing work. The expression of Dr.
Parkhurst, often quoted, puts the matter in exactly the
right light, "The pastor's congregation is not so much
his field as his force." The pastor is expected to exercise
the direction of his people, not only in immediate soul
saving, but in all those Christian labors that look to the
regeneration and reorganization of society.

So it is that the pastor's distinctly evangelistic preaching assumes a somewhat different type from that of the professional revivalist, while it seeks the same end, often reaches it by more desirable methods, and secures more permanent results.

The evangelistic sermon deals with the following subjects: (1) The nature, guilt, and consequences of sin; (2) The grace, power, and faithfulness of Christ; (3) How to escape sin in all its forms; (4) How to apprehend salvation, and how to "work it out" to its best results in subsequent life. Professor Garvie, in his "Guide to Preachers," has a number of excellent chapters covering these various subjects. They form the second section of his book, with the general title, "How to State the Gospel." They deal with the following special subjects: The need of the gospel, the penalty of sin, the nature of salvation, the grace of Christ, repentance, conversion, and others. We make no extended quotation from them, but they are earnestly recommended to the reader.

It will be seen that careful students like Professor Garvie and Dr. Patterson lay very special stress upon the necessity of presenting to the full in evangelistic preaching the first group of subjects mentioned above— the nature, guilt, and consequences of sin. It is particularly important that these should receive the pastor's attention in this particular age of the world when there appears to be in some quarters what one has called "a vanishing sense of sin." It will also be found that there is no more distinguishing mark of the New Homiletics than the return to the consideration of these subjects. In this respect the history of modern preaching has followed very much the same course as that exhibited in connection with instruction. The preaching of the eighteenth century had very much to do with the exceeding sinfulness of sin. The preaching of the nineteenth century largely ignored it, for the same reason that it largely omitted instruction, because it had been already pressed upon the consciences of the Church and of the world. But within the last few years the more earnest preachers of our country, and the best authorities upon homiletics, have perceived the need of a return to the earnest and faithful preaching of the Law. It may be that to some extent the neglect in this direction was due to the extreme severity of the preaching of the eighteenth century. Perhaps the people of our own age would not be so likely to be moved by it as our forefathers. Jonathan Edwards is the most distinguished illustration of this form of preaching at the time when it was in vogue. The principles which he maintained are absolutely sound and just. He himself said: "A minister would miss it very much if he should insist too much on the terrors of the Law and neglect the gospel, but yet the Law is very much to be insisted on, and the preaching of the gospel is likely to be in vain without it." No evangelical minister of the present age would probably dissent from this position. "The Great Awakening" (1735-1750) was to a large extent due to the leadership of Edwards. He was its most conspicuous figure. While we may not follow his style of discourse, we must follow the principles upon which it was founded in order to be successful evangelistic, pastoral preachers. His most remarkable sermon was entitled "Sinners in the Hands of an Angry God." One has said concerning it: "This was the sermon which New England has never been able to forget." The text was taken from Deut. 32:35, "Their foot shall slide in due time." He represented God as holding sinners in this life only so long as it suited His purpose, but He holds them on slippery ground, on the edge of a pit where they can not stand alone without His gracious help. They are already under a sentence of condemnation. When God lets go they will drop. The close of the sermon was in these words: "If we knew that there was one person, and but one, in this whole congregation that was to be the subject of this misery, what an awful thing it would be to think of. It we knew who it was, what an awful sight would it be to see such a person. How might all the rest of the congregation lift up a lamentable and bitter cry over him. But, alas, instead of one, how many is it likely will remember this discourse in hell! And it would be a wonder if some that are now present should not be in hell in a very short time, before this year is out, and it would be no wonder if some persons that now sit here in some seats of this meeting house, in health, and quiet, and secure, should be there before tomorrow morning." It was such preaching as this which awoke New England from its torpor, overcame the immorality of the age, and led the way to modern evangelism. Surely more of this kind of preaching is needed at the present time.

But, on the other hand, no pastor can be successful in winning souls to Christ who does not present the love of Jesus, and the grace of God in Him, with the most tender urgency. In this respect Spurgeon is the great example of the preaching of the nineteenth century. He was as great a soul-winner as Edwards before him, but while Edwards presented the terrors of the Law, Spurgeon presented the attractiveness of the Gospel. He himself selected from over sixteen hundred of his printed sermons twelve which had been most instrumental in leading souls to Christ. They are bound in a separate volume entitled "Twelve Soul-Winning Sermons," and the author says with regard to them, "These discourses have been already sealed with the highest approval, for they have been used by the Holy Spirit to lead many to Jesus." In not one of these twelve sermons are the terrors of the Law specifically presented, nor is there a single sermon among them in which the guilt and nature of sin are presented as the leading theme, although much, of course, is said with regard to them incidentally. We do not think that two men can be found in the ranks of modern preachers who will furnish better illustrations of the kind of preaching which is calculated to win men to Christ than Jonathan Edwards and C. H. Spurgeon, and we fully believe that every one who desires in his pastoral work to bring large numbers to the Savior should be a diligent student of their respective methods.

We pass now to consider some of the special features of the evangelistic sermon.

I. It should be addressed to the conscience. This should not always be made manifest by the preacher at the outset of his discourse. Sometimes considerable art may be employed to conceal this fact. Sinners do not wish to be touched in their consciences, and their antagonism is apt to be aroused if the preacher's purpose be made too plain.

More than this, sinners are not generally directly reached through their conscience, but through some other avenue by which their conscience is indirectly approached. The preacher, therefore, who at the outset of his discourse attempts to press home the truth to the conscience may find his very purpose thwarted, and yet his object is never to be concealed from himself. Truly and persistently he attempts to reach the conscience, to arouse it, to bring it into immediate action.

In order to do this he must ever keep before himself certain fundamental principles. In his evangelistic preaching he must recognize nothing but the awful fact of sin, the blessed offer of salvation, and the solitary revelation of sin and the Savior which is made in the Word of God. He will be likely to fail in reaching the conscience if he looks upon certain misdeeds and bad habits of those whom he addresses as due to nothing more than environment, heredity, or something else which would seem to relieve the sinner of a certain amount of responsibility. "'All unrighteousness is sin." Skepticism is sometimes inherited and sometimes associated with unfortunate training, but it still must be treated from the pulpit as sin, positive, willful sin, if the sinner is to be reached. Drunkenness, is sometimes truly a disease, but it is much more and worse, and must be treated by the evangelistic preacher in the same way.

More than this, the preacher who would win souls must make no special discrimination between sins and sins, as though some were very much more heinous than others, or as though some were not so likely to lead to the condemnation of God and His just judgment as others. To lay undue emphasis on certain sins, especially those that are gross and offensive, such as drunkenness, gambling, and adultery, is to give a very false impression concerning sin to many other sinners. The preacher must not seem to admit for a moment that there is any such thing as respectable sin, or sin that may be condoned because of its social or commercial character. It is not well even for the evangelistic preacher to deal much with specific sin of any kind, but rather to show the secrecy and subtlety of all sin, the inward guilt which corrupts the whole nature, the unclean motives by which all sinners are exercised, and the offense to an infinitely holy God of any spirit or practice which is contrary to His most holy law.

In like manner the grace of Christ must be shown as

necessary for all kinds of sinners, and as abundantly sufficient for them all. The preacher must never depart from his position that nothing else can change a man's nature, and make him sober, clean, honest, and true. It is by such methods that sin is exposed and the conscience is reached, and it must all be done by frequent reference to the testimony of the Holy Scripture, the "Thus saith the Lord" of the inviolable Word.

II. Evangelistic sermons should be positively instructive. We have already foreshadowed this remark, but we mean something more than that which we have already said. They are not to be polemic or apologetic. In this sense they should not be argumentative. The only argument which they present should be personal and pressing, moving at once to action. But for the most part they should be occupied with the explanation of Scripture. Such are the soul-winning sermons of Spurgeon to which we have referred: they are properly expository. Dr. Louis A. Banks, in a chapter in Dr. Torrey's book already referred to, gives doubtful advice when he says, "It is a common thing for the great evangelists, and the ministers who have great success in winning men to Christ, to be criticized by the so-called eloquent and profound preachers who never have any revivals of their own as being only story-tellers and not being strong preachers. This is all nonsense." We do not think, however, that it is so great nonsense as Dr. Banks imagines. He says a sermon is strong only when it is powerful to produce the effect for which a sermon is made. Very true. But by what means does a sermon preached by a pastor to his regular congregation become powerful to produce the effect for which it is made? Dr. Patterson, who certainly has had "revivals of his own," says with regard to this matter, "What is evangelistic preaching, or what does it mean to do the work of an evangelist? It is not being able to tell anecdotes in an interesting manner or to clothe stories with beautiful language; but it is the presenting of the truth to men in such a way that they will see themselves as sinners, and then presenting Christ to them as the Savior of sinners in such a way that they will receive him as their personal Savior and thus be saved."

The pastor addresses his evangelistic sermons to the intelligence of thinking people, and in order to reach them he must define and explain the teaching of the Word of God. This must be illustrated from history and experience, from the events of actual life, but beyond all, the pastor must rest his case on the presentation of the doctrines set forth in the Word of God. His people must feel that behind every appeal are weighty and well-considered reasons, and that they have been made to understand the divine philosophy of guilt, penalty, and pardon.

III. The evangelistic sermon must be exceeding simple. If there is a tendency upon the part of the preacher sometimes to deal with abstruse themes, nothing of the sort must appear when he attempts to bring men to an immediate decision for Christ. Gypsy Smith has remarked that we are sometimes "more intent upon saying the smart thing than the saving thing." In the evangelistic sermon we must resist with more vehemence than at any other time the disposition to say the smart thing. We must be determined to say nothing but the saving thing, and that in the plainest possible terms. Dr. Banks well says with regard to this, "No man who wants immediate effect in the conversion of sinners ought ever to say anything in a sermon that a boy, ten years old, brought up in a Christian family, would not easily comprehend." He likens the preacher to a lawyer before a jury on the last day of the trial. His whole desire is to make such an impression on the jury that he may secure the verdict. If he once thinks of his own reputation, or of any future case which he may have with them, he will defeat his own object. He must make the jury understand only the case which is before them, and must not use a single word which may not be comprehended by the simplest mind of the twelve. The minister who is not content to lower the literary or philosophical standards of his sermons in order to win souls to Christ will not be likely to win many.

IV. The evangelistic sermon must be experimental. In preaching it the minister is first of all a witness for Jesus Christ. He speaks because he has himself believed, and found peace and joy in believing. He wishes to lead others to the same Savior whom he has found. He must show them the grip that the truth has upon himself, if he would grip others with it.

Of course, there is a certain danger in this experimental aspect of the evangelistic sermon, because self may be thrust too far to the front, and the preacher's own personality may be made offensive. Some men are too fond of telling of their own conversion, and of the method in which it was wrought, and it is perilous for the preacher to make himself prominent. It may seem to those who hear him to savor of vanity, or even of unreality. So, while the preacher must be a witness and speak of that which he himself has experienced, it must be in such a way as to direct attention to the Savior rather than to himself.

V. Evangelistic sermons may display great variety in form: it will be better for the pastor to cultivate this variety. The narrative sermon, the expository sermon, the doctrinal sermon may all be also evangelistic. The preacher who ministers continuously to one congregation will be likely to exhaust himself if he does not cultivate this variety. Only let him be Scriptural, taking such passages as suggest themselves to him, and treating them evangelistically.

He will find, morever, that his evangelistic sermons will be universally useful. It is a mistake to suppose that they are of benefit only to the unconverted. They invariably minister to the most mature Christians. Sufficient evidence of this is found in the fact that the meetings of revivalists are usually crowded with professing Christians, to such an extent sometimes that they are invited to stay away in order to make room for those who are not Christians.

It is, therefore, of doubtful wisdom, in preaching evangelistic sermons, to address them directly to the unconverted, specifying the class. Preach the evangelistic sermon to all classes: preach to the entire congregation. Some will be aroused; some will be converted; but all will be helped, stimulated, and comforted.

The reason for this is that everything which the Gospel brings to us rests upon our sense of God's grace and mercy in Christ Jesus. We have no hope and no comfort but in this. The hymns which the most experienced Christian loves the best to sing are evangelistic hymns. The texts of Scripture which he most frequently quotes are those which speak of the grace of God in Christ Jesus.

VI. Evangelistic sermons should not always be preached at certain services, the evening service for example, or at times when the unconverted are supposed to be in the majority. While it may be well to preach the larger number at the evening service, they certainly should be preached many times to the morning congregation.

VII. And they should form a large part of the pastor's

preaching work. He should be his own evangelist. If more pastors would cultivate the art of evangelistic preaching, and depend more largely upon their own efforts in this respect, there would be less call for the services of the peripatetic revivalist; there would be more permanent results, and a much larger blessing.

Let the pastor remember, however, that all preachers are not equally gifted in this respect, and all can not expect to have the same success. There is an old story of a certain minister of mature years who was somewhat sharply criticized by a younger brother, who had had considerable success in his evangelistic work, because of his apparent lack in this respect. But the older minister replied to him, "My brother, when the Lord started us upon our mission he gave me a cruse of oil and you a quiver of arrows. Shoot your arrows: I will pour out my oil."

Indeed, one will be the more likely to succeed in winning souls to Christ, provided he has the evangelistic spirit and desire, if he does not take himself too severely to task for his apparent lack of success, because what he should seek for is not mere success, but the glory of the Master. Sometimes there is a temptation upon the part of the minister to seek mere success in winning souls to Christ for the sake of the success or for the sake of his own reputation. Under these circumstances his efforts are likely to be defeated, and his success to be the longer postponed. Let him do his work earnestly, faithfully, and look to the Lord for his blessing. Souls are never won except through the influence of the Holy Spirit of God. Let him use the means which the Holy Spirit is pledged to bless, and rest there. "It is told of a missionary who went to China in the early days of Gospel effort in that country that after some fifteen years

of earnest work he became dicouraged. He wrote home
to his board and to friends who supported him that he
had done his best and preached Christ to the heathen,
but he had become convinced that his ministry was a
failure as he knew of no conversions. The church at
home, however, thought otherwise; it stood by him loyally,
increased his allowance, and wrote urging him to remain
at his post and to continue his faithful labors, which
would be supplemented by the prayers of God's people
at home. Next year, the unexpected happened—the miracle came. Conversions by dozens and scores and hundreds astounded the missionary. His doubts fell away
like an old garment; he saw clearly now that the seed
he had planted and which had been so long in ripening
had come to the harvest and that cumulative blessings
had attended his long and faithful ministry."—*Christian
Herald.*

There is a story of a man who was engaged to hammer upon a rock. He was paid good wages, and his
hours of service were distinctly specified. After a time
the master returned to the workman and found him
sitting idle. "What is the trouble?" inquired the master.
"Oh," said the workman in a tone of despair, "I have
hammered upon the rock a long time, and it does not
break." "Ah!" replied the master, "I did not engage
you to break the rock. I engaged you to hammer on it.
Go to work again."

THE SPECIAL SERMON.

IV.

THE SPECIAL SERMON.

The term defined.

It is produced by

I. Careful selection of texts.

1. Reading large passages of the Bible at one sitting.
2. Devotional literature.
3. Comparison of homiletic ideas with others.

II. Rumination upon the passage.

Special parallel passages.

III. Special arguments and illustrations.

IV. Present and positive helpfulness.

V. Illustrations.   Horace Bushnell.

Textual analysis.

Read Jefferson's "Minister as Prophet," III; Bushnell's "Sermons for the New Life."

IV.

THE SPECIAL SERMON.

This term, the "special sermon," does not mean a sermon for some special occasion, or one of some strange category. It means a sermon in which some special view of the text is obtained, or in which the text is employed with a special application, but it is not implied herein that any other meaning is derived from the text than that which it is plainly intended to convey. In fact the special sermon is one in which the undiscovered beauties of the text are revealed, its hidden meanings, its more remote but more impressive uses. It is a sermon, therefore, which commands special attention, stimulates special inquiry, stirs the conscience to an unusual degree, and proves a positive spiritual power.

Many sermons rehearse the old platitudes in the same old terms for the same old purposes. The superficial truths which lie upon the surface of a given passage, and which are perfectly plain to the simplest minds, are set forth perhaps with considerable emphasis and suitable illustration, but the depth of the passage is not sounded, and its distinctive teaching is scarcely revealed. Such preaching is conventional, humdrum, and uninteresting. To be sure it is very useful; we can not do without it. A large part of the influence which is derived from preaching is connected with such work, but preachers who proceed no further than this will not exert any signal usefulness. This may be the case even when they show great learning, when they exhibit a profound knowledge of history, philosophy, and kindred branches, and yet their preaching may be traditional, formal, and dry. They do not really see the deeper truth, nor are they able to express it. Jesus said of the Pharisees that "seeing they saw not;" he spake to his apostles of "the mysteries of the kingdom of heaven;" he exhorted them to be like householders who brought "forth out of their treasures things new and old." The men who can justly be called "great preachers" have always been those at whose hands the Word of God took on fresh meaning and came with unexpected power. Their hearers were prompted to say, "I never saw that in the text before;" "I never realized what that passage meant." "I have learned a lesson for which I was entirely unprepared." The sermon conveyed the truth to the mind and heart through new avenues, for new uses, to edification, conversion, comfort, and service. It is the sermon that does this which may be called the special sermon.

The special sermon is produced in accordance with the following principles:

I. There must be, first, a skilful selection of the text. This is a very important part of the process. The text must be one which has been brought to the attention of the preacher by his own immediate contact with the Word of God. There must be that view of truth in connection with this passage which enables him to say somewhat after the manner of the Apostle Paul (Gal. 1:11.) "I make known to you, brethren, as touching the Gospel which was preached by me, that it is not after man. For neither did I receive it from man, nor was I taught it; but it came to me through revelation of Jesus Christ."

In such sermons, beyond all others, and particularly beyond all of the conventional kind, the text is the sermon. This truth we have already emphasized; but it receives unusual emphasis in this connection. When the preacher finds such a text, or rather, as we have said before, when such a text finds him, he has also found his special sermon, at least in its incipient stages. This text has found him because it has brought to him something new and peculiarly strong, and when he discourses upon it, if he does so in the proper manner and spirit, that same new and peculiarly strong element in the text which found him will find those to whom the sermon is addressed.

Sometimes so soon as a text takes possession of the mind, the preacher sees a whole sermon in it. It may be that the details are not all apparent to him, but the subject, its main divisions, certain of its leading illustrations, and the particular use which it be made of it, come in one great, over-mastering revelation, and for once, when that sermon is delivered, he will be a preacher indeed.

This is not the case in preaching alone, but in much that is not called preaching which partakes of the same character. Many an address on religious subjects, and particularly many a fine poem or hymn in which spiritual truth has been inculcated, has been stricken off by the author at a single sitting. The very form, as well as the substance of the thought, came to mind in one supreme, composite inspiration. It was so with Julia Ward Howe's "Battle Hymn of the Republic." It was so with Bishop Heber's great missionary hymn, and a multitude of other instances will occur to the reader.

In such a case the text thrusts itself upon the preacher. He does not select it: it has such a grip upon him that he can not shake it off. It has transported him to another scene; it has filled him with a new life; his soul has been refreshed as with heavenly manna; and the message is like fire in the bones. Happy the preacher to whom such experiences are frequent.

But the preacher must put himself in the way of multiplying such experiences. This he may do by schooling himself to be on the alert for the incoming of these special revelations of the deeper meaning of the Word of God.

1. He may read through certain entire books of the Bible at one sitting for homiletical suggestion. It is true, as we have already observed, that the way to obtain texts is in connection with the devotional reading of the Word of God, and it is not intended to set this principle aside. The book should first be read devotionally before it is read for any homiletical purpose, and when it is read with a view to the homiletical suggestions which it may contain, the homiletical intention is not to be emphasized by the preacher, and scarcely to come into mind. What we intend to imply is this, that a poor way to find texts is to turn over the leaves of the Bible, hoping to have the eye fall some passage which shall present itself to the mind in passing as a suitable text. Put the homiletical intention aside, and yet put it where it may be, so to speak, upon call. Then read an extended passage, an entire book for example, and note the texts that suggest themselves to the mind, whether it be emphatically or not. Nothing of any great importance may be derived from a single reading of this kind. No matter. Much of vast importance to the preacher may result at some other time, but by such a handling of the Word of God the preacher puts himself into the way of texts finding him for special purposes.

2. The same thing may be done with religious books, particularly devotional books, and religious poetry. Considerable importance is to be attached to the value of

fugitive poetry. It has this much at least in its favor that it is generally applicable to the present season and to present conditions. The preacher should always scan very carefully all the little poems that are found in his religious periodicals. The vast majority of them he may reject, but among them he will occasionally find some rare gem of spiritual expression out of which will come homiletical suggestions of immense value.

3. The preacher should take as frequent opportunity as possible to hear the sermons of other men. He should also be a reader of sermons. This is because every good sermon has its undeveloped side lines, perhaps barely suggested, and yet in these suggestions may be wrapped up much that will furnish him unusual thought. The preacher should frequently exchange homiletical ideas with other preachers. Much time might be given to such work which in ministerial associations is consumed with the discussion of abstract themes.

In this way special sermons are invited, if not at least created, and it must be apparent that this is a very different method from that of the man, who searches for fanciful texts, treats them in a sensational way, and looks for such results as a special knowledge and treatment of the Word of God alone will furnish.

II. When the text has presented itself to the preacher's mind in the way which has been indicated, let him ruminate upon it for a while. Let him look all about his text to begin with; let him study it in its immediate and remote context; let him consult the passages parallel to the text, and do such other work as has been already suggested. This work takes on a new form in connection with the special sermon. The preacher having obtained a special view of the particular text will connect that special view with the context and with the parallel passages.

The same light which has been shed upon this passa
will illuminate other passages also.

In this way the preacher will be the more likely
find that distinctive teaching which makes the spec
sermon what it is. It is special because he has discover
in the passage that which is not to be found in a
other passage of Scripture whatsoever. It has somethi
peculiar to itself. The view which he has obtained
a kind of "perspective" view, an oblique view, where
the ordinary sermon upon this text approaches it on
from the ordinary direction, and sees only its "façad
as it is ordinarily presented to the observer.

III. As it is with the context and with the paral
passages, so it will be with all the material of whi
this sermon is composed. The arguments which a
employed will be special arguments, the illustrations w
be special illustrations. Everything which enters in
the composition of the sermon will be of the same grad
The sermon indeed should not be finally completed un
such special material has been obtained. It is sure
come if the preacher will be diligent and patient. A
when it does come it will repay all of his work a
waiting.

IV. Finally, a special sermon is not to be tested a
judged by what may appear to be its originality or an
thing of the kind, but by its present and positive hel
fulness. Will it really give those to whom it is address
a more profound sense of their need, their sin and the
portion in Jesus Christ? Will it bring to them unusu
help, or unusual comfort? Will there be an urgen
in it which is not commonly connected with the preache
work?

V. A few illustrations of texts and subject of
special character may be given in closing this chapt
The best example of the use of the special serm

known to the writer is Horace Bushnell. He has exerted an unparalleled homiletical influence upon the American pulpit. There are many quotations in common use among ministers to-day, who are ignorant of their source. The following are illustrations: Is. 45:5, "I girded thee, though thou hast not known me." Bushnell's subject is "Every Man's Life a Plan of God." Matt. 25:28, "Take therefore the talent from him." Subject, "The Capacity of Religion Extirpated by Disuse." Heb. 7:16, "Who is made, not after the law of a carnal commandment, but after the power of an endless life." Subject, "The Power of an Endless Life." Luke 9:13, "But he said unto them, Give ye them to eat." Subject, "Duty Not Measured by Our Own Ability."

It will certainly be seen that Bushnell has derived from these texts no subjects that are not absolutely true to their original meaning, but they are such subjects as would not occur to the average preacher. Yet the average preacher can learn somewhat of the art by taking lessons from such preachers as Bushnell. Watkinson is not far behind him. To some of his subjects we have already referred.

Sometimes the special subject appears from an examination of the text in the original, when it could not possibly appear if the preacher confined himself to the English translation. Textual analysis, as we have seen is the most prolific source of such sermons. The fourth chapter of John in its account of the Savior's interview with the woman of Samaria, uses the word "well" five times. We have observed that when the Savior uses the word he uses a different term in the original from that which the woman of Samaria employs. ($\pi\eta\gamma\dot\eta$ and $\phi\rho\dot\epsilon\alpha\rho$.) The difference in the two terms gives the foundation for a special sermon.

Rev. 22:2, (see also Ezekiel 47:12), "The leaves

of the tree were for the healing of the nations." The original shows that there was a use for the fruit and a use also for the leaves, but the word "healing" in the original is θεραπεία, which is always used in the Greek in a medicinal sense. Here is a suggestion for a special sermon upon the effects and influence of the Gospel. Body and soul; leaves and fruit. It is this special study of special texts which yields special homiletical results for the careful student.

THE DOCTRINAL SERMON.

THE DOCTRINAL SERMON.

I. Its supreme importance.

II. What is a doctrinal sermon?

Negatively.

    1. Not an exposition of one or more doctrines.

    2. Not the proclamation of one doctrine to the exclusion of others.

    3. Not the presentation of the entire aspect of any doctrine.

Positively:

    1. That which sets forth truth.

    2. The distinctive truth of revelation.

    3. For purposes of edification.

III. How prepared.

    1. Select a text which presents truth rather than duty.

    2. Be governed by the text and subject.

Read Broadus, Part I, Chap. III.

V.

THE DOCTRINAL SERMON.

The doctrinal sermon is the culmination and crown of all sermonizing. Those sermons which are distinguished by other names may be somewhat doctrinal in character, but the sermon to which we refer as a doctrinal sermon is that in which the doctrinal character is pre-eminent. On the other hand the doctrinal sermon may partake of narration, exposition, and evangelism, and still be a doctrinal sermon because this is its distinguishing characteristic.

I. Note first its supreme importance. It is of the very highest rank: there is nothing beyond it. With this all the best modern authorities upon the subject of homiletics are agreed. This is because it has to do with those sublime revelations which God has made to man. It does not present our own speculations or theorizings. It is not the product of our own reasoning, but it is the result of the profound study of the mysteries of the kingdom of heaven as set forth in the Word of God.

All the great preachers of the Christian Church, beginning with the Apostle Paul himself, have been doctrinal preachers. If the student desires illustration of the method he has but to turn to one or more of the following: Spurgeon, Chalmers, Bishop Simpson, Bishop McIlvaine, Phillips Brooks, John M. Mason, Francis L. Patton, Benjamin M. Palmer, or others like them.

No other preaching has such permanent effects.

Other kinds may result in temporary excitement and produce temporary influence, which for the time being may seem to surpass that which is produced by the doctrinal sermon; but it is this which effects thought, determines policy, settles the creed of the church, and changes the currents of history.

In the last analysis, indeed, there are only two kinds of preaching and two kinds of preachers—the ordinary and the extraordinary. There are two homiletical levels related to each other as two great plateaus upon the earth's surface. They have their own elevations and depressions, but the highest point of the one is very far below the lowest point of the second. This higher level is unquestionably doctrinal. It resembles the plains of Thibet which are called the "roof of the world," and this is the roof of homiletics. On this high level stand the great doctrinal preachers. Such preachers may not always preach distinctively doctrinal sermons. They may not usually do so, but all their preaching is affected by their homiletical altitude.

II. What then is a doctrinal sermon? While its high place is generally recognized by the best modern authorities, and earnest exhortation is given with regard to it, there are substantially no rules offered for its production. Men who enter the pulpit are not adequately trained in this matter, consequently they are the subjects of some serious misconceptions in consequence of which they fail to produce that for which they strive.

1. Let it be understood that the doctrinal sermon is not the exposition of one or more doctrines, however, important they may be. It is not a theological treatise, and, therefore, it is not accomplished when one selects a given doctrine, determines to preach upon it, and prepares it after strictly theological formularies. Such a

plan is more apt to defeat the preacher's purpose than to accomplish it. Often the hardest thing which the young preacher has to learn is to avoid this theological method. This is not strange; because so long as he is in the theological seminary he is very subject to it, and it requires some experience and practice before he is able to escape from its shackles. When he attempts to preach a doctrinal sermon he uses technical terms and conventional phrases, and seems to think it important to set forth his dogma in its various relations to other dogmas after the manner of systematic theology. It is no wonder that such a method awakens some animosity in those upon whom it is practised, and leads to the expression of dislike for doctrinal sermons.

Theology, of course, is of the utmost importance in order to the preparation of such a sermon. One can never become a doctrinal preacher without it. But a theological treatise is no more doctrinal preaching than the suitable mixture of colors is painting, or a proper arrangement of light and shade drawing, a book on logarithms, astronomy, or a course in anatomy the sum total of medical practice.

Theology is the tool, not the product. It is related to the preacher as botany is related to the florist, tactics to the soldier, and political economy to the statesman. Just as an expository sermon is not an exhibition of exegesis, so also a doctrinal sermon is not the presentation of systematic theology. Theology "theological,"—as it has been styled—is not preachable. However, good and important it may be it is of man, while doctrine is of God; just as geology is of man, while the rocks are of God.

2. Neither is the doctrinal sermon one in which a single doctrine is proclaimed to the exclusion of others.

This also is a frequent source of embarrassment to the preacher. He imagines that it is the doctrine found in the text which governs the sermon. He imagines that in order to be truly doctrinal he must confine himself entirely to that one particular doctrine. Such, indeed, may be the case if no other doctrine is suggested in the text, but only in that case will he follow such a rule. Indeed, it will be better for him not to follow the rule at all, and not to have any respect to the doctrine in its theological form while the sermon is being prepared or delivered. He must be governed by the passage and by the sermon subject derived from it, just as he is governed in the other kinds of sermons which we have considered. It may be that a number of doctrines will present themselves without impairing the unity of his sermon, in which case he will give each its proper place as demanded by the sermonic treatment of his text.

3. Nor is it important that the entire aspect of any doctrine should be presented, nor the entire aspect of any set of doctrines. He is not called upon to co-ordinate them or to show their mutual relations.

4. Nor is it important for him to defend the doctrine in an apologetic or polemic manner. Instruction should be his object, and not primarily the defense of the truth against those who hold to error—except on very special occasions.

In brief, everything is a misconception in which the emphasis is placed upon the doctrinal idea rather than upon the sermonic idea. The doctrinal sermon is first of all a sermon, after that it is a doctrinal sermon.

To answer the question positively, we should say a doctrinal sermon is one which sets forth the distinctive truths of revelation to the edification of those that hear. Let us note the separate points in this definition.

1. "Truths." Truths rather than duties. The Shorter Catechism in answer to the question, "What do the Scriptures principally teach?" replies, "The Scriptures principally teach what man is to believe concerning God, and what duty God requires of man." This answer combines truth with duty, but "What man is to believe concerning God" is prior to "What duty God requires of man." Truth has the precedence. It is more important to understand truth than to know duty, but it requires more careful study to apprehend the truth, and greater skill to present it. Therefore the doctrinal sermon is superior in quality to the practical or experimental.

If, then, truth has the right of way in a doctrinal sermon rather than duty, the truth should be to the fore. The sermon as we have indicated may be expository, evangelistic or biographical, but the important truth of the Word of God is to be placed in the stronger light, and is to receive the special emphasis.

2. "The distinctive truths of revelation." That is to say the truths which are peculiar to revelation. That is not a doctrinal sermon which discourses upon truth derived from any other quarter than the word of God. The preacher may be very faithful to truth, and present very much of it, without being a doctrinal preacher.

One was asked concerning a certain minister, recently set over an important congregation, as to the character of his preaching. The reply was in these words, "He preaches truth, but not *the* truth." It is THE truth which makes the doctrinal sermon. "Things which eye saw not, and ear heard not, and which entered not into the heart of man," but that which is the exclusive property of the Holy Scriptures. Such truth it is the purpose of the doctrinal sermon to commend and to explain.

3. "To edification." To instruction, indeed, but not to mere instruction. Because the pulpit is not a professor's desk nor a lecturer's platform. It is the throne of the ambassador of Jesus Christ, where the preacher in the name of Christ, cheers, counsels, and stimulates the people of Christ, warns and wins the erring. Nothing is so effective for these purposes as the distinctive truths of the word of God. Says Phillips Brooks: "Preach doctrine, preach all the doctrine that you know, and learn for ever more and more, but preach it always—not that men may simply believe it, but that they may be saved in believing it."

III. What plan shall be pursued in preparing the doctrinal sermon?

1. Select a text which sets forth truth rather than duty. The subject may be the same in two different texts, while one will be adapted to the doctrinal use and the other to the evangelistic use. For example, 1 John 1:9, "If we confess our sins, He is faithful and righteous to forgive us our sins, and to cleanse us from all unrighteousness." And Matt. 3:2, "Repent ye; for the kingdom of heaven is at hand." The subject is the same in both texts, but the truth preponderates in the first and duty in the second. A sermon upon the first text should be doctrinal; a sermon upon the second text should be evangelistic. And so also with the doctrinal sermon as compared with other kinds of sermons which we have considered.

2. The text having been selected, the preacher is to be governed by the text no matter what his theological conception of the form of the doctrine contained in it may be, and this will appear in his subject, his divisions, and his application. His subject will not be stated in the doctrinal term which he has in mind in connection

with his text, unless that term itself appears in the text. His statement of his divisions will be governed by the same rule. His theological studies will be of special help to him in this particular, but they will be only as instruments which shall not themselves appear in the finished product. His theology will be the grist, the sermon will be the fine flour, ground, bolted, and purified.

We do not mean to indicate in this that technical terms are never to be employed, but that they should not form the staple of the discourse. Sometimes it is well to emply a technical term in order to teach those who listen its meaning and its place in doctrinal thinking, but ordinarily technicalities are to be avoided. So also with regard to the application. The preacher has been engaged with truth, but his application is not in this form, "Such then is the truth," nor even in this form, "Such is the very truth of God," provided nothing more be added. This would be distinctly to violate the maxim of Phillips Brooks. But the application is rather, "This is God's truth to you and for you, for your counsel, your comfort, your warning, and your hope." The application is for the heart more than for the head, though the heart is reached through the head. It is for the conscience and for the life.

If the preacher proceeds upon this plan he will find that the most abstruse doctrines, and even those that are sometimes considered the most obnoxious, will hold in themselves the most precious comfort for the people of God, and the most decided impulse for those who have not yet received the Savior. This is where the trained theologian has the superiority over those who have not received a suitable education. In the course of his training he begins with Scripture in Scripture form. He proceeds thence to theology. But from his theology he returns again to Scripture in Scripture form, and presents the doctrines concerning which he has studied, after the example of the ancient prophets, the apostles of the Savior, and Jesus Christ Himself. What has he gained from his study of theology? Anything in addition to Scripture truth? No, by no means; but very much more of that very truth, knowledge of terms and propositions, knowledge of proportions and relations.

The subject is well illustrated by the remarkable advance which has been made in present-day methods of farming. At first the old-time farmer, who had learned but little concerning his own work from books, was suspicious with regard to the training given in certain schools and colleges. Agricultural chemistry seemed to him unprofitable and foolish. At first he was loath to have his boys lose the time that was necessary to take such a course of training. But he has learned better in recent days. Agricultural chemistry has come to stay; and no one rejoices in it more heartily than the old-time farmer himself. His boys grow up upon the farm; they proceed thence to the agricultural college. They study the nature of soils, fertilizers, nitrates, and the like. Then they return to nature in natural forms again. They come back to the farm and are farmers worthy of the name. They work scientifically and methodically. The old folks' fields produce twenty-five and even fifty per cent. more than they did formerly, and the product is of a superior quality. So it is with theological training.

THE ILLUSTRATED SERMON.

THE ILLUSTRATED SERMON.

A pictorial age.
   The magic lantern.
I. The Illustrated Sermon not substantially different from others.
II. Rules for illustrations.
   1. They must be dignified.
   2. Simple.
   3. Made for this one purpose.
   4. Not shown until needed.
   5. Used for illustrative purposes only.
   6. Not exhausted at once.
   7. Sermonic.
III. Materials employed.

VI.

THE ILLUSTRATED SERMON.

We do not refer in this title to verbal illustration, but to visible, to that which is addressed to the eye rather than to the ear, and to that which is ordinarily known as "object illustration." It may be a map, chart, picture, or material of any suitable kind by which the mind is assisted in apprehending the truth by means of the concrete.

This is a pictoral age. The facility with which illustrations are produced and reproduced have multiplied them to such an extent that our daily papers are filled with them, and even an advertisement is scarcely complete without their use. It would seem, therefore, that they may well be employed in pulpit work. Indeed, there is considerable in the line of preaching which can not be well done without such helps. This is generally admitted with regard to addresses of another character. The magic lantern, for example, employs the results of photographic art to a great extent and has come into very general use, and there are few who essay to appear before the public in the rôle of lecturers who think of doing so without its aid. There are some ministers, indeed, who seem to think that it is every way proper to introduce the magic lantern into their regular Sunday services, but it is a very serious question whether this is either proper or profitable. It appears to the writer to savor too much of the spectacular, to divert the attention of the people, and to turn what should be the solemn worship of Almighty God into a kind of a show. The magic lantern may well be employed in the informal exercises of the congregation and upon a week-day evening. It is invaluable in connection with the work of missions, and other kindred subjects, but it does not seem to be in place in the stated Sunday services of a congregation. The objections that seem to obtain with regard to the use of the lantern, however, do not hold with regard to other pictorial illustrations which are used without the darkening of the room, and those other accessories which are necessary to the use of the magic lantern. Such illustrations, however, are very seldom employed. This may be because the preacher is ignorant of the proper method both in preparing and utilizing them. It may be because of a certain timidity which he suffers with regard to a process which he has never employed; a dread of the unusual; or perhaps the wholesome fear of being regarded as sensational. But such illustrations may be employed with entire success and absolute propriety. The method of preparation is not hard to learn, nor is the efficient use of them difficult to attain. Some suggestions are, therefore, given with regard to the preparation and use of illustrated sermons.

1. In general. The illustrated sermon does not differ materially from any other sermon. It is prepared in very much the same way. But when it is finished the preacher finds that the illustrations which he has sought to convey in mere words would be much more effective if concrete objects were employed. He therefore makes use of such objects in order the more clearly to set forth to the eye that which can not fully or precisely be conveyed to the ear.

The sermon, therefore, is not arranged for the sake

of the illustrations, but the illustrations are arranged for the sake of the sermon. Herein some are very likely to go astray, especially in connection with the use of illustrations which are furnished to the preacher ready made. This mistake is most likely to occur in connection with the use of magic lantern slides. Very few preachers can prepare such slides themselves, and must depend upon those which are bought from the dealers. The address which accompanies them must be arranged with reference to the material. The pictures thereby become the chief element in the discourse and the service degenerates into a mere entertainment. But when the illustrations are, in a certain sense, the aftergrowth of sermon work, the meretricious features are absolutely removed. The sermon is prepared with sole reference to the truth contained in the passage of Scripture which is being expounded. The illustrations are subsequently found and arranged in their proper place. Sometimes it may be necessary to rearrange the sermonic material in order to obtain the proper relation between the thought and the illustration, but such rearrangement does not violate the general principle.

II. In particular the following rules should be observed.

1. The illustrations should be entirely dignified. They should be of such a character as to accord with the divine truth elaborated by the preacher. What has been already said with regard to the quality of verbal illustrations applies equally with regard to visible ones.

2. They should be simple. The idea of mere ornament should be entirely excluded. It is not even necessary that they should be well executed, according to the artist's standard. If a map is exhibited it may be very crude and imperfect, but if it serve its purpose it is as well

for the sermon as though it were the work of an experienced draftsman. So also with regard to charts or pictures of any kind. Many ministers are doubtless deterred from using such things because they are not experienced draftsmen, and they hesitate to place before an audience that which has no artistic merit whatsoever. The force and beauty of the illustration, however, for such purposes does not consist in its artistic beauty, but in its adaptation to the purposes of illustration.

3. Such illustrations should be made by the preacher himself, or by some one under his immediate direction. Each illustration should be made for the single sermon with which it is to be employed, and should rarely be applicable to any other sermon. Many times it will be better for purposes of illustration if the map or chart be made in the sight of the people, and while the sermon is being delivered. This, however, might occupy too much time or prove only a source of embarrassment to the preacher. Such being the case his illustrations may be prepared in advance.

The reason why he should make them himself, or have them made under his immediate direction, is in order that they may show nothing more than that which he proposes to use. A standard map, for example, is of very little service to the one who knows how to prepare a map for special use. It contains too much. It may give emphasis to the very thing which the preacher desires to obscure, or fail to emphasize that upon which the preacher places the most emphasis. The map prepared by the minister himself will show no more than he wishes to treat in his sermon, and such other points as may be necessary to indicate relations. A map of Palestine exhibiting all its scenes—such as cities, rivers, mountains and plains, which are mentioned in the four

Gospels would be most inappropriate to the preacher's use if he were discussing some scene in early apostolic history. Suppose, for example, he desires to show the movement of the apostles when they were scattered abroad after the persecution following the death of Stephen. This will include the departure of Philip to Samaria, and his journey thence to the south where he fell in with the Ethiopian, and thence his removal to Azotus and to Cæsarea. Perhaps he desires to show in addition the movement of the Apostle Peter, who followed Philip to Samaria and afterward came to Lydda, Joppa, and Cæsarea. It will be seen that they journeyed in very nearly the same course to the same city of Cæsarea. The preacher will prepare a special map in which their respective journeys will be traced in suitable colors, say, for example, Philip's with a blue line, and Peter's with a red line. Very little appears upon the map in addition to the places which have been mentioned, and the map covers no other section of the country than that which is embraced in this particular history. This map will serve a purpose altogether different from any standard map and be of manifestly greater service. The same principle applies to all the illustrations which are used.

4. The illustrations should not be shown until they are needed in the development of the discourse; otherwise they will distract attention and anticipate the development of the preacher's thought. They should be exhibited in connection with that portion of the sermon which refers to them. The provision required for this purpose will appear further on.

5. The illustrations should be used for illustrative purposes only. They should not be displayed merely to catch the eye, or to furnish some attractive addition; but they should be for the positive enrichment of the

thought, its illumination and addition, just as in the case of verbal illustrations.

6. The illustrations should not be exhausted at once, but used at intervals throughout the sermon. Of course, there may be occasions when only one illustration is employed, and when the preacher desires to use it but for a moment, but he will find that ordinarily when he needs such illustrations at all he will need more than one. It is better that it should be so. They are not to be shown in advance and the audience informed that their use will appear later on, but they are to be used and used again as the necessity of the sermon requires. If a single illustration is shown its separate features are to be reserved for the proper time in like manner.

7. The illustrations should be used for sermonic purposes. The most difficult part of the art lies just here. It is quite easy for the preacher to learn to use these illustrations for narrative purposes, for the explanation of geographical, political, or social features in his discourse, but it is not easy for him to learn to make illustrations which shall themselves convey, in connection with the truth which is discussed, a useful, spiritual lesson. Yet this may be done with even so simple a thing as a map. Take, for example, the text found in 1 Sam. 14:23, "So Jehovah saved Israel that day: and the battle passed over by Bethaven." This verse closes the history of Jonathan's remarkable victory at Michmash. He and his armor-bearer descended into the deep ravine which separated the army of Saul from the army of the Philistines. Jonathan had said to him, "Come, and let us go over unto the garrison of these uncircumcised: it may be that Jehovah will work for us; for there is no restraint to Jehovah to save by many or by few." Jehovah did work for them. They climbed up the steep

cliff upon the other side, showed themselves to the garrison of the Philistines, succeeded in accomplishing their alarm and flight. King Saul, perceiving from a distance what had been done, led his army to the assistance of Jonathan and his armor-bearer. The rout of the Philistines was complete; they fled in confusion. So says the text, "Jehovah saved Israel that day: and the battle passed over by Bethaven." A suitable map will show the situation. It must be a physical map, very plainly exhibiting the elevations and depressions of the country, the great central ridge between the Jordan and the Mediterranean, the chasm which Jonathan and his armor-bearer crossed, and the relative positions of Michmash, Geba, and Bethaven. But the whole force of the text resides in the words "passed over," "the battle *passed over* by Bethaven." The map will show that Michmash and Geba are upon one side of the central ridge. Bethaven is on the other side. The Israelites chased the Philistines over the ridge, pursued them down the hillside to their own country. It was a down-hill battle. It proved to be a decisive victory. The spiritual lesson is plain, and is made the more so by the map. The map itself conveys a spiritual lesson because there may be a time in the life of any man when he obtains the upper hand of his spiritual enemies. It is when in all weakness he determines to give them battle. When he does so with the same faith which Jonathan exercised then it is that the same thing is accomplished in his life which was accomplished in the history of Israel. He obtains a decisive victory; the battle passes over the central ridge, and becomes for him forever after a downhill fight with sin.

It sometimes occurs with the preacher that he desires to use an illustration which might produce an unhappy effect upon the audience if it were presented by itself without suitable introduction. A certain preacher upon one occasion was speaking of the influence of Christianity in the households of the Roman emperors. He desired to refer to certain discoveries made in recent years in the explorations on the site of the imperial palaces. One of these was a certain "graffito" scratched into the plaster on the walls of a room occupied by the pages in attendance upon the Emperor Claudius. He occupied some time in telling the congregation about these discoveries. He said that the one to which he was about to refer would be quite shocking if its character was not well known in advance. He explained that all sorts of slanders were charged against those early Christians, some of them being sacreligious and scurrilous. They were accused, for example, of worshiping a white donkey. He then said that he was about to show them a copy of this particular picture, and that they would observe that while it represented a donkey nailed to a cross, yet it was proof positive that in the very palace of Claudius the crucified Savior was adored. All this was done with the greatest care, and when the chart upon which the picture had been reproduced was exhibited the audience was solemnized to the last degree. It represented a man with the head of a donkey stretched upon a cross. One of the young pages of Claudius appears before it, his hands raised in the attitude of adoration, and beneath it are scratched the words "Αλεξαμινος σεβετε Θεον" —"Alexaminos worships his God." Such an illustration as this must be very carefully prepared in advance, but it is evident that it will minister some strength and beauty to all which the minister may offer in connection with it.

III. In order to the preparation of such illustrations

certain materials may be suggested as the most suitable to be employed. The paper should be that which is known as "detail paper." It is usually cream colored, heavy, and tough, so that it is not easily torn. It has the quality of what is known as "laid" paper, that is to say there is no gloss to it, by which the light is objectionably reflected. It comes in large rolls of various widths. The preacher can obtain it of such a width as suits his purpose. If paper is employed which comes only in sheets it must be pasted together both horizontally and perpendicularly. On this account it will not roll well, but will buckle and wrinkle. Detail paper may be cut to any desired length and pasted only horizontally, removing the objections of which we have spoken. This paper may be mounted upon a large spring roller such as is employed in hanging shades in large windows. It should be so prepared as that it may be easily placed in the roller or removed from it. The roller brackets may be fastened permanently in a suitable place, and the roller taken down when not in use. After the chart has been prepared and placed in the roller it is rolled up out of sight and may be drawn down when desired.

The colors to be employed are ordinary fresco colors. These are soluble in water and are very cheap. They should be mixed with a little mucilage or glue to insure their adherence to the paper, but if too much glue be employed the color will flake off. A number of paint brushes of different sizes should be procured, one of them a large, flat camel's hair brush to be used in blending the colors when that becomes necessary. If the preacher desires to prepare a picture of some kind this may best be done with ordinary charcoal crayons, as they are easily brushed off the paper if a mistake be made in the drawing. When the picture is complete the charcoal may be permanently fastened to the paper by spraying it with dilute shellac. Special atomizers for this purpose are for sale at all artists' material stores.

The preacher may sometimes use the blackboard to great advantage, especially when he desires to draw his chart in the presence of the congregation. He should have a number of colored crayons. The best for his purpose are known as "exhibitors' crayons." They are square, about an inch in diameter and three inches long, and come in all colors. The colors are not to be employed on the blackboard for the sake of ornament, but only when the distinction between one line and another is to be observed. If the preacher finds himself very incapable with regard to this work he may procure a pantograph of large size, with arms three to five feet long. The salesman will show him how to use it, and by its means a very complete reproduction of the picture or chart which he desires to make can be obtained, enlarged to any desirable size.

With regard, however, to this matter of visible illustration it should be said that, while the writer has considered that this subject should be included in this work, it can not be thoroughly taught without a living teacher. So much depends upon the proper handling of material, that the preacher who desires to become proficient in such matters should not rest content with what he may learn from books, but should seek the advice and assistance of one who has attained success in this work.

SERMONS IN COURSES.

SERMONS IN COURSES.

"Series" and "Course."

Special value in systematic instruction.

I. Requirements.
  1. Unity in the entire course.
  2. Positive advance.
  3. Each sermon complete in itself.
    Diagrams.

II. Subjects.
  One course related to another.

VII.

SERMONS IN COURSES.

The delivery of a number of sermons under one general title is commonly known as "Serial Preaching." But we should distinguish at the outset between a "series" and a "course." By a "series of sermons" is meant a succession of sermons upon separate themes, in mechanical order and with a very loose relation, if any, to each other. By a "course of sermons" is meant a succession of sermons upon one comprehensive subject, in logical order and with an intimate relation to each other.

There is no call for special instruction with regard to the composition of a "series." Each separate sermon is prepared upon the principles governing single sermon construction.

But the construction of a "course" requires special skill; because in addition to the principles governing the single sermon, there are others which govern the relation of the sermons to each other, their distinct character, their combined effects, and their cumulative influence.

This subject has received next to no consideration by homiletical authorities, and the writer is unable to refer the reader to more than a few scattered and unsatisfactory paragraphs.

And yet it is a subject of great inportance. If the chief element in sermonizing is instruction, it can not be adequately supplied by a succession of sermons which have no connection with each other, in which the preacher passes by abrupt transition from one topic to another, and in which, as is sometimes said, the one "drives out" the other.

Such a course of instruction would be considered the height of folly in a secular school. Students might thereby come into the possession of many disjointed facts; but they would acquire no genuine knowledge and no real discipline.

Even so in the pulpit. If the people are to be taught the things of God preaching must follow a plan. The preacher, even when he does not formerly announce a course of sermons, should proceed according to a definite system, and frequently be engaged in what is really a course of spiritual instruction, though he may not advertise the fact in any way. Such a course may be, for example, doctrinal. Once in two weeks, let us say, he will deliver a sermon upon this plan. What is called "Theology," "Anthropology," "Soteriology," and so on will be taken up in order. It will be of great advantage to the preacher himself. It will promote careful and consecutive study; it will enrich his own mind and heart and it will thereby affect favorably all his other preaching. It will also be of great advantage to his people; it will sustain their interest; suitably indoctrinate them; and safeguard them against many evils and mistakes into which the uninstructed Christian is prone to fall.

The same advantages will appear in connection with formal courses of sermons, duly announced as such. It is with these that we deal particularly in the present chapter.

I. What is required in order to the construction of a course of sermons? We answer, The same qualities in the course, as such, which should obtain in a separate and single sermon.

1. There must be unity. There should be a real relation between the separate subjects and between them and the general subject. The general subject must be inclusive of the separate subjects. The discussion of the separate subjects must be kept absolutely subservient to the discussion of the main subject. This must be made clear from start to finish. The general subject must ever be given the greater prominence. It has been chosen because of its wider range and more comprehensive character, and because it can not be adequately discussed in a single sermon. The single sermons are but parts of the whole. They bear the same relation to it that the divisions of a separate sermon bear to its subject. Therefore they must have the same character. They must coordinate and combine, so that, when completed the result is itself a single, complete, symmetrical whole.

2. There must be progress. The second sermon must be a positive advance upon the first, and so on. A broader, better view of the general subject should be obtained with each successive sermon. If it is not so the "course" is only a "series" after all, and there is no reason in it. In order to such progress there must be careful prevision. Anticipation should be much more carefully guarded than in the composition of a single sermon. The balance of thought must be maintained—not too much ground in this sermon and too little in that. There should be an eye to reserve—the withholding of material for its suitable logical place.

And yet this progress must be of a peculiar kind. It is not that something is added, sermon to sermon; more taught and advance made; but

3. Each separate sermon must be in a measure complete in itself. It is part of a whole, yet it is a whole part. As in a wagon the wheel is only a part, yet the

wheel is a complete thing. Do not show it with the tire lacking or some of the spokes missing. He who hears but one of the sermons of a course should carry away a distinct idea of some aspect of truth. The preacher must finish up as he goes on. A course of sermons is not one long sermon divided into separate portions so that it resembles a serial story in a magazine—"To be continued in our next." The preacher should not say "We arrest our studies at this point and continue next Sunday." On the contrary he finishes this sermon to-night. Next Sunday's sermon will be found to include it, go beyond and also finish; and so on to the end.

This may all be illustrated by means of diagrams:

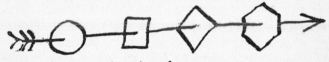

A series of sermons.

A course on the wrong plan.

A course on the right plan.

It is no easy task to construct a course of sermons possessing these qualities. The difficulties increase with the number of sermons, and in almost geometrical proportion. It is twice as hard to prepare a course of two sermons as to prepare a single sermon. But it is four times as hard to prepare a course of four sermons as a course of two. The adjustments require much study. It may be necessary to revise the plan again and again; but the course should not be announced before it is matured, and should not be brought into the pulpit until the sermons have all been fully planned.

II. Subjects. The general subjects for sermons in courses are manifold. They correspond closely to those which we have considered. They may be narrative, expository, evangelistic, and so on. Only they should not be mixed. This would be to destroy the unity of the course. If the general subject, for example, be narrative, let the course be narrative throughout.

A course of sermons, however, furnishes opportunity for great variety within these bounds. If the course is narrative, each separate sermon may proceed along its own special line and the unity of the entire course be all the more emphatic and beautiful. There is more room for analysis. The Bible character or scene employed may be viewed from different sides for different purposes. This will render the instruction all the more interesting and complete.

Take, for example, a course upon Nehemiah. The preacher might proceed on the lines of the consecutive historical events and, let us say, announce his subjects as follows: I. "The Persian Court." II. "Defenseless Jerusalem." III. "The Rebuilding of the Walls." IV. "Ezra and the Law." V. "The Progress of Reform." This would be instructive and profitable. But how much more so would be such an arrangement of subjects as would set forth the distinctive traits in the character of Nehemiah and his peculiar qualifications for his great work, as follows: I. "Nehemiah's Training in Administrative Affairs." II. "Nehemiah's Spiritual Life." (His frequent prayers, etc.) III. "Nehemiah and the Law." IV. "Nehemiah and the Sabbath."

There are many other general subjects which may be used. The distinct epochs in religious history. Their relation to that which precedes and that which follows—causes, influences, outcome. This class of subjects requires the cultivation of a true historical instinct; because history is not the mere recital of successive events. This is only "Annals" or "Chronicles." History takes note of the under current, the controlling principle, the invincible drift. History is philosophy in the concrete and the history of religion is philosophy at its climax. That preacher who is a true historian has an opportunity which all might well covet. A course of sermons under his hand is not easily surpassed in all that makes for the good of men and the glory of God.

It is not necessary to proceed further in this line. Subjects for courses may be of any kind applicable to single sermons.

These various courses of sermons should be related to each other, just as the separate parts of each course are so related. It may be well also to vary them by sometimes introducing courses of religious "lectures," in which certain side-lights may be introduced or history related to Bible history but not included in it. For example, a course on Nehemiah and the later history of the Old Testament might be followed by a course of lectures on the Maccabean Period, and this again by a course of sermons on the Life of Christ.

These courses should not be confined to the evening services; but sometimes be introduced at the morning hour. There is more apt to be lack of system in the morning preaching any way. The skillful preacher may often so arrange it that a morning course may admirably complement an evening one.